THE ATLAS OF
OCCULT
BRITAIN

THE ATLAS OF
OCCULT BRITAIN

CHARLES WALKER

HAMLYN

Half title page *The demon-head knocker on the north door of Durham Cathedral (see page 143).*

Title spread *The ruined chapel of St. Michael, at Rocke Cornwall (see page 52), where the cursed Jan Tregeagle sought refuge.*

Designed by Christopher Matthews

First published in 1987
by The Hamlyn Publishing Group Limited,
Bridge House, 69 London Road, Twickenham,
Middlesex TW1 3SB, England,
and distributed for them by the
Octopus Distribution Services Limited,
Rushden, Northants, England.

ISBN 0 600 50354 2

Printed in Hong Kong by Mandarin Offset

Contents

Introduction 7

Glossary 22

The West Country 29

London and Southern England 61

Eastern Counties 85

Central England 101

Wales and Western Counties 113

The North 137

Scotland 157

Bibliography 187

Index 188

HIGHLAND

GRAMPIAN

Scotland

TAYSIDE

CENTRAL

FIFE

LOTHIAN

STRATHCLYDE

BORDERS

DUMFRIES
AND
GALLOWAY

NORTHUMBERLAND

1

DURHAM

2

CUMBRIA

The North

NORTH YORKSHIRE

LANCASHIRE

HUMBERSIDE

3

5

4

6

G W Y N E D D

CHESHIRE

DERBY-
SHIRE

NOTTINGHAM-
SHIRE

LINCOLNSHIRE

CLWYD

STAFFORD-
SHIRE

LEICESTERSHIRE

NORFOLK

SHROPSHIRE

**Wales and
Western Counties**

**Central
England**

Eastern Counties

7

CAMBRIDGE-
SHIRE

SUFFOLK

POWYS

HEREFORD
AND
WORCESTER

WARWICK-
SHIRE

NORTHAMPTON-
SHIRE

8

DYFED

GLOUCESTER-
SHIRE

OXFORD-
SHIRE

BUCKINGHAM-
SHIRE

HERTFORD-
SHIRE

ESSEX

10

GWENT

GREATER
LONDON

11

12

AVON

WILTSHIRE

9

**London and
Southern England**

SURREY

KENT

SOMERSET

HAMPSHIRE

The West Country

DEVON

DORSET

WEST
SUSSEX

EAST
SUSSEX

ISLE OF
WIGHT

CORNWALL

1 TYNE AND WEAR
2 CLEVELAND
3 WEST YORKSHIRE
4 SOUTH YORKSHIRE
5 GREATER MANCHESTER
6 MERSEYSIDE
7 WEST MIDLANDS
8 BEDFORDSHIRE
9 BERKSHIRE
10 WEST GLAMORGAN
11 MID GLAMORGAN
12 SOUTH GLAMORGAN

The entries in the atlas are divided into seven geographical areas as indicated on the left. Each of these areas is introduced in the relevant sections by a map which shows the nature of the site indicated by one or more of the symbols below. Within the regional areas, each of the sites is arranged alphabetically according to the placename. This name is followed by its corresponding county and the graphic symbol (or symbols) which indicate the type of occultism found there. The reference letter and number (in bold type) indicate the square on which it is located on the area map, and its Ordnance Survey grid reference. Following each of the entries is a brief description of how to get to the site. At most sites there is something specific to see. Some, however, merely have associations with people or events from the past.

Symbols

♀	Fairies	◖	Dragons
⚇	Stone Magic	✡	Symbols
△	Witchcraft	♉	Demons
⊕	Astrology	♂	Hauntings
⊡	Mazes	⚵	Alchemy
✕	Myths	—⊢	Magic
◉	Occultists	◉	Holy Well

Introduction

There is scarcely a village or town in Britain which does not have its occult or secret history, told in the chance survival of stones, symbols, images and curious lore.

What is 'occult', in this context of Britain? So far as this book is concerned, the occult world is that which concerns itself with what is normally hidden from the ordinary realm of man. That is what the word was intended to denote, for the Latin 'occulta' originally meant 'hidden things'. The realm of the occult is a vast one, for the hidden things are myriad, and so the realm has for centuries been classified into many different categories. We may trace in occultism the fascinating world of Secret Symbols, that search for the inner and outer gold, which is still called Alchemy, the vast and puzzling realm of Astrology, the darker realm of Demonology and Witchcraft (as well as the modern pseudo-sciences of the psychics, which are not so far removed from demonology as one might suppose), Stone Magic and the related field of what is now called ley-line research, a subject not unrelated to the ancient system of Holy Wells which lined the old pilgrimage routes through Britain, and which are glanced at in the following pages because of their connection with magical powers. These, and many more, are the occult subjects which we shall examine through the symbols and stories which are discovered in different parts of our strange and fascinating land.

It is the main purpose of this book to chart some of the more interesting ancient remains of witchcraft, magic, occult lore, divination and the undying stream of secret symbolism and to set out for the general reader a clear picture of just a few remnants of this occult history, in the hope that he or she may then personally discover other survivals from the fascinating realm of myth, magic and occult legend.

More often than not, the magic lore behind our patch-work history is recorded in symbols or stories – a whole tale of occultism may be traced in the faint lines of an obscure carving, from the shape of an old stone, in the secret words of a fading manuscript, or behind the hidden meaning of a well-told legend or outrageous myth. Since these symbols and relics belong to a secret history which is now almost forgotten, it is usually necessary for an occultist – the so-called 'initiate' – to point out their significance to those who know nothing of the occult lore. In the majority of cases, such symbols and remains are now so well disguised that their original meaning has been lost, and in many cases even the stories connected with them have been discarded. An outstanding example of this is the curious witch-stones (see Glossary on page 22) that are found in many parts of Scotland, for example in the village of **Auchencrow**, where one stone is almost hidden in a field wall (figure 1), and another, totally overgrown by brambles, is still the object of a curious ritual by schoolchildren. They mutter a protective rhyme against 'Peg Tode', even though they no longer know that this Peg Tode was once a local witch, who taught rats to sow seeds in order to grow corn. If one did not know these stories, one might easily walk by such a stone without sensing its secret relevance to a magical past. Such symbols are silent testimony to an age and beliefs which have almost passed away.

Figure 1 *A witch-stone, set in a wall at Auchencrow.*

Figure 2 *A zodiacal image on the roof of the Fitzjames Arch at Merton College, Oxford.*

Figure 3 *Detail of the 'Witchcraft Tomb' in Bottesford Parish Church.*

Figure 4 *A demonic gargoyle from the parish church at Littleborough, with strange carvings on its side.*

Figure 5 *Detail of zodiacal carving on the wall of the Bank of Scotland in George Street, Edinburgh.*

Figure 6 *A Masonic symbolism on the tomb of Laurence Newall, former Deputy Provincial Grand Master, in the parish church at Littleborough.*

In other cases, however, the occult symbolism is all too apparent, even if it is generally ignored, or passed by without any real awareness of its true meaning. Examples of this form of occulta abound: how many people who walk the roads which skirt **Littleborough** church have reflected on the meaning of the strange symbols carved on the sides of its gargoyles (figure 4), or how many ask why there should be zodiacal symbols on so many Victorian buildings, as in the magnificent double range of twenty-four zodiacal images on the George Street branch of the Bank of Scotland, in **Edinburgh** (figure 5)?

Such carvings and symbols are clearly 'occult', even to the eyes of the uninitiated, and a book of this kind mentions the main series of similar secret symbols and magical lores which are to be found in Britain. Among the most striking examples are the wonderful mediaeval astrological images in **Merton College**, Oxford (figure 2), a city which is filled with carvings, details of symbolism and (safely preserved in museums) works of art which speak of a world of astrological, occult and alchemical lore which has long since disappeared from the modern world of thought. A great deal of nonsense has been written about the Merton College zodiac by astrological 'experts' – some of whom insist that it is a horoscope, a schema of the heavens for a particular moment in time – but this should not obscure the fact that whatever its meaning, and whatever the secrets of its orientation on the Fitzjames Arch, the images themselves are of great beauty, and do indeed point to a secret lore, which is no longer really understood, even by experts.

Equally recognisable as 'occult' are many of the symbols in British graveyards. One need not puzzle over the secret symbols on the gravestones of those whose lives were in one way or another involved with occultism, as for example on the famous witchcraft tomb at **Bottesford** (figure 3), or on the tombs of well-known Masons (figure 6), designed specifically to incorporate occult lore. However, anyone who has a feeling for symbolism should at least wonder why so many ordinary people – those who appear to have no connection with occult lore – should have secret designs carved on their tombs or memorials, as may be seen from the magical Seal of Solomon on the gravestone from St Tudno's ancient church on the **Great Orme** (figure 7).

Some occult symbols are hidden to those uninitiated into the occult lore, while other symbols and devices are clearly linked with occultism, even if the precise meaning of these escapes the modern understanding. It is the purpose of this book to look into good examples of both these different categories, in the hope that the selection of symbols, myths and secret lore which demonstrates so clearly the continuance of an occult stream of thinking in Britain, will encourage the readers to look with new eyes on the other remnants of our past, and perhaps even begin to discover similar occult and secret symbols for themselves.

Figure 7 *The occult 'Seal of Solomon' on a gravestone in St Tudno's Churchyard, on the Great Orme.*

Symbolism

Occult symbols are found almost everywhere in Britain, but (as with so many things) one has to develop the eyes to see them for what they are. As like as not, few would deny the magical origin of the amulets which were originally fixed to doors, barns, windows and house fronts, as in the over-done door at **Quainton** (figure 9), but not everyone is able to see the magical power of other images derived from the amuletic tradition, which may be discovered, for example, on many of the houses in the strange and powerful village of **Erlestoke**.

The most persistent occult symbolism has flourished through the impact of the secret devices of heraldry, even in those cases where the heraldic origins have been forgotten, and where the occult basis for heraldry is no longer known. It is heraldry which accounts for such surprising images as the rhinoceros at the foot of the effigy of Sir Robert Gardener at **Elmswell** (figure 11), and it is heraldic symbolism which explains why three trefoils should figure on a coat of arms at the Triangular Lodge at **Rushton** (figure 10), as a further play on the *Tres* (Latin for three) in the name of Sir Thomas Tresham, who dreamed up and built this most extraordinary three-cornered structure.

But while the secret symbolism of heraldry, with its recondite play with numbers, names and sounds, is found in coats of arms, memorials and isolated symbols, it survives more intimately in our daily life through the names of pubs and even houses. On a superficial acquaintance we might take the Rose and Crown as a reference to the coat of arms of the Tudors, and in some respects we would be correct in doing this. Similarly, the Red Lion, or the Green Lion might just as easily be traced to coats of arms and heraldic sources. But if we look into the matter more deeply, we find that the

heraldic symbols themselves were more often than not replete with hidden symbolism derived from the occult lore, especially from alchemical symbolism. The Rose and the Crown are Christian and Jewish Cabbalistic symbols, respectively; the Rose was one of the symbols for the life-power of Christ, perpetuated in the rose-windows of our cathedrals, or in the rose of the alchemical diagrams, and hidden in a multitude of forms intended to represent the life-power of the rose-flower in the cross (figure 8), while the topmost level of the Tree of Life is called 'Kether' in Hebrew, which is usually translated as 'Crown', and linked also with what in modern occultism is called the 'Crown Chakra'. The red lions (figure 12) which grace so many of our modern pubs have an ancestry in alchemical diagrams, clearly marked in the ancient texts as Red, Black or Green Lions, symbols of different stages in that secret 'Great Work', which was the transforming power of Alchemy (figure 14). The 'Red Lion', says one of the English commentators on the work of the magician and alchemist Paracelsus, is the 'name given to the terrestrial and mineral matter which remains at the bottom of the vessel after sublimation of the spirits, called Eagle.' We see, then, that The Lion and the Eagle is far more than a pub-name derived from heraldry, but symbolises a secret meaning of the alchemical search. Thus these places carry names which were once hermetic, sealed in with magical power, even if this magic has now run dry or been forgotten.

From the 'aqua vitae' (water of life), to the bitter waters of death, the symbols have their sway. Even our word for 'alcohol', the 'aqua vitae' consumed in these pubs which

Figure 8 *The Rosy Cross, the symbol used by Stanilas de Guata, for his Cabbalistic Order of the Rosy Cross. The arms of the cross bear each of the four Hebraic letters of the Tetragrammaton (the Holy name of God), while the pentagram inside the cross bears the same four letters along with the Hebraic letter 'Schin', which represents 'spirit', or the 'Quintessence'. For all the Hebraic symbolism, the image of the Rose and Cross is entirely Christian, the basic symbol of the Rosicrucian movement.*

Figure 9 *A doorway in Quainton, to which have been affixed numerous magical amulets.*

Figure 11 *A rhinoceros on a 16th-century memorial tomb at Elmswell.*

Figure 10 *Trefoils on coat of arms of Sir Thomas Tresham, at Rushton.*

Figure 12 *A red lion above the porch of the 'Red Lion' pub at Henley on Thames.*

Figure 13 *A bench-end carving in the Church of St James, Kilkhampton, Cornwall, perhaps of a pedlar, which may be linked with the symbolism of 'The Fool'.*

THE FOOL

Figure 15 *The unnumbered Tarot card, 'The Fool' from the so-called Marseilles Pack.*

Figure 14 *The 'Green Lion', devouring the sun, a standard alchemical image of a process in the manufacture of the Philosopher's stone. From a 16th-century alchemical document.*

bear secret names, came from the ancient word for a demon, a word which still survives in our version of the Arabic 'Al Ghoul' (the demon) – alcohol was the 'demon', and a corruption of the name is preserved in the evil star which the modern astrologers call Algol, and visualise as a demon in the constellation of Perseus. The death's-head skull, which was used by the pirates, and which still stands as warning of death on numerous notice-boards throughout the British Isles, also came to us from alchemy, as a symbol of the last residue of life, as the rejected and useless form. Its frequent presence in our graveyards should remind us that the Christians took it as a symbol not of death, but of resurrection, and (as may be seen from the example at **Glendevon**) of the coming life which surely follows on death. To make from a popular symbol of death a symbol of spiritual life is occult work indeed. Almost every graveyard in Britain is a happy hunting ground for those who find themselves interested in occult symbols, and while it is beyond the compass of a book of this kind to mention even the most important occulta of the burial grounds, there are sufficient examples given for the reader to take up the cue, and do his or her own research. There are, of course, many other different forms of symbolism reflected in the occult places of Britain which point to non-heraldic origins. A surprising example of this is the strange bench-end from **Kilkhampton** (figure 13), which requires no great imaginative effort to link it with one of the arcane cards of the Tarot Pack (figure 15).

Astrology

Without any doubt, the most persistent survival of occult symbolism in Britain has been through astrology. This is perhaps not surprising, as astrology, in Britain and in Europe as a whole, was once the most coherent and spiritualised of all philosophies, linking as it did every aspect of the material wo ld with its spiritual prototypes, which were re ,ard ' as being the planets, the signs of the zodiac or the star imes past everything was sensed as meaningful fragments cut from the vast arc of the zodiac, and t' we've signs, most ofteı represented as a circle of hermetic images (figure 15), were linked with the human body (figure 17), with the design of buildings, with the secret symbolism of the Church, and so on. There are many examples of this 'astrological man' symbolism in Britain, and very often the symbols reach into very deep levels of esoteric lore, as may be seen in fragments of sculpture at **Toller Fratrum**, or in a grave-slab in the aisle of **Christchurch**. This occult lore of astrology was not as simple as the modern newspaper 'star readings' would have us believe: in its heyday astrology was a most demanding study, requiring a thorough knowledge of philosophy, history, alchemy, symbolism and magic, as any survey of the astrological notebooks of such men as Thomas Smith (preserved in the manuscript department of the **British Museum**), or William Lilly (whose birth is noted at **Diseworth**) will indicate. It is therefore not surprising that an approach to the occult symbols of Britain would require some knowledge of the symbolism inherent in the horoscope figure, in the planetary images, or in the zodiac. To savour fully the occultism of Britain it is not really sufficient to know that there are twelve signs of the zodiac, and that there were seven planets (truths which are again and again reflected in the numerological symbolism of the twelve and

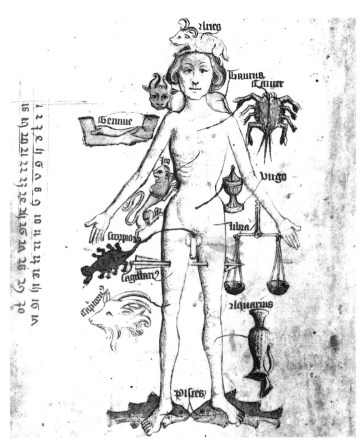

Figure 17 *The zodiacal Man (the so-called 'Melothesic Man'), with the symbols of the zodiacal signs aligned to parts of the body. Note the symbol for Virgo, given here as a chalice. From the 16th-century manuscript, 'The Guildbook of the Barber Surgeons of York', British Museum. (See Table 1).*

the seven in a variety of surviving occulta): one has to know what the ancient texts call 'all the ancient things'.

If one really wishes to appreciate to the full some of the wonders of the occult centres in Britain, then one has to know a little about the secret connections established between the stars and the world as a whole: one has to be aware that in the past it was believed not only that individuals were guided by particular angels, and misguided by particular demons, but also that towns, cities and even localities were under the control of particular zodiacal and planetary forces (see chart on page 14). This Atlas cannot provide a rounded view of the whole of astrology, of course, but it can give some indication of how deeply astrology influenced the symbolic lore which lies behind many of our monuments, and architectural gems. The very least information which one must have to begin to appreciate something of the richness of astrological lore in our private buildings, churches and cathedrals, is set out in Tables 1 and 2, on page 15. The first table lists the traditional images, sigils and 'parts of the body' ascribed from ancient times to what is now called the 'zodiacal man' (figure 17) and the second lists a further, and perhaps less frequently encountered, system of astrological correspondences in British symbols.

Even a perfunctory survey of astrological symbolism in Britain will reveal that the most enduring and popular symbol derived from this 'circle of animals' (the zodiac) is the fishes of Pisces, which was widely adopted as an arcane symbol for Christ, and is accordingly found in many occult centres – especially in churches. Indeed, it is quite extraordinary how many of the modern tapestry kneelers in churches

Figure 16 *A zodiacal circle, with the twelve signs of the zodiac arranged around a schema of the stars, the space occupied by the planets, the lunar sphere, and the earth. The placing of the Sun next to Libra may well have something to do with the fact that it was widely believed that Christ's horoscope was Libran.*

(in which occult symbols have preserved a most powerful life of their own), are involved with the image of the fish, or with the image of three fishes. However, the pair of fishes which are found in early churches appear in the most unlikely places, often apparently divorced from a zodiacal context, as for example in the marvellous Norman carvings on the south door at **Kilpeck** (figure 34), as well as high on the north side of this remarkable church. A brief note of the significance of the symbol for Pisces (called a 'sigil' by specialists) is revealed in the entry under **Christchurch** – but this is given merely as a good example of the *kind* of secret symbolism which may be found in other churches and buildings. The survival of this fish-symbol may be noted in many different places and in many guises, as fish-men or mermaids, and sometimes one must be prepared to use one's imagination to grasp its significance fully. For example, the strangely-shaped brass memorial plates which one finds in some late mediaeval churches, in the form of children in swaddling clothes, is really making a secret use of this fish-symbolism, for the shape of the memorial plate is in the outline of a fish, and the entire plate proclaims the spirit of the child to be 'with Christ', who was himself the Fish.

More recondite astrological symbols, usually derived from mediaeval art figure to a large extent in British occult centres, and are accordingly noted in the following pages. For example, the goblet is one of the secret symbols of zodiacal Virgo, the astrological counterpart of the Virgin Maria, and no doubt links with the Holy Grail legends developed in the mediaeval period. It is surely this merging of the ancient Egypto-Babylonian lore of astrology with the Grail legends, which accounts for the strange use of the chalice as an image for the Virgin, in figure 17, but it also appears in a curiously disguised form in the rebus-shield in St Benignus Church at **Glastonbury**.

The most frequently used of the astrological symbols in British (and Continental) art are those of the four fixed signs of the zodiac, which have been representations of the four Evangelists from very early Christian times (figure 18). The essence of this symbolism is set out in Table 2, but we should note in passing that the Eagle is the esoteric symbol for 'redeemed Scorpio' (that part of the Scorpionic nature which can fly skywards, rather than being held down in the arid desert, like a scorpion), which is why it is adopted as the symbolic 'beast' of St John. The Centaur is one of the earliest forms for Sagittarius, though this is more and more displaced by the horseman. Both centaur and horseman invariably shoot a bow and arrow, and appear in this guise in the most surprising places in British churches. In classical astrology Capricorn was usually a goat-fish, and a fine level of secret symbolism was contained in this curious image: in modern times he has been demoted to the status of goat, and the loss of his fish-tail corresponds to the loss of understanding about the nature of this intriguing sign and constellation. The dolphin symbol is really another example of the Pisces of astrology, and is therefore linked with Christ. Both goat and dolphin are found in this symbolic guise in the **Oxford** zodiac in Merton College.

One form of astrological symbolism which appears from time to time in British occult images is derived from an astrological tradition which links the twelve lost tribes of Israel with the zodiac. Perhaps the finest example of this tradition is found on the 17th-century pulpit at **Giggleswick** (figure 19).

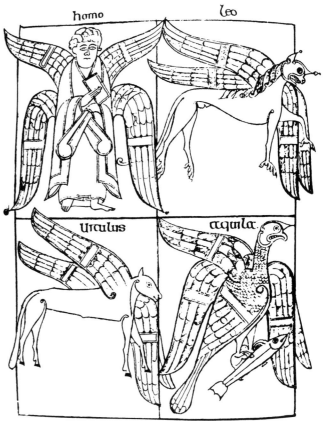

Figure 18 *Symbols of the Four Evangelists, derived from the four fixed signs of the zodiac. After the Book of Armagh, in Trinity College, Dublin.*

Figure 19 *The symbol for the Israelite tribe of Dan with its supposed badge-symbol of a basilisk, which is really an astrological association with the sign Scorpio. From the Pulpit of St Alkleda's Church, Giggleswick, dated 1680. The astrological tradition of associations between the Twelve Tribes and the signs of the zodiac is ancient, but received ecclesiastical sanction in the 13th century in the works of William Darandus.*

BRITAIN as a whole was said in the ancient astrological texts to be ruled by the sign Aries, but in later texts ENGLAND only is given to Aries, SCOTLAND to Cancer, WALES to Capricorn (though some say Gemini), and IRELAND to Taurus. The West of England is given in the ancient texts as being under the rule of Gemini. The CITY OF LONDON is said to be ruled by Capricorn, but LONDON town (west of the city) is ruled by Gemini: for an interesting example of this, see LONDON –

THE CITY. The astrologer William Lilly (see DISEWORTH) says that the 18th degree of Gemini is London's Ascendant degree, and points out that the 25th degree of this sign is also important to England. Lilly foretold the outbreak of the plague of London, in 1625, in which over 35,000 people perished, and the beheading of King Charles in 1649, from consideration of this London degree.

CHART OF PLACES IN BRITAIN FOR WHICH
ASTROLOGICAL RULERSHIPS HAVE BEEN GIVEN IN
ANCIENT MANUSCRIPTS

Place	Sign	Place	Sign
Bath	*Leo*	**Nottingham**	*Sagittarius*
Birmingham	*Aries*	**Oxford**	*Capricorn*
Bournemouth	*Pisces*	**Portsmouth**	*Leo*
Brighton	*Aquarius*	**Reading**	*Virgo*
Bristol	*Leo*	**St Andrews**	*Cancer*
Cheltenham	*Virgo*	**Salisbury**	*Capricorn*
Dover	*Scorpio*	**Sheffield**	*Sagittarius*
Dublin	*Taurus*	**Sunderland**	*Sagittarius*
Farnham	*Pisces*	**Taunton**	*Leo*
Leicester	*Aries*	**Tiverton**	*Pisces*
Liverpool	*Scorpio*	**York**	*Cancer*
Northampton	*Sagittarius*		

(REF: *For further information, see* F. Gettings, Dictionary of Astrology, 1985, *under 'Chorography'.*)

TABLE 1

Zodiacal sign	Image	Sigil	Part of body	Function
Aries	Ram	♈	Head	Thinking
Taurus	Bull	♉	Throat	Speaking
Gemini	Twins	♊	Arms, lungs	Expression
Cancer	Crab (Crayfish)	♋	Rib-cage	Protection
Leo	Lion	♌	Heart	Emotions
Virgo	Woman	♍	Womb	Nourishing
Libra	Scales	♎	Small of back	Balance
Scorpio	Scorpion	♏	Sexual parts	Sexuality
Sagittarius	Horseman archer	♐	Thighs	Locomotion
Capricorn	Goat-fish	♑	Knees, Skeleton	Structural
Aquarius	Waterman	♒	Lower Leg	Dissemination
Pisces	Fishes	♓	Feet	Spiritualisation

The following table should make the main astrological associations clear, both for the Giggleswick pulpit and for other examples which one may find in Britain.

The tribe name in lower-case is mediaeval, that in upper-case the mediaeval name adopted in the Giggleswick pulpit.

TABLE 2

Zodiac	Zodiacal symbol	Evangelist	Tribe	Symbol
Aries	Ram		NAPHTALI	Deer
Taurus	Bull	Luke	JOSEPH	Bull
Gemini	Twins		Simeon-LEVI	Book
Cancer	Crab/Crayfish		ISSACHAR	Ass
Leo	Lion	Mark	JUDAH	Lion
Virgo	Virgin (Goblet)		ASHER	Goblet
Libra	Scales		Dinah-SIMEON	Sword
Scorpio	Scorpion (Eagle)	John (Eagle)	DAN	Basilisk
Sagittarius	Horseman/Centaur		GAD	Standard
Capricorn	Goat-fish (Goat)		BENJAMIN	Wolf
Aquarius	Water-pourer	Matthew	REUBEN	Waves
Pisces	Fishes (Dolphin)		ZEBULON	Ship

Demonology and Angelology

The demons play a most important role in the esoteric centres of Britain. A hellish cast of devils peer down from the walls of many parish churches, and every occultist knows that these are far from being merely decorative, for their secret language speaks of the demonic strain in man, of his own inner weaknesses. In earlier times there was a highly-developed lore of demons, which has now been lost. Just as there were angels charged with specific rule over individuals, or over particular human activities and parts of the world, so there were individual demons who were charged with particular roles in the affairs of men. The demons who grimace down at us from the churches are more than merely reminders of the demons within – very often they are containers of a particular symbolism, as in **Littleborough** or, less obviously, in **Southwell**, though all too often the power of this symbolism has been forgotten.

Just as one often finds the four Archangels (Michael, Gabriel, Raphael and Uriel) on each of the four corners of church towers, symbolically representing the spiritual world triumphant, so one also finds demons in the lower registers, who are symbolic of the inner demons in man. The imagery of these archangels appears in many forms in British art, and so it will be useful to note the main pictorial traditions in Table 3.

The demonological symbolism inside some churches is almost too obvious, for below a complex series of angels within the roof beams, one often finds an equally complex series of demons in the bench-ends or finials of the pews (figure 21). Such symbolism proclaims quite openly that while the angels dwell in the high heaven, the demons dwell on earth, at the same level as mankind. A superb example of this is in **Woolpit**, and a slightly more impressive one at **Swaffham**. In fact, the angels of the early occult

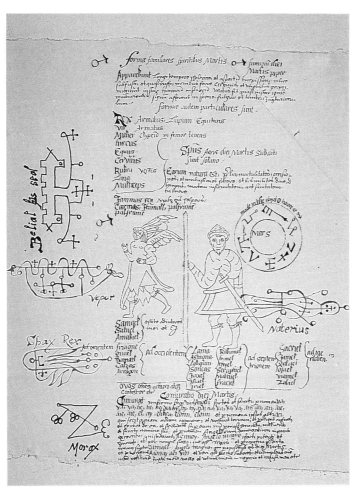

Figure 20 *A 16th-century Latin text on demons, with sigils of the spirits added in a later hand.*

Figure 21 *Sixteenth-century benchend finial or poppyhead of a demonic creature in St Mary's, Woolpit.*

TABLE 3

Archangel	Symbol	Element	Planet	Direction
Michael	scales and golden sword	Fire	Sun	East
Raphael ·	sometimes a fish, or musical instrument	Air	Mercury	West
Gabriel	the lily, sometimes a book	Water	Moon	South
Uriel	(often named)	Earth	Earth	North

tradition were often intermixed with the devils in demonological texts, as figure 20 indicates. This manuscript, from one of the numerous private collections of occult lore, charts some of the characteristics of the demon linked with the planet Mars, and is covered with marginal scrawl and drawings which set out some of the sigils for certain of the more important named demons (such as Morax and Shax). Surely it does not demand much imagination to see the symbols incised into the body of the gargoyle from **Littleborough** (figure 4) as being derived from a similar sigil in a demonological text.

Witchcraft

The lore of British witchcraft is preserved most poignantly in the awful histories told by the ancient books, and in the crude woodcuts designed to embellish such texts (figure 22), yet a few more directly material remains still litter the British landscape. Among these, the most interesting are the so-called witch-stones, that mark the places where witches were burned in Scotland, or where they were otherwise put to death by the mob during that terrible period of the witchcraft frenzy that came to a head in Britain during the 16th and 17th centuries. The surviving relics are found also in the forms of smoke-dried carcasses (figure 24) and the often quite charming witchcraft poppets in our museums (page 88), as well as in a whole batch of witchcraft legends

Figure 24 A mummified puppy or kitten, found as part of a charm against evil of witchcraft, stuffed in a chimney. In the Moyse's Museum, Bury St Edmunds.

woven around villages and individual stones. Among these is the fine example of the witch-stone in **Forres**, which marks the last resting place of a witch who was (according to local custom) incarcerated in a barrel of tar, fired, and rolled down a hill.

Stones

There is not always a clear distinction between witch-stones and some of the standing stones which we find in Britain: indeed, in some instances the ancient menhirs have themselves been saddled with the witchcraft lore, as one notes in connection with the stone on the headland above **Kempock**. There are many good reasons why the occultists include in their area of study the menhirs and stone circles which are still found in almost every region in the British Isles (some 500 still survive in England and Scotland alone). Indeed, it has become a commonplace for popular writers to assume that all the stone circles and standing stones are somehow 'occult'. This probably arises from the occult tradition which insists that the stone magic was linked with the lost power of Vril in the quite un-fabled Atlantis, a land-mass which is said to have perished mainly because of its involvement with the darker side of magic. I have restricted myself to mentioning only a few favourites of my own with a view of revealing something of the variety of occult lore which has attached itself to the stones. The grandeur of **Stonehenge** (figure 23) is now somewhat diminished by the modern fencing and turnstiles, and although I was familiar with this magnificent circle before its atmosphere was destroyed by insensitive officialdom, I must now consider **Callanish** or **Avebury** as the finest examples of stone circles.

Figure 22 A witch being carried by the Devil. After a woodcut from the 1555 edition of Olaus Magnus.

Figure 23 Stonehenge in the 18th century.

However, there are a number of lesser known circles, such as **Sunhoney Circle**, that deserve a mention for a variety of different reasons – Sunhoney, because of the way the cup-and-ring marks have been linked with the constellation of the Great Bear in the skies. Similarly, Long Meg and her Daughters at **Little Salkeld** find their way into this text because they illustrate so well the growth of myths and legends which have always been associated with the ancient stones.

Geomancy and Ley-lines

Occult symbolism reaches into almost every walk of life. The simple diagram in figure 25 is from a book by the English occultist Fludd (see **Bearsted**), and reveals some of the main divisions of occult research. Here we see 'Genethlialogia', an old term for astrology, as the squared horoscope within the segment indicates. There is also 'Chriomantia', or the study of the lines of the hand: 'Physiognomia', the study of the face; 'Geomantia', the use of earth for purposes of prediction, and so on. It is this last word, the old form for 'Geomancy', which should remind us of the modern wide-spread interest in what are now called ley-lines. The word was first suggested by Alfred Watkins in connection with his work on old trackways, and some of his findings are noted under **Hereford** (his native city) and **Dinedor**. In modern times this notion of ley-lines has developed beyond anything which Watkins would recognise. If you visit the ancient stone circles at all frequently you are bound to meet people playing around with divining rods or pendulums: usually they are plotting out what they take to be ley-lines, as invisible earth-currents. While such invisible earth currents doubtless exist, and may be charted, they have nothing whatsoever to do

with the ley-lines of Watkins, just as they have nothing to do with Geomancy. As the segment on Geomantia in figure 25 indicates, the art of geomancy was the art of establishing (by means of throwing stones or earth at random) a meaningful figure, on this case presented on a shield, which could be used as the basis for interpretation of a question about the future. This geomancy – which is preserved in very many interesting documents in the major museums of Britain (figure 26) has nothing to do with ley-lines. I have therefore made passing references to some of the more important ley-lines traced by Watkins, but have not misused the word geomancy to cover this field of research.

Figure 26 *Personification of the Moon, with geomantic symbols on either side of her head. After a 13th-century manuscript.*

Wells

The sacred wells, some of which are said to heal still, and many of which have been demoted to wishing wells, play an important role in occult lore, for many of them are the most extraordinary survivals from a past age which took its inspirations and its fears from magic. I have therefore included a few notes on those which, for one reason or another, I find the most impressive of the very many wells in Britain – over 500 in Wales alone. The most beautiful magical well in Wales is undoubtedly that at **Holywell**, the waters of which gave a name to the town (figure 27). The finest English well is probably at **Bath**, but the watery origin of this place-name has long since been forgotten, so, instead, I will point to the splendid **St Clether's** well in Cornwall. The well which I prefer in Scotland has also lent a name to a village, and although the outer structure of the well is newly restored (with considerable taste and feeling), the magical bubbling of underground waters into the cistern at **Scotlandwell** (page 183) is surely sufficient to mark this as

Figure 25 *An esoteric diagram – 'A Man as the Ape of the Gods', from Robert Fludd's* Cosmi Utriusque Maioris . . . *of 1617.*

the finest of the northern wells. If the amazing structure of the **Burghead** well were really nothing more than a well, then this would surely take pride of place: I have no doubt, however, that it was an initiation chamber.

Figure 27 *The interior of St Winifride's Well, Holywell.*

Figure 29 *The holy well at St Cleer in Cornwall.*

Figure 28 *An 18th-century engraving of St Winifride's well by Nathaniel Buck.*

Birthing places and museums

There must be something personal in a book of this kind, and this is revealed in the passing notes I make of the localities and myths which I have enjoyed during my life-long study of occult lore. Among these personal loves are the curious 'birthing places' of important ideas from occult sources – as for example the strange birth of modern abstract art from occult images on **Parliament Hill Fields** (London), or the quiet creative force in Milton's House at **Chalfont St Giles**, which saw the growth of *Paradise Lost* and the conception of *Paradise Regained*, those exemplary works of British occultism. Such places as these carry still a feeling of the intensity of those important moments, when the spiritual world poured its forces into the material realm with more than its customary bounty. In addition to these 'personal places', I note also the 'public occult places', to be noted in certain parts of the country – of these, the best-known is **Glastonbury**, with the legend-woven Tor, and the mythology spread (perhaps a little too thinly for an occultist's taste) around the abbey and the town itself.

In fact, the greatest remains of British occultism now reside in our museums. The large number of Roman and mediaeval amulets and magical spells, the enormous numbers of occult, astrological and magical texts, and the witch charms, curse-dolls and poppets are preserved in many museums, and I hope that what is set out in the following pages will enable the reader to discover such things for himself. In fact, it is unlikely that there is a museum in Britain which does not in some way or another preserve or exhibit occult remains, even in those cases where the occult basis for the exhibits is not recognised. Initial research found no fewer than eighty collections where interesting occulta might be found, but for want of space, I have provided information on only half a dozen or so of the more accessible collections, and libraries. I have limited myself to only the most remarkable collections and libraries of occult books, of which pride of place must go to the British Museum, the Bodleian and the Ashmolean, the last almost born from an interest in magical lore, as even the official history of the place admits.

Hauntings

The other subjects covered within the text include haunted houses and castles, a number of interesting psychic photographs, and a few mazes. Some occultists would undoubtedly say that 'hauntings' and 'psychic photographs' (the materialised fragments of hauntings) have nothing to do with the occult). However, since the genuine cases are without doubt examples (however distasteful) of the interpenetration of the normally invisible astral world into our ordinary physical world, there is definitely a sense in which they might be called occult.

Mazes

One might argue that mazes have nothing to do with the occult, but all the indications point to the ancient mazes being ritual dance-patterns, linked with an aspect of the Christian and pagan religions which has almost been forgotten. Mazes in such cathedrals as **Ely** and in churches such as **Bourn**, point to the religious origins of at least the non-labyrinthian mazes. Since my purpose is merely to present a sort of anthology of occulta, with a view to encouraging readers to find for themselves other examples,

I have included in this Atlas only a handful of the mazes which interest me personally – the most lovely internal maze is that at **Ely**, while the most original is the one at **Hadstock**: the external maze at **Saffron Walden** is perhaps the most lovely. It is interesting to see how the idea of mazes spills over into the community. At Saffron Walden, the maze has been used more than once in other designs within the town – most notably in the lovely kneeler in the parish church, while the **Alkborough** maze has spread even more, for the external maze (page 140) has been translated into the porch floor of the village church, a smaller version is found in an east window of the same church, and in the village cemetery a brass plate maze has been set into a gravestone. The Alkborough maze is of a fairly traditional formal pattern, and is not strictly speaking a maze at all (one may scarcely lose oneself in its meander pattern), and the remnants of other patterns, such as those found in **Rocky Valley**, or in Wisley (figure 30) or **Skewsby** appear to be far older in design, and may even belong to the concept of the Cretan maze, as some modern esotericists suggest.

Figure 30 *Plan of the Wisley Labyrinth. This is an example of a fairly standard 'maze' used in gardens and rock-carvings. It is not a pattern in which one may get lost – it is more of a formal pattern, said to have been used originally as a dancing ground.*

Lost meanings

In making this selection of what I regard as the most interesting of British occulta, I hope to encourage the reader to look at the British landscape and its history in a different way. Understanding the multi-layer significance of these symbols fully is difficult, but I hope the information in this book will cultivate an awareness of the vast array of occulta around us. The curious collection of amulets nailed to the door in **Quainton** (figure 9) is certainly something of an excess, and would scarcely escape anyone, yet the more subtle secret symbols on doors, lintels and thresholds sometimes need a practised eye for their significance to be revealed. One needs a deeper awareness of the occult lore to understand other connections, however, for example, the curve of the horseshoe linked with the crescent moon is not immediately obvious. By fixing such a crescent to a door one drives away the demons, but precisely why should the moon-symbol repel the evil forces, and why should it be linked with demons in such a way? From the very earliest time occultists have held that demons dwell invisibly in the sphere of the moon, which bathes the earth itself, as the simple diagram in figure 16 indicates. This sphere of the moon is the ancient astral realm of occultism, the realm so often figured as demonic, and linked through a thousand images and traditions with dragons. It is no accident that the alchemical images of the moon so often portray dragons in their symbolism (figure 31). Such a footnote in occultism should lead us to see, for example, the village of **Mordiford** in a different light: many people know the myth which has

Mordiford plagued by a dragon (the story is echoed in the name 'Serpent Lane', used of the trackway below West Hill), but how many people realise the significance of the pub in the village which looks on to this West Hill being called The Moon. It is in such seeming accidents that the true occultism in the British landscape and villages resides. My anticipation is that anyone who reflects on the messages contained in this anthology of occult sites will quickly learn to appreciate such subtle connections and 'accidents', and begin to see how such symbols speak a language of their own. Whether one agrees or not with all that is claimed for occult symbolism in this book, one thing at least will be clear – that there are more secret places in Britain than is generally imagined.

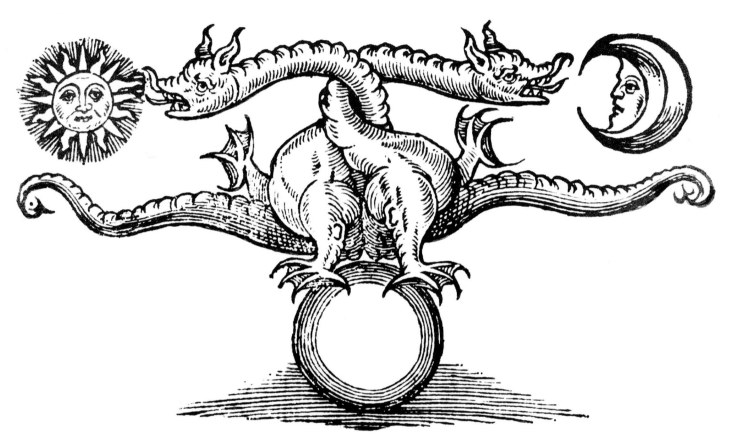

Figure 31 *Lunar dragon between Sun and Moon, from a 17th-century alchemical text.*

Glossary

Alchemy
Occultists recognise that the practice of alchemy (which was in some cases merely a search in a very materialistic sense for the secret of making silver or gold from dross materials) was itself a secret science, involved with attempting to so refine the inner man as to allow the dross of the darker passions to fall away, and leave the pure gold of higher being free. Many of the alchemical symbols reflect the various stages of this perfecting of the inner man, and are linked with Christian and astrological symbolism.

Amulet
A protective device, used to reject the curses or harmful emanations of a witch, warlock or evil-worker.

Ascendant
The point of the zodiac arising (ascending) over the horizon at a given moment. In the horoscope or birth-chart, this ascendant is expressed in degrees of the zodiac, and is probably the most important single point within the figure.

Astral
Literally 'starry', but used by occultists to denote a higher and invisible realm, peopled by a wide variety of different beings without physical bodies: such beings include **elementals**, fairies and demons.

Atlantis
A continental mass, and the civilisation which existed on it, which is said to have sunk beneath what is now the Atlantic, many thousands of years ago. (See for example Perranuthnoe.)

Basilisk
A fabled serpent which could kill merely with the power of its evil glance.

Chakra
A term of Sanskrit origin used to denote the (invisible) **astral** and **etheric** power-centres on the surface of the human body.

Clairvoyance
Literally 'clear seeing', but used to denote the capacity for seeing clearly into the hidden realms of the **astral** or the **etheric** planes. A true clairvoyant usually has the ability to see into the future.

Constellations
The images traced in the skies by imagining connections between stars and stellar groups. The constellations must not be confused with the **signs**, for while they sometimes have the same name as signs they do not cover the same extent in the skies, nor are they in the same areas.

Curse-doll
A witch **poppet** made as an image to accompany a written or spoken curse on a named individual.

Deva
This occult term was originally taken from the Sanskrit, in which it was used to denote a mighty spiritual being that dwells, unseen by men, in the spiritual realm. In popular western occultism, however, the same word has recently been used to denote fairies – especially those fairies linked with the elements, such as the undines, sylphs, salamanders and gnomes.

Devil's Mark
A part of a witch's body insensitive to pain. Those who were appointed to search out witches would locate such imagined spots, press into them a pin or bodkin, and note whether the witch felt pain.

Devil's Teat
An unnatural deformation in the form of a pimple or a teat on a witch's body from which (it was believed) her familiar or devil might suck her blood.

Dragon
In occultism, the image of the dragon is very often used as a protective device, as a sort of cosmic **amulet**. The dragon is also associated with the power of **initiation** – inititiates were once called dragon-men. Many of the dragon images which survive in Britain are really remnants of initiation symbols.

Elements
An important doctrine of alchemy is that the material forms of nature are supported by the spiritual activity of four elements, which are named, Fire, Earth, Air and Water, but which do not themselves consist of the material equivalents of these (which is to say that the element of Fire is not itself an incandescent gas, but a principle of life). Associated with these elements are the so-called 'Elemental Beings', the Salamanders being linked with Fire, the Gnomes with Earth, the Sylphs with Air and the Undines with Water. The four elements, and their numerous associations, play a most important role in occult symbolism. The most frequently used symbols for the four elements are:

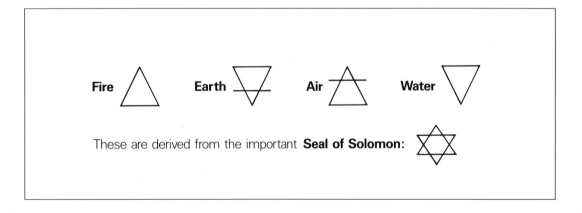

Etheric
The **quintessence**, the fifth element or life-force which animates all living things. It is often symbolised by a **pentagram** or by a sun cradled in a lunar crescent.

Fish
In occult symbolism, the fish is generally a representation of Christ, and connotes the connection between Christ and the age of Pisces, symbolized by an image of two fishes. The fish is also a symbol of spirituality, even of the spiritual world.

Geomancy
A method of divination which (originally at least) was based on the random throw of pebbles, stones or earth, by means of which a table or formal pattern was constructed, and then interpreted according to certain rules. See also **Ley-Lines**.

Gnomes
The beings of the **element** earth: they are often depicted as grotesquely formed mannikins.

Gorgon
A demon whose eyes could petrify or kill any living creature on which they looked. The face of the Gorgon is sometimes used as an **amulet**.

Figure 32 *A 'Green Man', from a mediaeval misericord in the Priory Church of St Margaret, in King's Lynn.*

Green Man
A particular form of symbolic head, in which greenery (often in the form of vine-leaves) issue from the mouth of a male head. Some occultists insist that, for all they appear frequently in ecclesiastical architecture, such images are nevertheless pagan, representing nature spirits (figure 32).

Grimoire
A grimoire is a collection of demon-names, and descriptions of demons, often accompanied by lists of secret symbols ('Seals') and sigils for the demons, as well as a number of black magic spells, incantations and charms (figure 20).

Initiation
There are many different forms, and various stages, of initiation, but the essential purpose behind the undertaking is to lead the initiate into a vision and understanding of those higher worlds inaccessible to man by ordinary (natural) means.

Lemniscate

This occult symbol is a figure of eight, though it is to be conceived as being drawn in three dimensions. It is much more than a sign of 'eternity', for it is linked by occultists with the basic rhythm behind the planetary and stellar forces.

Ley-Lines
A term originated by Alfred Watkins to denote linear connections between ancient sites, churches and places of importance. In modern times the ley-lines are regarded by many as consisting of hidden lines of force, which may be mapped out by psychic means. Page 125 gives examples of ley-lines in the sense originally used by Watkins. The science of leys has been confused in recent years with **geomancy**.

Luck
A fairy gift, usually to a family as a protective amulet or talisman.

Mark Stone

A term used by Watkins (see **ley-lines**) for a man-made or natural boulder located meaningfully in the system of ley-lines traced across the land, or used to denote unnatural boundaries.

Maze

A complex series of pathways in which it is possible to lose oneself – a labyrinth. However, many formal patterns found in cathedrals (see **Ely**, page 91), churches, and formerly on several village greens, were dance patterns, in which it was not possible to lose oneself, and which always led to a centre.

Mermaid

Most images of half-fish humans, or even of half-dragon humans, are occult symbols of **initiation**. The notion in the curious symbolism is that the initiate is free to live in both the physical world (that is the human half) and in the spiritual world (that is the **fish** or **dragon** half) at one and the same time.

Mithras

A sun-god of Babylonian origin, whose ancient mysteries had a great influence on the development of Rome: there were several Mithraic temples in Britain during the Roman occupation. The imagery of Mithras is largely derived from astrology and, since it involved the annual ritual slaughter of a bull, it was linked with Taurus.

Ogham

An ancient alphabet of simple linear characters (surviving mainly in lapidary forms) used by the ancient British and Irish tribes. It is generally believed that there is the same magical ethos behind these simple characters as behind the **runes**, which is why the term 'oghamic' is used to denote a secret form of speech.

Ouraboros

The alchemically-derived symbol of the snake (sometimes a winged dragon) biting its own tail, so that its body forms a circle. It is often intended as a symbol of time, and (rarely) as a symbol of eternity.

Figure 33 *An ouroboros from the 12th century Norman doorway of Kilpeck Church.*

Pelican

The image of the pelican piercing its own breast with its beak to feed its young is both an alchemical symbol and one derived from early Christian images. Its occult symbolism is linked with the notion that the spiritual development of humanity (the ultimate search of **alchemy**) cannot be a selfish activity.

Pentagram

A magical five-pointed star, linked in occultism with the **etheric**. Some occultists say that it is an image of one of the spiritual bodies of man, the four lower points representing his limb extremities, and the upper point his head. The inverted pentagram, on the other hand, is sometimes said to represent the Devil.

Phoenix

An alchemical symbol of great mystical importance, linked in a very simple way with the notion of healing, which is why the bird was adopted as the symbol of chemists (see Launceston). In occult circles, however, the same symbol is often used to denote the principles of **reincarnation**.

Pisces

The name of the 'Fishes', the twelfth sign of the zodiac, which rules over the feet of the human body, and which is linked with Christ, who is the **fish** (figure 34).

Poppet

A small figure made from cloth, paper, wax, and so on, in the image of a particular individual, usually by a witch who intends to deform or in some way 'torture' the doll in order to damage that person. A good example of a poppet is on page 88.

Quintessence

One of the names for the magical fifth element, sometimes called in occultism the **etheric**.

Rebus

An enigmatical device, designed to represent a name or word by means of images or pictures. An example is mentioned under Quainton – Brudenell House (page 109).

Figure 34 *Pisces, as the symbol of Christ, from the Norman doorway of Kilpeck Church.*

Figure 35 *An esoteric symbol of the Quintessence, from a 17th-century bench-end in the parish church of East Quantoxhead.*

Reincarnation

Occultists insist that the human spirit is periodically reborn into physical bodies. Only initiates of a very high order are normally able to remember preceding incarnations, however. A frequently used symbol of reincarnation in occult symbolism is that of the **Phoenix**, reborn from its own self-engendered flames.

Runes

The letters of a number of Nordic alphabets, believed by many to be of a magical nature. Each of the runes has a name, a **sigil**, a sound and a secret meaning.

Sabbat

The supposed gathering of witches to worship the Devil and to receive from the demons orders for evil-working.

Salamanders

The beings of the **element** fire, often symbolised in the form of newts or lizards.

Sciomancy

The raising of the shades of the dead (often wrongly called necromancy). The purpose of such dealing is usually to learn about the future. See Walton-Le-Dale (page 154).

Seal of Solomon

An occult symbol, sometimes used as an **amulet**, of two interlocking triangles. It is this seal which accounts for the symbols used to denote the four **elements** of fire, earth, air and water. The space inside these interlocking triangles is said to represent the invisible fifth element, the **quintessence**. A good example of this symbolism is found at East Quantoxhead (figure 35). See also Bloxham (page 103).

Second Sight

One of the many terms used to denote clairvoyant vision.

Sigil

A graphic symbol used to denote a secret principle. An example of the secret use of a sigil for the zodiacal sign Pisces is given under Christchurch.

Signs of the Zodiac

The twelve equal-arc divisions (each of 30 degrees) of the ecliptic, or imagined path of the sun. Figure 16 sets out the twelve images associated with these signs, from Aries (the Ram) to Pisces (the Fishes).

Swimming

A method of establishing a suspected witch's guilt or innocence: the suspect was usually tied, fingers to toes, and dropped into deep water. If she swam, she was a witch (the waters of baptism rejecting her evil), but if she sank, and therefore sometimes drowned, she was innocent. For an example of such swimming, see St Andrew's – Witch Hill (page 182), and Tring (page 99).

Sylphs

The beings of the **element** of air: they are usually represented as diminutive, winged creatures.

Sympathetic Magic

Sympathetic Magic is that branch of practical magic involved with attempting to influence a person or a thing, for good or evil, by means of images or symbols which resemble that person or thing, as a result of which a 'sympathy' is believed to exist between the symbol and the thing itself. The use of a **poppet** in witchcraft is an example of sympathetic magic, for the doll is believed to resemble a person (to establish a 'sympathy' with that person), as a result of which it is possible to transfer hurt from the poppet directly to the person. A more crude example of sympathetic magic is when a witch or a magician takes a stone, or a piece of wood, and, after naming this after a person, then damages it, in the belief that this damage would be transferred to the person whose name it bears.

Undines

The beings of the **element** of water: they are usually represented as diminutive creatures with fluid-like bodies, sometimes with wings.

Vesica Piscis

The two words are Latin, meaning approximately 'fish bladder', but in occult symbolism it is used to denote a particular structure, the magical form of which has a deep numerological and geometric significance. It was used as an occult symbol in ancient Egyptian art.

Virtue

The name once given to the secret **astral** or **etheric** principle inherent in a material form. It was believed that such virtue came from the stars, or from the stellar realm, and was the link between spirit and matter. See Trellech (page 135).

Vril

An extraordinary occult nature-power, said to have been used in **Atlantis**. For an account, see Knebworth (page 94).

Witch

A person (according to some mediaeval legal definitions) who agrees to aid the Devil in his evil ways. Sometimes this agreement is by means of written Pact.

Witch Pricking

The practice (especially in the 17th century) of pricking suspected witches on their supposed **devil's marks**, to prove that they were indeed witches. Distinguish from **witch scratching**, however.

Witch Scratching

Drawing the blood of a witch or warlock in the belief that they could afterwards do no harm. A modern example of this belief is recorded under Sidbury (page 53).

Witch-stone

Any memorial (especially in Scotland) linked with witchcraft, either legendary (as at Kempock) or historical (as at Forres).

Woodwose

One of the names for a satyr or faun of British mythology: a wild-man of the woods. The origin of the term is obscure.

Zodiacal Man

An image of the human being in which the twelve signs of the zodiac are linked with twelve parts of the body (figure 36). Table 1 (page 15) in the Introduction sets out the traditional associations between the zodiac and the human frame.

Figure 36 *Zodiacal man, from a French 'Shepherd's Calendar' of the later 15th century.*

The West Country

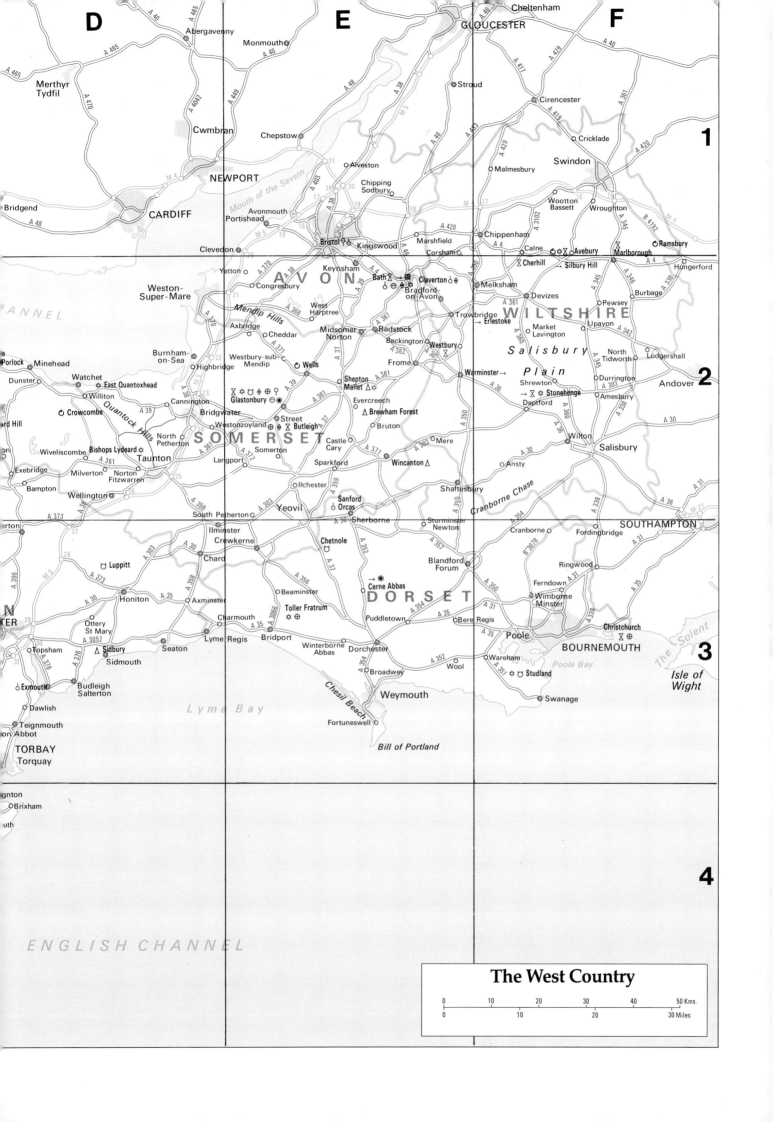

The West Country

0	10	20	30	40	50 Kms.
0		10		20	30 Miles

Avebury, Wiltshire

F1 SU 0969

The village of Avebury not only nestles into a huge complex of stone circles, earthworks and avenues over 1,400 yards/1,280 metres in circumference, but many of the houses (as well as the church) were partly built from stone pillaged from this ancient site. It is likely that there were originally well over a hundred standing stones on this 29-acre/12-hectare site, but only twenty-seven remain, the places of those missing being marked by ugly concrete stumps, favoured by those given to the excavation and restoration of such sites. The interesting thing about Avebury is that each standing stone appears to have a personality of its own – not merely in terms of shape and texture, but also in terms of the 'feeling' which it exudes. This may be a result of the stones being unshaped by human hands, but some say it could also be a result of the ancient practice (mentioned still in some occult books) whereby the priests would charge individual stones with a guardian spirit or earth-being (not to be confused with the earth elemental, popularly called the 'gnome'). I have heard of people receiving electric shocks when touching these stones in certain places – the 19th-century occultist A.P. Sinnett sets out why this should be so, when he wrote of manipulation of 'magnetic currents'.

Although it is not a lintelled monument like **Stonehenge** (The West Country), Avebury is probably the most impressive of the circled remains in England.

The variety of the surrounding related sites, such as Silbury Hill (said to be the largest man-made hill in Europe), the Kennet Avenue (50 feet/15.2 metres wide, marked by pairs of sarsens 80 feet/24.4 metres apart), Windmill Hill (a causewayed enclosure and cemetery), and the West Kennet long barrow, as well as the numerous processional ways marked by sarsens, earth-work mounds and causeways in the immediate vicinity, point to Avebury being one of the most important of religious or ceremonial centres of the ancient western world.

In the parish church is a 12th-century font which is carved with the image of a winged serpent, which is either paying homage to a bishop, or biting his foot. Such images of the winged serpent are often seen as relating to the so-called 'serpent power' of the pagan world, but in fact the serpent, dragon and related basilisk were used as Christian symbols of the Devil from very early times.

■ *Avebury is on the A4361, south of Swindon.*

Sarsens from the megalithic circles, alignments and avenues at Avebury.

Silbury Hill, Wiltshire →

F1 SU 1169

Almost a mile/2 km from **Avebury**, on the Marlborough–Chippenham road, which wisely deflects to go around it, is a huge man-made mound called Silbury Hill. While it is the largest such mound in Europe, and is certainly linked with several leys which cross Salisbury, no-one is sure why it was constructed, though it has been calculated that it would have taken gangs of up to 700 men ten years to move and pack the 1.25 million cubic feet/354,000 cubic metres from which it is constructed. The earliest part of the mound was erected just over 4,000 years ago, and it seems to have been enlarged at three or even four different points in history. Inevitably, stories of vast treasures buried beneath it have circulated for ages, and it was largely to discover such hidden wealth that the earliest attempts to dig into the mound were made, in 1776 (with a vertical shaft) and 1849 (with a horizontal shaft). A modern shaft was also dug between 1967–70, though for archaeological purposes: these researches showed that the mound was built on very similar principles of inner-platform construction as that used by the ancient Egyptians in pyramid-building.

■ *Silbury Hill is to the north of the A4, to the west of Marlborough, a few hundred yards or metres from the A4361 turning to Avebury, from which road an excellent view of the hill may be had.*

Weathered standing stones of the prehistoric Avebury Circle.

Bath, Avon ⧖ → ⌸ ☿ ☉ ☿ ✡

E2 ST 7464

Bath, like the city of **Wells** (The West Country) is one of the few cities in Britain with a name which points to its mythico-magical origins, for it is said that it was the site of a curative healing spring which removed the leprosy of King Bladud. It was this Bladud who longed to fly, and who manufactured wings with which he leapt from the top of the Temple of Minerva (thereby anticipating the presence of Rome in Bath by about a thousand years), whence he fell to his death. In the Roman Museum is the so-called Medusa Mask, a protective magic amulet much used by the Romans, which is probably not an image of one of the Gorgons as some maintain (the hair does not appear to consist of intertwining snakes, as in the genuine Gorgon images against the evil eye), but a pagan sun god. Perhaps of more immediate interest to occultists are the remains of a leaden curse, written in reversed Latin, intended to be thrown into a sacred spring to bring harm to an enemy. In recent times, a maze has been constructed on the east bank of the river, above the weir.

Abbey Church ✡ ☿ ☉ ☿

The Abbey Church at Bath has its own special connection with occult matters. After the abbey and lands had been surrendered to the rapacious Henry VIII in 1539, Prior Holeway, the incumbent at that time, continued to live in the Priory House in front of the abbey. Here he carried on his passionate study of alchemy, collecting around him an important school of alchemical research which included the alchemist Thomas Charnock, perhaps the most important student of Holeway. It is interesting to speculate to what extent they were aware that many of the symbols on the fabric of the abbey church were alchemical? One of the most famous are the ladders to heaven, climbed by angels on the west front. Six angels climb each of the two ladders, and one of the angels 'falls', to become a devil. It is generally believed that of all the angels a third 'fell', or rebelled against God.

During the First World War the image of a soldier's face developed on a wall in the abbey, near the recently established war memorial. It attracted such crowds of visitors to the place that the authorities took steps to efface the image. (For a similar instance, see **Oxford** [Christ Church]). In the north aisle of the abbey immediately in front of the porch entrance is the (broken) memorial stone to the Reverend Joseph Glanvill who died in 1680. As a result of his study of witchcraft, hauntings and allied phenomena, he has been dubbed the 'father of modern psychical research'. Later one of the early members of the Royal Society, Glanvill was among those deputised to report on the **Tedworth** Drummer haunting, and his experiences during the investigation increased his interest in such 'witchcraft'. Being a good churchman, he was convinced that such happenings as the Tedworth hauntings were the Devil's work, yet he also felt that the new methods of science could explain the supernatural. Eventually he wrote several books on the basis of his researches into the Drummer and other similar strange manifestations. In the meantime he gathered around him a band of like-minded people with the aim of systematically investigating hauntings, apparitions, and what are nowadays called poltergeists. The group met

regularly in Ragley Hall, Warwickshire, and was to have a considerable influence on the development of interest in psychic phenomena. The title page of his book *Saducismus Triumphatus* illustrated some famous cases of curious happenings, cases of witchcraft and hauntings in Britain. These include the Tedworth Drummer (page 83), a witch of Somerset, the levitation of Richard Jones at **Shepton Mallet**, the witch sabbat at **Wincanton**, and the case of a Scottish witch. Glanvill died a year before this famous book· was published.

■ *Bath is on the A4(T). The maze is most easily approached by way of the stairway towards the river weir, from Pulteney Bridge, and is best studied from the modern bridge over the weir. The abbey church is central, to the west of the River Avon.*

A detail of the West front of Bath cathedral showing angels ascending a ladder, an occult image derived from alchemy.

Higher Gunstone Lane, Bideford, the site of the meeting between a witch and the Devil.

Bideford, Devon △

C2 SS 4526

In 1682 Temperance Lloyd, a reputed witch, was accused of casting spells on one of her neighbours by means of sympathetic magic. She was searched for a witch-teat, and afterwards confessed that she had indeed met the Devil (who came to her in the form of a huge black man) on the 30 September, 'in a certain street or lane in the town of Biddiford aforesaid, called Higher Gunstone lane'. She also admitted that an evil spirit, in the form of a lion, would at times come into her house, and spend the night with her, using her body as it wished. Another suspect, Susanna Edwards, who admitted to being a member of the same witches' coven was tried in the same hearing at Exeter and also claimed to have met the Devil, this time dressed in black, in 'a field called Parsonage Close in the town of Biddiford'. Both Temperance Lloyd and Susanna Edwards were hanged on the 5 September 1682. Parsonage Close appears to have been swallowed up by 19th-century expansion, but Higher Gunstone Lane still exists, and shows traces of 17th-century buildings.

■ *Bideford is immediately to the south of the A39(T), west of Barnstaple. Higher Gunstone Lane runs up the hill to the west of the town.*

Bishop's Lydeard, Somerset ✡

D2 ST 1629

In the parish church there is a late 15th-century Green Man, the head and extensive foliations carved in wood relief against a painted red background of a bench-end.

■ *Bishop's Lydeard is on the A358, north-west of Taunton.*

Bodmin, Cornwall ◉

B3 SX 0767

The restored St Guron's well stands to the west of St Petroc's church: a late mediaeval relief (again restored in the 18th century) on the south face of the well-cover shows St Guron at the well. No records exist of examples of the well's healing power in modern times, but in the 18th century it was highly regarded as a specific against all eye troubles, and the official guide to St Petroc's points out that various streams run under the churchyard. It is therefore likely the well had been in use for some centuries before the introduction of Christianity to the area. St Guron is said to have established the first Christian monastery here circa AD 500, shortly before the Welsh prince St Petroc settled here, to make Bodmin the 'Abode of Monks'. There are some splendid demon gargoyles on the 15th-century tower.

■ *Bodmin is on the A30(T), and St Petroc's church stands to the north of this road, to the north-east of the town.*

Bodmin Moor, Cornwall ⋈

B3 SX 1975

The bleak moor is scattered with the flotsam and jetsam of ancient occultism and magic, sometimes more mythological than historical. The inevitable associations with King Arthur figure in the so-called bed on Trewortha Tor, which is more a coffin than a bed, weathered and hard. An ancient enclosure, still called King Arthur's Hall, dates from before any English king. We have also near Camelford the supposed site of Arthur's last battle, the site of his legendary palace, and the dark pool of Dozmary into which he threw his magical sword Excalibur. More historically reliable is the Doniert Stone between Redgate and Minions, for King

Bizarre rock formations above the Cheesewring, Bodmin Moor.

Doniert did exist: he was a chieftain, who was drowned in the river Fowey in 878. Even closer in time were the Knight's Templars, who had a chapel in the place still called Temple. Near the curious Devil's Cheesewring, which balances 18 feet/5.5 metres over the edge of a quarry beyond Minions, are the three ancient rings, some 3,500 years old, now called the Hurlers: legend says they were humans turned to stone for playing the game of hurling on a Sunday. The Trethevy Quoit, on a hill in St Cleer, is just as ancient, and is probably the best ancient burial chamber in Cornwall. The dark eye of Bodmin Moor is the Dozmary Pool, an alien reflection of darkness even on a sunny day, associated with Arthur and his dark-self, Jan Tregeagle. There are also less mythological ghosts on Bodmin, for the ghosts of a woman and a sailor (murdered quite separately) still haunt Rough Tor. See **Bolventor, Camelford—Dymond Monument, Cheesewring,** and **St Cleer.**

■ *Bodmin Moor is now cut by the A30(T), and stretches from Camelford (south of which is Rough Tor), down to the Dozmary Pool, as far as Warleggan.*

Bolventor, Cornwall   ⛌ ♂

B3 SX 1777

Dozmary Pool   ⛌

With a 30-acre/12.5-hectare extent, the largest natural expanse of water on Bodmin Moor, this brooding, reed-fringed and featureless pool is the centre of a complex mythology. In romantic literature it is the pool into which the dying King Arthur had his knight Bedivere throw his sword Excalibur. The sword was caught by a magical hand before it hit the waters – a symbolism which some may link with the esotericism of the zodiac, portraying the circle of space between the first sign of the zodiac (the sword of Mars) and the last sign Pisces (waters). In mythology, it is the bleak pool in which Jan Tregeagle, of Cornish mythology, is condemned to moan away his penitance, emptying the waters with a limpet shell. One of the ironies in the Tregeagle myth is that the waters were supposed to be endless, for the Dozmary Pool was long considered bottomless – until it dried up in 1869!

Dozmary Pool on Bodmin Moor, the lake into which Arthur's sword was thrown, after his death.

Jamaica Inn ☿

Dramatised and popularised by Daphne du Maurier in her novel of the same name as a setting for smuggling (which is at least historically true), romanticised for tourists by the present owners, Jamaica Inn is the site of a haunting by a sailor-smuggler who was murdered there in the 18th century.

■ *The Dozmary Pool lies to the south-east of Bolventor, and is signposted off the A30(T) along a minor road. The pool lies on the eastern side of the road to St Neot, and must not be confused with the Colliford Lake Reservoir, which is to the west. Jamaica Inn is to the north of the A30(T), south of Bolventor.*

Braunton, Devon ✡ ☿

C2 SS 4836

St Brannock's church

The 16th-century carved chestnut pews contain several occult and esoteric symbols, but perhaps the most interesting images are those on the roof bosses, highly stylised relief designs which remind one of Celtic coins. The subjects are mainly Christian, but there is also an image of a man being swallowed by a dragon, in the traditional initiation symbolism, a pelican feeding her young with her own blood (which, while Christian in symbolism, is derived from the ancient alchemical stream of imagery), and a striking triple-face, with only four eyes, a clever graphic commentary on the idea of 'three in one'. Among the roof bosses are some interesting esoteric images.

It is said that St Brannock (whose name lives on in the name Braunton) had a vision which told him to build a chapel where he first encountered a sow with her piglets. The vision was fulfilled at Braunton, and a gilded roof-boss shows a sow with several suckling young.

■ *Braunton is on the A361 north-west of Barnstaple.*

Brewham Forest, Somerset △

E2 ST 7236

Julian Cox, who was later hanged as a warlock at Taunton, in 1664, confessed to attending many witch sabbats in Brewham Forest, where he met the Devil 'in the shape of a black Man', and entered into written pact with him, in exchange for his own soul. The 17th-century historian Joseph Glanvill refers to these sabbats, and records that those who attended them were especially proficient in making wax figurines, which they then subjected to an evil 'baptisism' and used as deadly amulets. The witch flying through the air in the panel from Glanvill's book is said to be a picture of Julian Cox, returning from a Brewham Forest sabbat. For more information on Glanvill, see **Bath** (Abbey Church).

■ *Brewham Forest is to the north-east of Brewham, signposted off the A359, north of Bruton.*

Bristol, Avon ♀ ☿

E1 ST 5973

Thomas Parkes, who lived in the late 17th century in the Temple parish of Bristol was by trade a gunsmith, but he also made a little money casting horoscopes for locals. His interest in the occult increased, and he was soon using rather superficial grimoires in order to raise demons. Rather than demons, he appears to have succeeded in raising fairies, 'in the shape of little girls, about a foot and a half high', who spoke with shrill voices. In later attempts to raise spirits, however, monstrous shapes appeared in the forms of bears, lions and serpents. These were the forms in which the magical grimoires insisted that the devils would first appear. After that experience, 'he was never well so long as he lived'.

Another encounter with spirits in Bristol in the 19th century also appears to have resulted in demonism. It was arranged by some people working through a number of mediums, including a retired photographer called John Beattie. He appears to have been very sceptical of the numerous spirit photographs which were then all the rage, and so he undertook to make pictures of a sitting or seance held by a group of friends. The first two days of experiments produced nothing extraordinary, but eventually strange forms and shapes began to develop on his sensitive plates. This series of sittings between 1872 and 73 produced some thirty-two quite remarkable photographs showing 'extras' ranging from scarcely defined areas of light to frightening humanoid images. One historian described the pictures in the *Journal of the American Society for Psychical Research* as 'perhaps the most remarkable series of experiments ever made on this subject'.

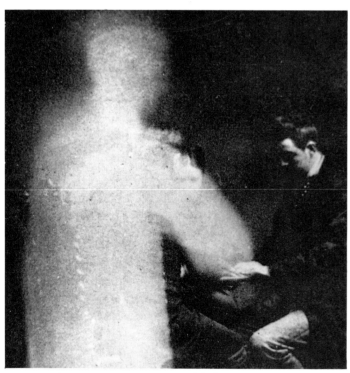

A spirit photograph taken at a seance organized by John Beattie in Bristol between 1872 and 1873.

Brown Willy *See* Slaughter Bridge

Butleigh, Somerset ⊕ ♎ ♊

E2 ST 5233

This village was chosen by Catherine Maltwood as the centre of her supposed earth-zodiac (misnamed the Glastonbury Zodiac), which covered a circle about 9 miles/ 14.5 km in diameter through Somerset with the supposed images of the zodiacal signs or constellations. By tracing lines and correspondences or connections between places, roads, ancient marks, tracks and field-systems on the Ordnance Survey map, she drew up what she took to be twelve images of the zodiac, as set out in diagrammatic form in the illustration. Since the constellations are not signs, and

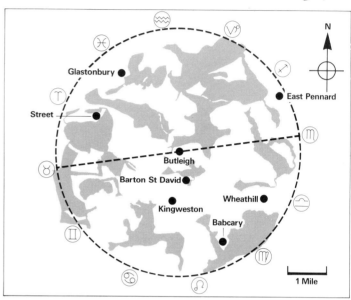

the images she traced bear no relation to the ancient images of the constellations she named, it seems that the 'zodiac' is a figment of her imagination. The figure certainly does not represent a zodiac, which consists of twelve equal-arc sectors, for it has on the periphery only ten images, each of unequal extent, within the outer radius. Maltwood called it 'a temple of the stars', but she made no attempt to correlate her figures with stellar patterns. Some writers link this supposed zodiac with a passing reference made by the occultist John Dee (see **Glastonbury Tor**), but it is likely that Dee was not referring to a zodiac as a vast earthworks, but to something which found a correspondence with the stars – a common enough notion in mediaeval esoteric lore. He wrote, 'thus is astrolgie and astronomie carefullie and exactley married and measured in a scientific reconstruction of the heavens which shews that the ancients undestode all which today the lerned know to be factes'. Such could be said of a prehistoric circle of stones, as for example may be seen in **Stonehenge** or **Callanish** (Scotland). Mrs Maltwood relates the identification of the supposed Glastonbury zodiac with Sumeria and Chaldea (though it is evident that she knew nothing of either Sumerian or Chaldean astrology), which she imagined was inherited by the Druids – yet another imaginative leap. In spite of the dubious nature of the earthwork zodiac, very many people believe in its existence, and the 'tracing of the figures' has become something of a pilgrimage.

■ *Butleigh is signposted to the east of the B3151, south of Glastonbury.*

Camelford, Cornwall ♂ X
B3 SX 1083

Some say that Camelford is the site of the ancient (and probably legendary) Camelot of Arthurian fame. The name of the village is scarcely the link, however, for it derives from the Cornish *camalan*, meaning bend in the river, a place where people forded. The word became 'camel', so that today one finds a golden camel on top of the town hall, the only camel to be born of a river. The scene of Arthur's last battle is traced for tourists to **Slaughter Bridge**, about a mile further up this same river.

Dymond Monument ♂

Among the many ghosts which are said to haunt Bodmin Moor the most well-documented is that of Charlotte Dymond, who, it is generally believed, was murdered in 1844, and whose shade has wandered the moors ever since. The Charlotte Dymond memorial, an inscribed upright stone, stands close to the Helland Bridge over the River Camel, on the edge of Bodmin Moor, about half a mile/1 km from Rough Tor. It was raised by locals to commemorate the supposed murder of this servant girl by one Matthew Weeks, her jealous lover. Recent research by Pat Munn has suggested quite convincingly that Charlotte committed suicide, and that Weeks was hanged for the crime as a result of a conspiracy. The area around the monument was once holy – a chapel, dedicated to St Michael, originally stood on the top of Rough Tor, though it has long been dismantled.

■ *Camelford is on the A39(T). The monument is on the moorland side of the Helland Bridge, below Rough Tor, which is signposted from the B3266 south of Camelford.*

The Dymond Memorial at Camelford, a memorial to a murder (or was it murder?) on Bodmin Moor.

Cerne Abbas, Dorset → ◉
E3 ST 6601

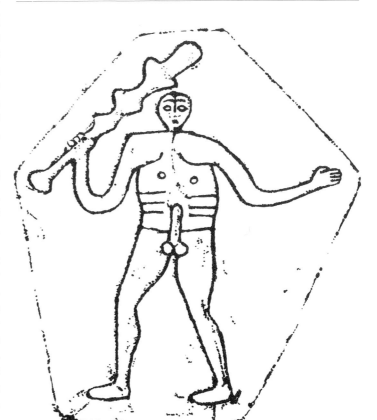

The Cerne Abbas Giant is a huge outline figure dug into the slope of the downs quarter of a mile/½ km from the village itself. The distinctive knobbed club in his hand, and the huge phallus, has suggested to some historians that it is Roman in origin, and perhaps an image of Hercules, with his club – though the Romans were not accustomed to cutting such figures into the hills. The figure is 180 feet/54.8 metres high and the phallus is 30 feet/9.1 metres long. In the 13th century the churchman Walter of Coventry noted that this part of the world had been the site of the worship of the pagan god Helith, which has led some people to suggest that the giant is his idol. The earliest known drawing of the figure (from 1764, in the *Gentleman's Magazine*) indicates that a few changes have been made to the outline, which is actually a two-foot/60 cm deep trench filled with chalk. There is a legend which connects St Augustine with the giant, for it tells how he and his companions came to convert the local heathens, but were driven away, tails having been tied to their backs, in mockery. Augustine prayed God to give all children born in Cerne Abbas village tails until such time as their parents embraced Christianity. Even today some young women will go to the figure (usually in secret) and walk seven times around the phallus in the belief that this ensures or increases fertility.

High beyond the giant is a rectangular earthwork called the Trendle, which many suppose to have been a sacred precinct connected with a fertility cult: folklorists are at pains to remind us that until recently the fertility cult was re-enacted by the maypole dancing on the Trendle.

The church has competed with all this pagan magic to some extent, by declaring the well at the end of the churchyard holy. It is said to have been declared a holy well by St

Augustine, though in modern times the waters have been demoted, so that now they merely grant wishes. Significantly, those asking a wish of the well should turn their back to the giant, and drink the waters from a laurel leaf, making the wish while facing the church. In this way, the pagan, classical and Christian requirements are all met.

■ *Cerne Abbas is on the A352 north of Dorchester. The giant is signposted to the east of the road.*

Chambercombe *See* Ilfracombe

Cheesewring, Cornwall ⚥ ♉

B3 SX 2671

The exotically weathered balancing act known as the Cheesewring on **Bodmin Moor** is so-named because of its association with the Devil: the imaginative see in it the petrified remains of the Devil's attempt to make cheese by squeezing curds in a cheesecloth. The 18-foot/5.5-metre high Cheesewring itself is set dramatically on the edge of the man-made quarry beyond Minions, and the remoteness of the setting has led to a bevy of legends attaching itself to the dramatically shaped stone: for example, it is said that at cockcrow the top stone revolves on its socle three times – though such a tale is told of many similar outlandish stones.

■ *The Cheesewring is best approached by driving or walking to the end of the cart-track to the north of Minions (signposted to the west of the B3254): the stones are visible on the north-east cliff of the quarry, and may be approached by the pathway to Stowe's Hill around the north edge.*

Cherhill, Wiltshire ⚥

F2 SU 0370

On the hillside to the south of Cherhill is a chalk figure of a horse, said to have been cut in 1780 by a Dr Alsop, who shouted instructions from the village green of Calne to the labourers (students from Marlborough College) through a megaphone. There is some historical reason to suppose that this hill figure was a new cutting based on a much more ancient one, something like that still preserved at **Uffington** (Central England).

■ *The horse, visible in many places between Calne and Cherhill on the A4, is best seen from the hills to the north of Cherhill.*

Chetnole, Dorset ♉

E3 ST 6007

The 16th-century tower of the church of St Peter has some of the most interesting gargoyles in the south of England. The finest of these is a vast demonic creature, with small human

heads in place of eyes, the arms of the humans doubling as the cheeks of the monster: another is a grotesque manikin, straining as though at stool.

■ *Chetnole is signposted to the east of the A37, south of Yeovil.*

Christchurch, Dorset ⚥ ⊕

F3 SZ 1592

The priory church at Christchurch has several myths attached to the story of its building, among which the most persistent is that a mysterious and unidentified carpenter who worked on the site was Christ himself. In the nave of the church is a tombstone (dated 1688) with an inscription which incorporates the sigil for the zodiacal sign Pisces. In the secret symbolism of Christianity, Pisces was linked with the Christ, perhaps because (as St Augustine pointed out in the 5th century) the Greek word for fish was used as a secret acrostic for Christ. In the Christchurch tombstone the sigil for Pisces is placed immediately in front of the word church, so that together the sigil and the word read Christchurch.

■ *Christchurch is signposted to the south of the A337: the church is to the south of the town.*

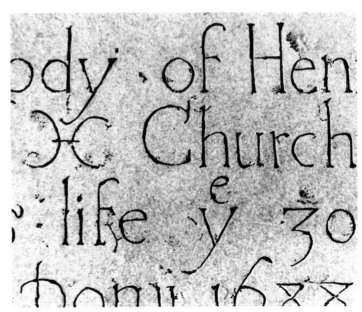

The secret symbol of zodiacal Pisces on a grave slab in the Christchurch Priory. The sigil for Pisces is used to represent the name of 'Christ', so that the secret word means 'Christchurch'.

Chun Castle *See* Madron

Claverton, Avon ♂ ☿

E2 ST 7864

In the churchyard of St Mary's church is the extraordinary mausoleum to the philanthropist Ralph Allen who died in 1764. Allen helped the architect John Wood in his creation of 18th century Bath. It is likely that Allen, like Wood, was a Mason; and his mausoleum is covered by a huge hollow pyramid. This would be remarkable in any situation, but what is particularly of interest is that in the grounds above the churchyard is the American Museum, formerly Claverton Manor. The Great Seal of America, designed as an occult device, mainly under the direction of Masons, has on the obverse an image of a pyramid, with thirteen layers of stone, in keeping with the number of original states in the Union. The number was so important to the designers that they dropped a letter from the Latin inscription (a quotation from Virgil's *Aeneid*) so that it consisted of only thirteen letters. It is interesting that although the pyramid over Allen's mauseoleum has fifteen layers of stones, only thirteen can be seen from the lower graveyard because there is a parapet (in the 18th century the upper graveyard did not exist as part of the churchyard). One wonders what secret thread connects this beautiful village with America?

Among the gravestones worthy of note in St Mary's churchyard is the oldest known, that of a churchwarden who died in 1727, which has what appears to be a skull and cross-bone on the west side. Analysis shows this to be much more than a skull and cross-bone, however, for there is a vertical band running through the skull to the hour-glass, a device which is found in several alchemical diagrams. A few of the soldiers killed in the English civil wars were buried beneath the church wall, and inevitably stories of hauntings have circulated.

■ *Claverton is to the west of the A36(T), south-east of Bath. The church is signposted from the Claverton approach road, and is on a hill to the west.*

Colebrooke, Devon ✡

C3 SS 7700

In the church of St Andrew in this hilltop hamlet are some highly symbolic Norman corbels and ancient bench-ends (probably early 16th century) the most interesting of which is a carving of a pagan woodwose.

■ *Colebrooke is signposted to the south of the A377, north-west of Exeter.*

Crowcombe, Somerset ☿

D2 ST 1336

The magnificent bench-ends in the parish church include a very impressive Green Man, and one or two curious symbols, but the most famous of these wooden reliefs depicts two men attempting to kill a monster, which has two legs, two heads and wings. In the lower left-hand corner another dragon is spouting grape-laden vines from its

The pyramid-roofed mausoleum of Ralph Allen (d. 1764) at Claverton.

mouth, perhaps in reference to some forgotten earth magic. Some authorities insist that the upper dragon is the Crowcombe Worm, which once lived in Shervage Wood nearby (on a diet of ponies, sheep and people) and which was killed by a woodcutter. However, the Worm did not have two heads, so the truth of the bench-end story is lost to us.

■ *Crowcombe is on the A358, north-west of Taunton.*

Culbone, Somerset

D2 SS 8546

Culbone church is the smallest church in England still in use. It has a leper window, to enable those stricken with this disease to watch services without coming in contact with the congregation within the church. See also **Porlock**.

■ *Porlock is on the A39. Culbone church is a (signposted) 2-mile/3-km walk to the west of Porlock Weir.*

Durgan, Cornwall

A4 SW 772277

In Glendurgan House gardens (National Trust) north of Durgan is a laurel-hedge maze which is said to have been designed in 1833. It is a genuine maze: it is quite possible to lose oneself in its narrow curvilinear design. See also **Wing** (Central England) and **Saffron Walden** (Eastern Counties).

■ *Durgan is on the north bank of the Helford river, 4 miles/6.5 km south-west of Falmouth. Glendurgan House is to the north of Durgan.*

East Quantoxhead, Somerset

D2 ST 1343

The parish church in East Quantoxhead has some of the most fascinating 17th-century symbolic bench-ends in England. The symbols range from pseudo-classical monsters to hermetic devices of a very high order of esotericism. The series of 'Seals of Solomon' on one bench-end are of particular interest because of the floral inserts at the centres of each of the seals. The Seal itself is made from two interpenetrating triangles, and in the occult symbolism this is believed to represent the four elements of earth, air, fire and water. The inner space within the interpenetrating triangles is designated the symbolic place of the invisible etheric, or fifth element (the quintessence) which, it is believed, holds together the manifestations of the four elements that lie behind phenomena. In this bench-end, however, the usually empty space is filled with a floral design, reminding us that in alchemical and hermetic circles the flower was frequently used as a symbol of the etheric. On this level alone the East Quantoxhead seals are of a very high order: however, the symbolism is of an even higher quality, for the appearance of a central circle or boss within the flower enables one to trace within the figures a numerological sequence – one central boss, two triangles, three points to each triangle, four petals to each flower, five for the quintessence, six points to the triangle, and so on, through to twelve.

■ *East Quantoxhead is to the north of the A39, west of Bridgwater.*

Edington *See* Erlestoke

An exotic 17th-century bench-end, at the parish church East Quantoxhead.

Spirit photographs taken by William Hope at Exmouth in 1924. There are four spirit 'extras' in the picture. (Inset) *The son's horse, Tommy.*

Egloskerry, Cornwall ✡ ☾

B3 SX 2786

The blocked-up door in the north wall of the church, with its early Saxon dragon, is almost certainly an early example of a Devil's Door. Esoteric symbols from many periods may be found within the church. The slate tomb in the south porch bears mermaids and unicorns in the decorative scroll-work, while even the modern stained glass (1905) deviates from the norm by showing all four Archangels of the Seasons and Directions – it is usual for Michael, Gabriel and Raphael to be shown in church symbolism, but less usual for Uriel, the Archangel charged with the continuance and health of the earth, to be presented in symbolic form.

■ *Egloskerry is on the minor road to the west of Langore and St Stephens, which is on the B3524 to the west of Launceston.*

Erlestoke, Wiltshire →

F2 ST 9654

Several of the houses on the road which passes through this delightful village have inset into their facades a number of stones, a few of which appear to have been so placed for magical reasons. Some of the figures are clearly 17th-century psuedo-classical carvings, as for example the image of Venus on one of the houses to the north of the road. Others are derived from patterns replete with magical significance, relating to initiation lore. One may presume, therefore, that while some are probably decorative, others were intended to ward off evil forces, as lapidary amulets.

The source of the carvings is not known, but local historians suggest that they came from a house at Edington, to the west along the B3098, dismantled in the 18th century.

■ *Erlestoke lies directly on the B3098. Houses to the north and south have the stones inset in their facades, though the best examples are to the south.*

Exmouth, Devon ☿

D3 TL 2545

William Hope of **Crewe** was probably the most famous English psychic photographer in the 1920s. The accompanying photograph (opposite, bottom right) was taken while on holiday at Exmouth, in 1924. It shows his psychic assistant Mrs Buxton, and her family, on the steps of their holiday caravan, along with a number of uninvited 'spirit extras'. Just above the head of Mrs Buxton is a wreath of ectoplasmic fluff (a characteristic of Hope's psychic pictures which has led many psychic investigators to doubt his genuineness) within which is the face of her son, who had died the previous year. To the left of this spirit boy is the head of a horse, Tommy, which had belonged to her son (a photograph of the living horse is inset for comparison). The one other extra (not wrapped in the ectoplasmic cotton-wool) is the face in Mr Buxton's waistcoat, to the right of her son. Mrs Buxton saw it in the face of her husband's brother, who had died in the previous year.

■ *Exmouth is on the A376, south-east of Exeter.*

Garrow Tor *See* Slaughter Bridge

Details of masonry transferred from older buildings and incorporated into 17th century houses for amuletic or decorative purposes. (See Erlestoke.)

Glastonbury, Somerset ◎ ◉ ✇ ✡ ♉ ⊕ ♀

E2 ST 4938

The connection drawn between Glastonbury and the legends of the Holy Grail, as with Joseph of Arimathea, is nothing more than pseudo-occult romance, stemming from romantic literature developed in the 13th and 14th centuries. The imagery attached to Arimathea and his chalice, and indeed to his thorn, is nonetheless widespread in this part of the world, and is found in many curious stone images, frescoes and stained glass.

Abbey ✡ ◎ ✇ ◉

The centre of the excavated grounds of the mined abbey is marked with a plaque where the supposed remains of Arthur and Guinevere were discovered in 1191. It is certain, however, that the 'discovery' was arranged by ecclesiastical policy-makers to put Glastonbury on the lucrative pilgrimage routes. The ploy worked, and to this day the pilgrims still come, and the legends are daily on the increase.

In fact, the most important occult connection with Glastonbury is quite modern, for one of the archaeologists concerned with the discovery of the ancient walls, as with the restoration of the site, was Frederick Bligh Bond, who used spirit-writings in seances during the early parts of the present century (working mainly in Bristol) to help him in his research – perhaps one of the most interesting examples of amenuensis 'spirit-writing' on record. It was Bond who designed the circular cover on the Chalice Well, with a 'Celtic' pattern involving two interlinked circles, intended to symbolise the interpenetration of the material realm with the spiritual. The waters of the well are reddish (due to the high iron content) and it is said that this gave rise to its distinctive name – however, the earliest mythology of Glastonbury is linked with the chalice or Grail.

The abbey grounds and ruinous remains are replete with occult symbolism which is often missed by general tourists. Note, for example, the mediaeval fish inscribed in the fabric of the western side of the high wall of the abbey. More interesting occult remains have disappeared, however, for in the mediaeval period, William of Malmesbury refers to two pyramids, well over 25 feet/7.5 metres high, with carved inscriptions from an unknown language, in the abbey's cemetery.

The Glastonbury Thorn, which is to the left of the main public entrance to the grounds, is said to have been grown from a cutting brought to England by Joseph of Arimathea, of whom Jesus was a nephew. The story of Arimathea, which is entirely romantic, is well recorded in the pseudo-occult vein by the Reverend L.S. Lewis, one-time vicar of Glastonbury, who marshals a fascinating array of documentation in support of his arguments. See also **Strata Florida** (Wales and Western Counties).

Abbey Barn ⊕

The beautiful 14th-century barn of Glastonbury Abbey is now used as the Somerset Rural Life Museum. The figures of the evangelists on the four walls of the building remind us of the esoteric notion that the four evangelists were linked with the four signs of the zodiac, and hence with directions in space. The lion of Leo is the lion of St Mark, the eagle of St John is associated with Scorpio, the bull of Taurus is the bull of St Luke, while the Human Face of Matthew is the human water-bearer of Aquarius.

St Benignus Church ✇ ✿ ♉

On the tower of St Benignus church is a gargoyle referred to by a spirit of a 16th-century monk, communicating through automatic writing during the investigations being carried out by Frederick Bligh Bond, in the first decades of the present century. The monk claimed that he had carved the figure during his own lifetime, in the early 16th century, and that for a joke he had made it look like a demon from the side, but like the head of his abbot, with his hat and neck-decoration, from the front. 'God wot, I meant no harm,' the monk wrote after explaining what he had done. The demonic gargoyle preserves this double image of the abbot and demon to this day.

Inside the church is a shield bearing the rebus of the Abbot Bere, with jugs (holding beer) on either side of a cross. This rebus figure has been claimed to be the 'arms of Joseph of Arimathea', with the beer jugs taken as chalices, reference to the Holy Grail. However, coats of arms had not developed in the early days of Christianity, and in any case the rebus device was recognised in the 15th century.

Glastonbury Tor ✇ ✡ ♀ ◎

The occultist Dion Fortune saw the spiral terraces of the 552-foot/168.3-metre high Tor as 'two great coils, which were beyond all question a processional path . . . such mounts as this were always sacred to the sun.' The remains of the St Michael's church at the top of the tor is a reminder that sometimes England does have earthquakes, for the shell is said to have remained in the present form since being destroyed by a quake in the 13th century. However, the tower is certainly later than the 13th century, but there has been a Christian settlement on or near the tor since at least the 4th century, although the story which claims St Patrick as the first abbot of Glastonbury is certainly spurious. On the fabric of the inner tower someone has scratched the runes meaning 'this is the place of the thorn', perhaps in reference to Christ's thorn.

It is widely believed by the locals that 'Gwyn', the king of the fairies, held (and indeed still holds) his court on the tor's summit. There is a story to the effect that the Welsh St Collen, who lived at the foot of the tor, once climbed the hill (an act which is linked in the secret lore of fairytales with the notion of travelling on the astral plane, which is where fairies are supposed to have their proper realm) in search of King Gwyn. On the top he found a beautiful castle, teeming with small people, with Gwyn seated in great dignity on a golden throne. Collen had been taught that the fairyfolk were really demons, so he threw at them the holy water he had carried up the hill, and the entire company disappeared. Gwyn ap Nudd is said in Celtic mythology to be the Lord of Annwyn, a sort of Celtic shadow-realm something like the classical Hades, and it is quite possible that this figure has been merged with that of a fairy king.

■ *Glastonbury lies at the junction of the A361 and the A39, south-west of Bath. The Abbey Barn is to the south-east of the Abbey grounds, in Bere Lane. St Benignus church, sometimes called St Benedict's, is to the west of the Abbey, to the north of St Benedict's Close. The tor is visible from all approach roads.*

Glastonbury Tor at sunset.

A boss at Glastonbury Abbey showing a shield bearing the rebus of the Abbot Bere, said by some to be the coat of arms of Joseph of Arimathea.

Helston, Cornwall ⧗ ☿

A4 SW 6527

Those who derive the name of this town from 'Hell's Stone', and refer to the granite block in the wall of the Angel Hotel in support of their derivation, are on dubious ground: the word Helston has nothing to do with either hell or stones. Equally, the story that the annual Furry Dance, celebrated on 1 May at Helston, has something to do with the Devil being furry, is just as groundless. The word 'furry' is certainly from the root which gave us 'floral', and probably refers to a May celebration of springtime growth. The furry dance is now said to celebrate the fact that St Michael drove the Devil from the town. The Devil had appeared in the shape of a dragon, but as he soared off, his wings failed and he fell into a lake.

■ *Helston is on the A394, south-west of Truro.*

Ilfracombe, Devon ♂ ✡ ◉

C2 SS 5147

The beautifully maintained 16th-century Chambercombe Manor is open to the public, and visited mainly because of the many ghost-legends surrounding its history. Of particular interest is the story of the female ghost connected with a skeleton which was discovered walled up in a concealed attic room (now visible through a removed section of the partition): this story may have arisen from a romantic tale first published in the popular magazine *The Leisure Hour* for 1865 (No. 721 ff), and repeated more or less verbatim in several later books. Postcards as early as 1904 depict the 'ghost' of Lady Jane Grey, however, and the 'Coat of Arms bedroom' is still pointed out as the room of Lady Jane, though there is no documentation of either her real or ghostly sojourn in the manor. A modern clairvoyant has claimed to have seen the ghost of a monk in the tiny 15th-century chapel. Of very real interest are the early Tudor wainscot chairs with ornate esoteric and rebus symbols carved on them. The well in the garden of the manor is said to have healing properties.

■ *Ilfracombe is on the A361, north of Barnstaple. Chambercombe Manor is signposted, about 1½ miles/2.5 km to the south-east of the harbour.*

The much-haunted Chambercombe Manor at Ilfracombe.

Kennet Avenue *See* Avebury

Kilkhampton, Cornwall ✡

B3 SS 2511

The 15th-century church of St James contains some of the most interesting esoteric and mythological images in any church of Cornwall. Of particular interest are the 157 ornate bench-ends and panels, for among the Christian symbols (themselves of great beauty), coats of arms and trade emblems are several 'grotesques' of occult significance including demons and a Green Man. By far the most intriguing, however, is one bench-end which, while it may depict a shepherd, is significantly like the esoteric image in the well-known unnumbered card of the Tarot Pack, the Fool. It is therefore intriguing to compare this 15th-century carving with an 18th-century version of the card (page 11). The notion of the 'pilgrimage through life' which is the esoteric theme of the Tarot card is not out of place in a church dedicated to the patron saint of pilgrims.

Note also the excellent early 19th-century windows which portray Joseph of Arimathea, King Arthur, and other British mythological symbols.

■ *Kilkhampton is signposted on the A39(T), north of Stratton.*

A stained glass window depicting Joseph of Arimathea of the Grail Legends at Kilkhampton.

Launceston, Cornwall ✡ ⚏

B/C3 SX 3384

Above a chemist's shop in the High Street, near the lavishly carved exterior of St Mary Magdalene's church, is one of the last surviving alchemist symbols of the phoenix, sitting in its pyre of flames. The phoenix or Hermes bird (so-named after Hermes, the founder of the hermetic art of alchemy and occultism), or the Arabian bird, as it was called by alchemists, is one of the most enduring of occult symbols, linked by some with the notion of reincarnation, by others with historical periods, and (within Christian symbolism, derived from the ancient occultism) with the notion of spiritual rebirth. The story of the Hermes bird is complex, but essentially it maintains that once every 500 years the bird makes itself a nest, somewhere in Arabia, – then, with its own breath, it kindles a flame, sets fire to its coracle, and is consumed in the fire. As soon as all is reduced to embers, a new young phoenix is born from the ashes, and the life-cycle begins again. The Launceston symbol is one of the last outer signs of the fact that modern chemistry was born out of the researches of the alchemists.

- *Launceston is on the A30(T).*

The phoenix in the flames. An old chemist's shop sign, derived from alchemical symbolism, at Launceston.

Launceston *See also* Perranuthnoe

Lewannick, Cornwall ✡ 🔲

B3 SX 2780

The church is famous in most guide books for its Ogham stone (a pillar bearing writing in an ancient Celtic alphabet), but should be more renowned for its wonderful Norman font, which has geometric patterns of esoteric and occult symbols on each of its six faces. Two of these are illustrated: the first is a pentagram, the second and more interesting depicts a maze, the pathways of which lead to the cross.

- *Lewannick is signposted to the east of the A30T, south-west of Launceston.*

A pentagram and a maze-like device on the Norman font in the parish church of Lewannick, Cornwall.

Lewtrenchard, Devon ◎ ✡

C3 SX 4585

A Tudor house in the village, which has been converted into a hotel, incorporates in its woodwork and stonework a curious selection of symbols 'plundered' by the Rev Baring-Gould, whose family home it used to be. This Baring-Gould had a profound interest in symbolism, occultism and psychic studies, and wrote several works of interest to occultists, often with particular concern for the mythology of churches, church-hauntings, and so on: his *Yorkshire Oddities, Incidents and Strange Events* of 1900 is still easily acquired in second-hand bookshops.

The church in front of the hotel was restored by his grandfather and Gould himself, and though the results may be disappointing to a church-historian, they are fascinating for anyone interested in symbolism. Of particular interest is the bench-end depicting Michael standing on the belly of the dragon, holding his golden blade aloft in his right hand, and weighing the souls of the newly departed in his left hand.

The symbolism of this figure is replete with occult nuances – the golden-bladed sword is held in the right hand because this side of the body is linked with the sun, which in turn rules gold: Michael himself is said to be the archangelic ruler of the sun. On the other hand, the left side of the body is linked with the moon, and in occultism it is taught that the newly deceased must pass through the sphere of the moon (that is, in Christian terms, through purgatory) before entering the realms of heaven: this is why the balance is held in the left hand. In modern occultism, the dragon of the Michael imagery is linked specifically with the demon Ahriman, who was the dark demon of lies in the Zoroastrian magical lore.

- *Lewtrenchard is signposted to the south of the A30(T), east of Launceston.*

Luppitt, Devon ♉

D3 ST 1606

The Norman font in this village church is perhaps even more worthy of note that the impressive gargoyles on the north side. Around the outer well of the font are carved curious grotesques, and a pagan centaur (note especially the priapus, which at first sight may be taken for a tail). It is possible that the image of the demon swallowing the top of the human head is a symbolic representation of demonic possession, the idea being that the demon is in charge of the thinking of the human being it is attacking.

■ *Luppitt is signposted to the east of the A30(T), north of Honiton.*

Madron, Cornwall

A4 SW 4531

The erect remains of the Lanyon Quoit, a neolithic chambered tomb is nothing more than the bare skeleton of stonework which was once covered by earth. It has been suggested that the structure was used in astronomical surveys, conducted in many of the surrounding prehistoric centres, such as the Nine Maidens, the Men-an-Tol, the Chun Quoit and Chun Castle.

■ *The Lanyon Quoit is signposted on the road from Penzance to Morvah, across Green Burrow.*

Marlborough, Wiltshire

F1/2 SU 1969

In the grounds of Marlborough College is a terraced mound on which the castle once stood. It is said that the magician Merlin is buried here, and some claim that the name of the town (hence that of the college) is from the name Maerla, a belief enshrined in the town's Latin motto. However, Merlin was originally called Myrddin or Emrys.

■ *Marlborough is on the A4, and lies south of Swindon. The college is to the west of the town.*

Minions, Cornwall

B3 SX 2671

This village is said to be the highest in the county, and its fame rests on its proximity to the three stone circles popularly called the Hurlers on the moorland beyond. The axis of the central circle of stones lies east-west, which would suggest that this complex was (like **Stonehenge**) involved with calendrical sightings. Further up the hill behind these frozen dancers is the curious stone formation known as the 'Devil's **Cheesewring**', which balances on the edge of Stowe's Hill quarry, and is itself a quarry for legends and imaginings: folk legends insist that the top stone revolves three times on the lower pivot of stones, at cock crow – though the stone is too far from any village for the crowing of cocks to be heard.

■ *The Hurlers lie to the north-west of Minions, which is signposted to the west of the B3254, north of Liskeard. The Cheesewring stands at the head of a large quarry, further to the north of the village, at the head of a rough approach road from Minions.*

Morvah, Cornwall

A4 SW 4035

The Men-an-Tol, near Morvah, is a distinctive, if not unique, prehistoric monument, consisting of four stones, one now fallen, with two uprights (about 4 feet 6 inches/1.4 metres high) orientated on a line with the most distinctive polygonal slab through which an almost perfect 'porthole' has been cut. The monument, or whatever the stones represent, is said to be over 4,000 years old. Many explanations are given for the presence of such stones near prehistoric burial sites and stone circles: while those interested in folklore have suggested that the uprights form centres for the practice of contagious magic. Some, such as the astronomer Norman Lockyer, have suggested that they have an astronomical or astrological purpose, and Lockyer himself has convincingly pointed to sighting lines connected with other distant stones, much on the same basis as the modern theory of ley-lines, as well as to links between these and important star positions. In historic times the holed stones have been used for a variety of purposes – one either crawled through the hole, or was lifted through, to cure illness, to ensure the beneficial outcome of numerous activities or enterprises, such as engagements, childbirth, marriage, or as cure for such ailments as infertility, and so on. Jacquetta Hawkes mentions that the stone was also consulted by people who wished to know about their future love life.

■ *The Men-an-Tol is signposted from Morvah, and is approached by way of a well-signposted track across farmlands and moorland.*

The Men-an-Tol holed stone is one of the most famous of the prehistoric stones near Morvah.

Newquay, Cornwall ☽

A3 SW 8161

Of particular interest to occultists are the 19th-century dragons mounted on the roof of the house (now a shop) at the corner of Bank Street and Manor Road. These show Chinese influence, and have much the same intention as their Chinese lung-dragon counterparts – that they drive away evil from the place.

■ *Newquay is at the junction of the A3075 and the A3058 to the west of Bodmin.*

North Brentor, Devon ♂

C3 SX 4881

The story is told how the locals intended to build their church at the foot of the hill, but each night their building materials were moved miraculously to the top of the hill, so at length they settled for this as their building site: this is why the conical hill is still topped by a mediaeval church. Some insist that the stones were moved by the Devil, but it is more reasonable to suppose that the good daemons (the angels) are concerned with where churches are built. There are of course many stories about the frustrations involved in siting churches – especially those on the top of hills.

■ *North Brentor is signposted to the west of the A386. The hill on which the church is built is visible from far around.*

Perranuthnoe, Cornwall ⚔

A4 SW 5329

This small village looks onto a sea beneath which (it is said) lies the lost land of Lyonesse. This Lyonesse was supposedly a vast land, so many seaside villages of Cornwall must look over it, yet Perranuthnoe gains special mention because of later tales. According to the Saxon historians, Lyonesse was destroyed in 1099, on 11 November. Even now the local fishermen say that they can hear the bells of the submerged churches, tolling warning of the dangers in the Seven Stones reef which was part of this lost land, and some say that on a clear night one may see the roofs of houses beneath the waters. Legend elaborates the tale, however, and has two creatures escaping the inundation of the Atlantic – a man from Launceston and his horse, who were swifter than the sweep of waves, and managed to scramble ashore at Perranuthnoe. Some records merge with a more ancient mythology known even to the Greeks: there was once a whole land beyond the seas where Perranuthnoe is now the land's end – it was a land with many great cities and splendid people. Are such myths racial memories of the lost Atlantis, or the islands which occultists call Ruta and Daiyta, the last traces of that ancient culture to be submerged?

■ *Perranuthnoe is signposted to the south of the A394, to the west of Helston.*

Perranzabuloe, Cornwall ⚔ ✡

A4 SW 7752

Legend says that St Piran came to Cornwall from Ireland, miraculously floating on a millstone. Perhaps in reality he came in a coracle, which would be almost as much a miracle, though the story is sometimes explained in terms of the circular portable altar which he might have brought with him from Ireland in the 9th century.

Since his day, the church of St Piran he founded has been moved inland away from the encroaching waters, and the present building is mainly 18th century, though the font is Norman, and has, on either side of the image of the Mother and Child, little men in the posture which art historians call the 'orans' gesture, but which occultists recognise as an early form of the pentagram-gesture. There are interesting grotesques on the carved panels, now at the west end.

■ *Perranzabuloe is on the A3075, south of Newquay.*

Porlock, Somerset ⚔

D2 SS 8846

The curious truncated spire of St Dubricius church has led to several interesting stories, of which the most amusing is that the top of the spire was blown off in the horrendous gales of 1703, and landed at **Culbone**. The joke is that Culbone church is reputedly the smallest church in Britain still in regular use, and that the tower, while of different stone, is approximately the size that would complete the Porlock truncation. However, the Porlock spire is octagonal, the Culbone circular. Another story has the workmen who were building the Porlock spire (circa 1490) leaving their work to follow the hounds. There is no explanation as to why they did not come back. Were they the Devil's hounds of British mythology? Saint Dubricius (*Dyffrig* in Welsh) is said to have crowned King Arthur, which would set Arthurian mythology firmly in the early 6th century. On the roof of the nearby Castle Hotel is a weather-vane dragon.

■ *Porlock, and the church itself, is on the A39, west of Minehead.*

Porlock Weir *See* Culbone

Ramsbury, Wiltshire ☽

F1 SU 2771

In the parish church at Ramsbury is a cross shaft depicting a dragon, said to be of 9th-century workmanship. Although the friendly looking monster is biting its own forked tail, it is quite unlike the traditional alchemical ouroboros, and indeed it is quite difficult to follow precisely the curvilinear movements of his interlaced body.

■ *Ramsbury is signposted to the west of the B4192, to the north-west of Hungerford.*

Redgate *See* Bodmin Moor

Roche, Cornwall ⚔
B3/4 SW 9860

The village takes its name from the outcropping of granite rocks behind the houses. What is of interest to the occultist is the 15th-century chapel of St Michael which is literally built into one of the higher pinnacles. There is deep symbolism in the myth which has the cursed Jan Tregeagle seeking refuge from his terrible penance at the Dozmary Pool at the hermit's cell on this rock, for it is nothing other than the emptiness of pagan life seeking sanctuary in the Christian faith. Tregeagle was removed to the northern coasts of Cornwall, and set to the endless task of making ropes from sand. In connection with Tregeagle, see however **Bolventor – Dozmary Pool.**

■ *Roche is signposted to the south of the A30(T). The rocks of Roche are to the south of the village, a few yards or metres down the road to Bugle.*

Rocky Valley, Cornwall ⌘
B3 SX 073894

Behind a ruinous building, incised into the rock face, is a curious maze-carving, which (in the tradition of mediaeval mazes) is more a formal dance pattern than a maze, as one does not get lost in the meander lines. It has been noted by Janet and Colin Bord in their book *Ancient Mysteries of Britain* that the Rocky Valley maze resembles Cretan designs, but one suspects that these petroglyphs are mediaeval.

■ *Rocky Valley is to the north-east of Tintagel, off the B3263 before Trevalga.*

Rough Tor *See* Camelford—Dymond Monument and Slaughter Bridge

St Cleer, Cornwall ◉
B3 SX 2468

The holy well at St Cleer is now covered by a restored 15th-century building, probably once used as a baptistry (the waters still run within the cistern). The well and the adjacent free-standing Latin cross were restored in 1864, and the well is generally regarded as being second in importance to the more complex holy well at **St Clether.**

Besides the holy well, the area is rich in antiquities around which a variety of legends have been woven: among these is the upright fragments of the 10th-century stone inscribed to King Doniert, said to be a memorial to a Cornish king who was drowned in the Fowey River around about AD 875: the inscription asks passersby for intercessory prayers for his soul.

■ *St Cleer is signposted off the B3254, before its junction with the A390. The well is 200 yards or metres down the hill to the east end of the parish church. The Doniert memorial is almost a mile/2 km from the village, on the St Cleer-Redgate road.*

St Clether, Cornwall ◉
B3 SX 2084

The holy well at St Clether is without doubt one of the finest stone-covered wells in the British Isles. The chapel, like the well, has been dedicated to St Clederus, and has been constructed and orientated to allow the water overflow from the well to pass through the end of the chapel, beneath the present altar, where the body of the saint was originally laid. Thus, what had been magical water in the past was rendered 'holy' by its contact with the aura of the saint's body – an interesting example of the use of what occultists might now call etheric forces. Although the flow of waters from the underground stream has been regarded as magical or holy since ancient times, it is unlikely that the flow was 'directed' as it is in the mediaeval well-head and the adjacent chapel. An engraving inside the chapel links St Clether with the Saint Cleder of Brittany, but there is much dispute as to whom Clederus was. It has been suggested that the name (like St Cleer) is a corruption of the Franciscan St Clare.

■ *St Clether is signposted to the south of the A395. The well is some considerable distance to the west of the church, tastefully signposted across hilly grasslands.*

St Ive, Cornwall ✡
B3 SX 3067

Above the south porch entrance of the parish church is a sundial, dated 1695 and bearing the Latin inscription *Quotidie Morior* (Daily I die), the whole design surmounted by an ouroboros image of a snake biting its own tail. This snake is ultimately from alchemical sources, and while in this instance it is meant to represent time (which eats even itself), it is more usually intended to represent eternity, as is explained on a grave-slab in the church at **Zennor.** The St Ive church has a blocked-up Devil's Door.

■ *The parish church of St Ive lies to the north of the A390, to the north-east of Liskeard.*

St Michael's Mount, Cornwall ⚔
A4 SW 5130

This sea-beleagered mount is one of the most holy places in Cornwall, and is said by some to take its name from a hermit who had a vision of the Archangel Michael while living on the mount. Like the northern isle of **Staffa** (Scotland), this mount is supposed to have been built by giants: it is said that before the ancient giant Cormoran came to Cornwall there was no mount off Marazion, and he built it as a base for his nest. Cormoran died when he was trapped by a human into rushing across a piece of ground into which a huge pit had been dug, and loosely covered with turf. Those who are interested in the inner meaning of myths and fairy tales take this as an illustration of the occult truth that the earthly world is an inverted image of the spiritual world: Cormoran built a hill by raising a mound of earth, but died when a hill of space (a deep hole) had been cut into the earth. In connection with the Cormoran legend in particular, one finds oneself wondering if the legends of the giants are derived from folk memories of lost Atlantis? The area of seas to the south and west of Cornwall are said to have been part of the lost land of Lyonesse, which was submerged before history began, and even reputable occultists write of the existence of giants in the early days of the Atlantean civilisation. See also **Perranuthnoe**.

■ *St Michael's Mount is off Marazion, signposted from the A394, east of Penzance.*

Sandford Orcas, Dorset ☿
E2 ST 6220

The manor house of this village is said to be one of the most haunted houses in England – at least, it has more than the usual retinue of ghosts, from the spirit of a pet dog, a phantom spinet-player, a 'Lady in Green', a 'Lady in Red' (said to appear punctually at ten minutes to midnight), a monk, an Elizabethan lady, the spirit of a man who committed suicide in the gatehouse, to the ghost of a previous owner, Sir Hubert Medlycott. At the last count, fourteen ghosts had been seen in the house.

■ *Sandford Orcas is signposted to the east of the B3148, to the north-east of Yeovil.*

Shepton Mallet, Somerset ✡ △
E2 ST 6143

The village is remembered in occult circles because of the stories of curious cases of levitation experienced by a local man named Richard Jones. The tale was preserved in the witchcraft literature through Joseph Glanvill's *Saducismus Triumphatus* of 1683.

There are no levitating witches to be seen in Shepton Mallet nowadays, but the magnificent wagon-roof in the church of St Peter and St Paul seems almost to fly skywards on its angel-decorated beams: on this there are some 300 bosses, each bearing symbols, of which some are distinctly hermetic and occult.

■ *Shepton Mallet is at the junction of the A37 (south of Bristol) and the A361, to the east of Wells.*

Shepton Mallet
See also Bath – Abbey Church (interior)

Shervage Wood *See* Crowcombe

Sidbury, Devon △
D3 SY 1391

This village was the scene of what was probably the last case of witch scratching, in 1924. The case is recorded in the *Evening News* by a Mr Britten, who tells the story of a strange event which befell one of his acquaintances. This man was cycling through the village of Sidbury and was stopped by a group of locals. He dismounted from the bicycle, and then, much to his surprise, one of the ringleaders pushed a pin into one of his legs, chanting: 'Prickee wi' a pin, and draw his blood, an' ee can't hurt ee.' Having done this witch scratching, they were perfectly friendly towards the stranger. (Witch scratching is different from witch pricking – see these terms in the glossary.)

■ *Sidbury is on the A375 to the south of Honiton.*

Silbury Hill *See* Avebury

Slaughter Bridge, Cornwall ✕
B3 SX 1083

This is the dramatic name given to another undistinguished bridge which marks the supposed site of King Arthur's last battle, from which the king, fatally wounded after killing Modred, crawled to throw his magical sword Excalibur into the dark Dozmary Pool: quite a crawl over Rough Tor, Garrow Tor and Brown Willy on **Bodmin Moor**, even for an epic king. The stone called King Arthur's Tomb nearby is far from Arthurian, for the inscription is in Latin, with one of the words repeated in the curious Ogham Script. It is likely that the site was in fact the place where the Celts and Anglo-Saxons met in battle in AD 823.

■ *Slaughter Bridge is 1 mile/2 km to the north of Camelford, signposted to the east on the B3266.*

South Hill, Cornwall ✡ ♀
B/C3 SX 3372

In the 15th-century church is a Norman font which is said to be decorated with salamanders, the fire spirits of occultism and alchemy, the symbolic life-force of the element of fire. The creatures on the font are two-legged, and the notion that they are salamanders probably started in 1937 with the genial travel-writer Arthur Mee, who knew little of occultism. Mediaeval salamanders usually have six legs (sometimes four), but never two. The South Hill 'salamander' is a conventional dragon grotesque, symbol of demonic forces.

■ *South Hill is signposted off the B3527, which runs off the A388, to the north-west of Callington.*

Stonehenge, Wiltshire → ⧗ ⊹

F2 ST 1343

What are the facts about this most remarkable British antiquity of Stonehenge? It seems to be agreed among the scientists that the oldest part of the structure is well over 4,000 years old: it consists of a circle and sacred avenue of enormous stones, some of them forming immense horizontal lintels (the henge stones) on pairs of uprights, within a huge circular earthworks, some 380 feet/116 metres in diameter. Most specialists are convinced that it was used in ages past for some kind of religious ceremonies, and there is no doubt that sophisticated building techniques were employed to make the structure perfect: how many casual visitors to the site realise that the henges are carried on tongue-and-groove joints, and that the surviving lintels are all dressed on a curve, and are designed to permit the eye to adjust for the natural foreshortening of perspective?

It is argued by some that the whole complex is linked with other stone circles by invisible lines of force, or by geometric principles, as far afield as **Avebury** in north Wiltshire, and (some say) even further. At least eighty of the larger stones were carried to the desolate Salisbury plain from distant Wales, recalling the mediaeval belief that the stones had been brought by magic from Ireland. Why did some priest or king consider it necessary to carry four-ton stones from Wales? What is the reason behind the building of this extraordinary place? In recent times, as the historian Jacquetta Hawkes records, a geologist has suggested that the Welsh blue-stones were not carried by men, but by glacial action. The occultists would dismiss this notion, and point to the ancient power of the vanished race, which had the secret of anti-gravitational force under their control. Indeed, it is because they lost control of this secret power of nature that their race came to an end, and their country was swallowed by the seas.

Is this circle built of the magic stones to which so many occult texts refer? In modern times stones are all deemed inanimate, but in classical times it was commonplace to distinguish between the living stones and the inanimate ones, for writers to declare some stones magical and others not. There are records of a Greek called Heraclius who was said to have the power to determine at a glance which stones were endowed with life and motion. It is recorded that some of the balanced rocking stones of ancient times were more remarkable than the logan stones of the present age, for they were moved not by the pressure of a hand, but by the persuasion of the mind alone. Such myths abound, and may be rooted only in the imagination, yet anyone sensitive to

The stone circle at Stonehenge near the time of midwinter sunrise.

the menhirs and ancient circles of Britain knows that they are not ordinary stones, and that many of them are charged with some majestic power of magic: it is still possible to get a shock, something like an electric shock, when you touch such stones in certain places. The occultists see Stonehenge as the last truly great link with a long-lost past, when men built magic structures to ask questions of the cosmos, and as a background for their most remarkable ceremonials of initiation into cosmic mysteries.

In ancient times Stonehenge was called *chior-gaur*, meaning approximately dance of giants, reminding us that even by the 12th century the chronicler Geoffrey of Monmouth still called the circle the Giant's Dance, though he knew as little of the meaning or purpose of the stones as we do today. The ancient Greek Hecataeus, whose writings have come down to us in a fragmentary state, says that Britain has a magnificent spherical temenos, which is a sacred precinct, dedicated to the sun, and visited by the moon god every nineteen years: this is near enough to the eighteen year, eleven-day Saros cycle for us to be certain that even the ancients knew that Stonehenge was, among other things, a calendrical computer. The occultist Blavatsky insists that Stonehenge and certain of the other cyclopeian circles were constructed by ancient giants: 'we say,' she writes, with disarming simplicity, 'that most of these stones

are the relics of the last Atlanteans.' If this is so, then the circle is well over ten times the age ascribed to it by scientists: this is one of the most interesting characteristics of the occultist notion of the stone circles – that they are far older than the modern scientists appear to realise.

Something of the mystery of the circles has been sensed in modern times: we now know that the design of the circles is far from accidental, and that Stonehenge in particular is based in a secret and sacred geometry. It is also possible to trace important ley-line connections between many stones circles throughout the British Isles, and to show that the major surviving circles, such as those at Stonehenge or **Callanish** (Scotland) in the north, are calendrical comput-ers, designed to study the lunar-solar cycles during the important Saros cycle, a knowledge of which was essential for a society involved with cosmically-linked rituals and initiation practices. The stones were raised by savages, by initiates, by wizards, by giants, by the Atlanteans, by the Druids. With Stonehenge, it is difficult to know where fact ends and fiction begins.

The experience of Stonehenge has changed more in the past twenty years than in the past two thousand. Those old enough to remember the stones when they were a remote mystery, set in a lonely landscape, find it painful to approach the circle now, demystified as they are by a

thoughtless tourism, and by the inelegant fencing. This is perhaps one reason why it is so much more pleasant to contemplate pictures of Stonehenge through the ancient engravings than through the sophisticated camera-work with long focus lenses which the modern barbed wire and fences have made necessary.

The popularity of the midsummer 'festivals', and the vacuity of the so-called Druidic rites in the sacred place, have not disguised the fact that the circle of hanging stones was not designed for festivities, and had nothing whatsoever to do with Druids, a religious cast which came to Britain when the stones were already a thousand years old. Little is known for sure about the reasons why Stonehenge was built, which is probably why it is so susceptible to strange theory and outlandish hypotheses, but the known facts are themselves pointers to a wonder which is almost beyond the conceiving of a materialistic age. Do these thousands flock to the circle as though in retreat from the superficialities of our modern age, in the conviction that there is something in these stones which is 'more real than real', a reminder of a different inner life in man?

■ *Stonehenge is visible to the north of the A303, to the west of the junction with the A360.*

Stonehenge ley-lines

Stonehenge is famous among ley-hunters for the richness of the leys which connected in a meaningful pattern so many of the important landmarks, stones, tumuli and forts which are scattered widely over this part of Wiltshire. It would be merely confusing to present all these leys on a single map, but the illustration below is designed to show two of the important leys which hinge on a fulcrum of Stonehenge itself. The north-south ley may be traced from the tumuli and barrows to the north east of Rollestone Camp, in direct line through Stonehenge itself, through the centre of Old Sarum (an ancient religious centre, the old Salisbury), through the Clearbury Ring, and down to the tumulus above North Charford Down Farm. It is possible that when the markers for this ley were still intact, they led northwards to Oldbury Castle, north of which is the Cherhill White Horse: at all events, a linear alignment may be traced between this horse and Old Sarum, through Stonehenge. The second ley, on an axis to this first one, connects Sidbury Hill camp with Grovely Castle, on the same fulcrum as Stonehenge.

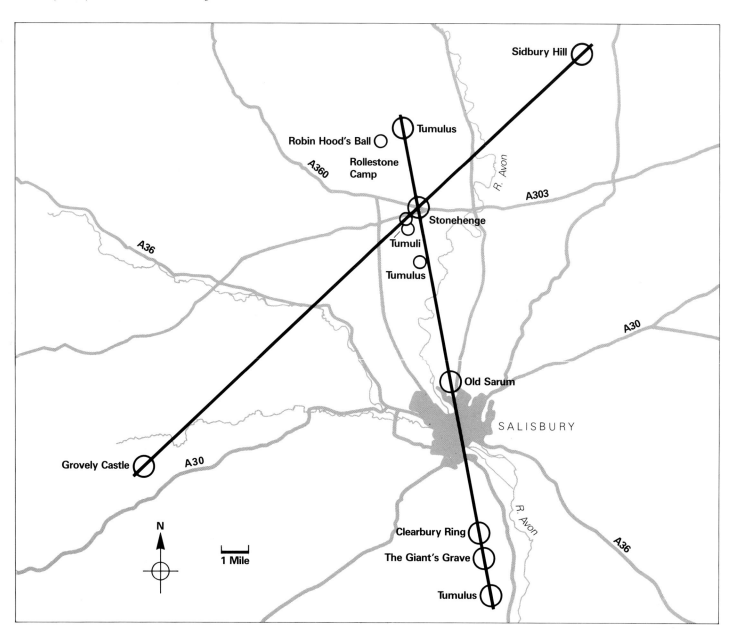

Tintagel Castle associated with the Arthurian legends.

Tintagel, Cornwall ☒

B3 SX 0588

The fame of the village rests almost entirely on the Arthurian legends woven around it, for the nearby castle, perched precipitously on the fiddle head of rocks called Tintagel Head to the west is said (on little historical authority) to have been the castle of King Arthur, the famous Camelot of mythology, a claim made by several villages and towns. So far as Tintagel is concerned, the claim is fantastical, as Arthur, to the extent that he was a historical figure at all, would have lived in the early 6th century and records show that this castle was built in 1145. The nearby Merlin's Cave on the shingle beach below is just as much a romantic fantasy. There are indications of 6th- and 7th-century Celtic Christian settlements in the area, but not on a scale to equate the area with the palace of a king.

■ *Tintagel is on the B3263, south of Boscastle. The castle ruins on Tintagel Head are well signposted along a rough track from the village.*

Toller Fratrum, Dorset ✡ ⊕

E3 SY 5797

The name itself conceals a secret, as the Fratres (brothers) were the Knights Hospitallers (the Knights of St John of Jerusalem), an esoteric movement concerned, among other things, with introducing methods of healing into Europe from the East. The House of Toller may have been used by the brotherhood from about the time of their foundation in 1070, but it was rebuilt in Tudor times, probably after the Knights had been driven by the Turks from the fortress island of Rhodes: the last Grand Prior of the order was Sir Thomas Tresham. See also **Rushton** (Central England). Even so, there are still many interesting early finials replete with occult symbolism – note for example the monkey, chained and holding a mirror, and the griffin.

The small church of St Basil, behind what used to be the refectory, has a rare fragment of carved stone, showing Mary Magdalene washing Christ's feet: an image of a gesture taken by most occultists to symbolise the coming age of Pisces, inaugurated by the Christ under the symbol of the fish. To grasp this symbolism correctly, one must recall that in the zodiacal image of man, the feet are ruled by Pisces. In washing His feet with the hair of her head, it is said that Magdalene was admitting that the age of Aries (ruling the head) was giving way to the age of Pisces. Such an image, even in fragmentary form, is clearly linked with the idea of 'healing' in a very deep sense, not merely because the woman is washing and healing the feet, but also because Pisces has rule over hospitals.

■ *Toller Fratrum is signposted to the south of the A356, north-west of Dorchester.*

Studland, Dorset ✡ ☿

F3 SZ 0382

The roof corbals of the 13th-century church of St Nicholas consist mainly of interesting grotesques, but one is especially remarkable, being apparently a pair of lovers in pagan abandon.

On the heath towards Poole Harbour is the curious Agglestone, which is said to have been thrown by the Devil, standing on the Needles at Alum Bay, to the west of the Isle of Wight. It would seem that the Devil had intended to hit Studland church, but missed his mark.

■ *Studland is at the eastern end of the B3351, to the east of the A351, north of Swanage.*

Temple (Cornwall) *See* Bodmin Moor

Trewortha Tor *See* Bodmin Moor

Truro, Cornwall ⬦

B4 SW 8244

On the north-east corner of the fabric of the cathedral is a beautiful image of a pelican feeding her young with her own blood – originally this was an alchemical symbol.

■ *Truro is on the A390, and the centrally located cathedral is visible from almost every vantage point around the city.*

An alchemical symbol of the pelican feeding its young with its own blood at Truro Cathedral.

Warleggan, Cornwall ♀

B3 SX 1569

The church of St Bartholomew, in what is reputed to be the loneliest village on Bodmin Moor (the name seems to be from the Welsh *Worlegan*, meaning a high place), appears to have been bedevilled by some of its clergy from early days, and is famous among tourists for its ghost-stories. Ralph Tramur, the son of the second rector, was generally regarded as a heretic and a witch even in the 14th century, while the curate of 1774, Francis Cole, is said still to haunt the road outside Trengoffe, where the wheels of his carriage are heard at night. Modern inhabitants of Warleggan claim that the adjacent Old Rectory (a back gateway gives access

into the forecourt of the church), now turned into flats, was badly haunted – images of figures and faces have appeared on the old walls; several different ghosts have been seen.

There are some delightful vertical animal-images on the Norman capitals inside the church (possible rebus symbols), and signs of an ancient Devil's Door in the northern fabric. The steeple which once stood on the tower was struck by lightning in March 1818, doing much damage to the church fabric. This sorry tale reminds us that there was still much reluctance in England to reject the notion that lightning, being the effect of a diabolical agency, might be deflected by the angels (especially the Archangel Michael) or by bells. The lightning rod, which is based on the notion that lightning flash is an electrical discharge, was not attached to an English church until 1762, and even St Paul's Cathedral in London was not protected with a rod until six years later. The story of the reluctant move from diabolism to physics is outlined by Andrew White (see Bibliography).

■ *Warleggan is isolated between the A30(T) and the A38(T), almost immediately east of Bodmin. It is perhaps best approached by way of the minor road between Cardinham and St Neot.*

The haunted village church at Warleggan.

Warminster, Wiltshire

E2 ST 8644

Warminster is famous among UFO hunters for sightings of unidentified flying objects, messages, 'space ship' landings, and so on. The town is said to lie on the intersection of over a dozen important ley-lines (being even more powerfully located than **Hereford** (Wales and Western Counties) and is one of the few British cities to have a book devoted to its space visitors: Arthur Shuttleworth's *The Warminster Mystery*.

■ *Warminster is on the A350, north of Shaftesbury.*

Wells, Somerset

E2 ST 5445

The city is said to take its name from the seven underground streams which surface in what is now the gardens of the Bishop's Palace: it was here that Bishop Jocelyn is said to have driven back the terrible dragon which had been attacking and devouring the locals.

■ *Wells is on the A39, south of Bristol.*

Westbury, Wiltshire

E2 ST 8751

The horse cut into the chalkland near Westbury is said by some to be the oldest in Wiltshire, though in fact it is by no means as old as the one at **Uffington** (Central England). This distinctive creature is claimed (on what authority, it is not clear) to have been cut to commemorate King Alfred's victory over the Danes in AD 878. Its present form, to a large extent persuaded into fantasy by the pathways made by innumerable visitors, is an 18th-century remodelling, and it is possible that originally the figure was a dragon.

■ *The White Horse lies on a hill to the east of Westbury, south of the B3098 – it is most easily seen when driving eastwards, towards Bratton.*

The White Horse cut through the turf on the escarpment above Westbury.

West Kennett *See* Avebury

Wincanton, Somerset　　　　△

E2 ST 7128

A sabbat of witches held at Trister Gate, Wincanton, is celebrated in one of the six panels of the frontispiece of Joseph Glanvill's *Saducismus Triumphatus* of 1683.

■ *Wincanton is signposted to the north of the A303, north-east of Yeovil.*

Wincanton *See also* Bath – Abbey Church (interior)

Windmill Hill *See* Avebury

Winsford Hill, Somerset　　　　

D2 SS 9034

The Caractacus Stone on Winsford Hill is said to belong to the Devil, who uses it as a weight to hide his secret treasure which is buried beneath. Although the stone has been moved some distance in recent years, the tradition of the secret treasure still persists.

■ *Winsford Hill is to the west of Winsford, to the east of the B3223.*

Zennor, Cornwall　　　　X ⟶ ⁘

A4 SW 4538

In the parish church of St Senara at Zennor, is the figure of a mermaid which is probably the most famous in Cornwall, and which is without doubt the most impressive. It is carved on a plank which was once part of a mediaeval bench-end, but which, during the restorations of 1890, was made into part of a chair – though this is still used in the church. The story runs that a woman in a long dress used to attend services to listen to the singing of the chorister Matthew Trewhella. One Sunday she managed to lure him down to the village stream, and then down to Pendour Cove, where Matthew disappeared, to become the husband of the mermaid. Tales are told of sailors meeting the mermaid of Zennor, and even of their seeing the sea-children fathered on her by Trewhella.

The stained glass windows on the south side of the chancel show the patron of the church, St Senara, concerning whom virtually nothing is known, but around whom many myths have been born. Legend claims that she is the

Princess Asenora of Brittany, condemned to be burned because of a false accusation of infidelity to her husband King Goello. The executioners discovered that she was pregnant, so nailed her into a barrel and threw her into the sea, but she was miraculously saved by an angel, who washed her up on the Irish coast. She bore a son, who eventually became the abbot of St Budoc.

The cross on top of the south porch of the church lay on the ground for some years, and is said to have healing powers: an old woman placed it on her bed during an illness, and cured herself.

■ *Zennor is signposted to the north of the B3306, to the west of St Ives.*

Detail of the mediaeval carving of a mermaid on the 'Mermaid Chair' in the Church of St Senara, Zennor.

London and
Southern England

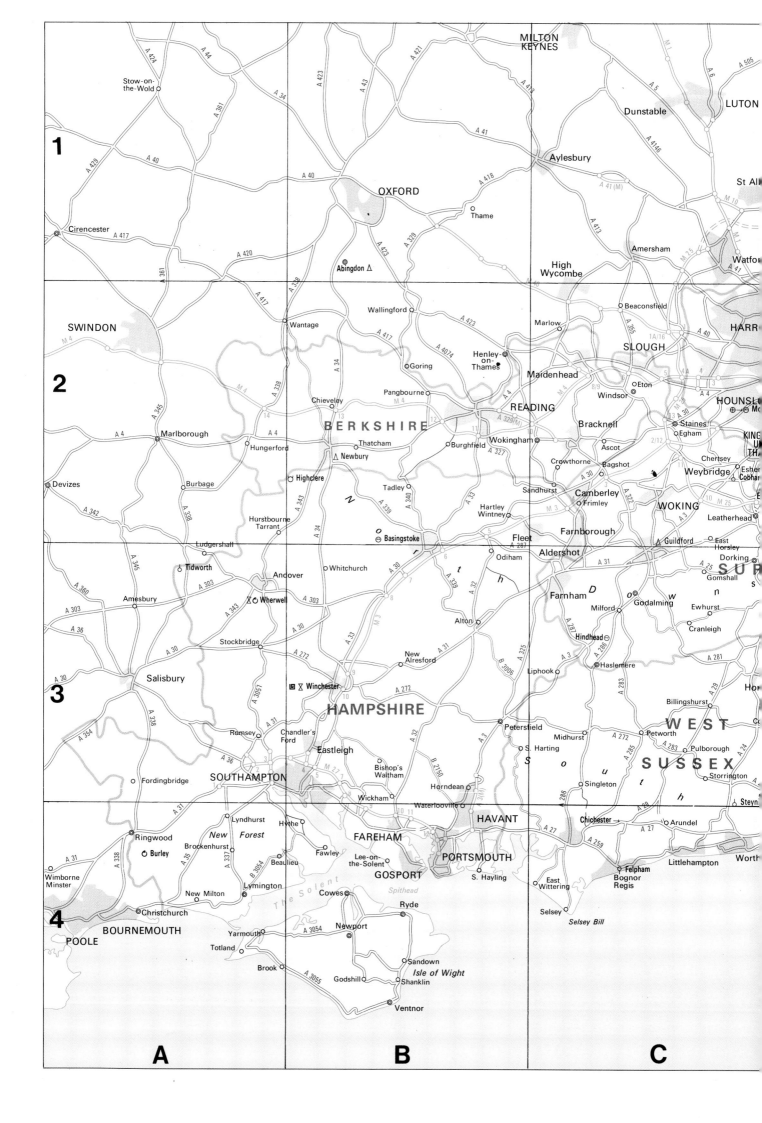

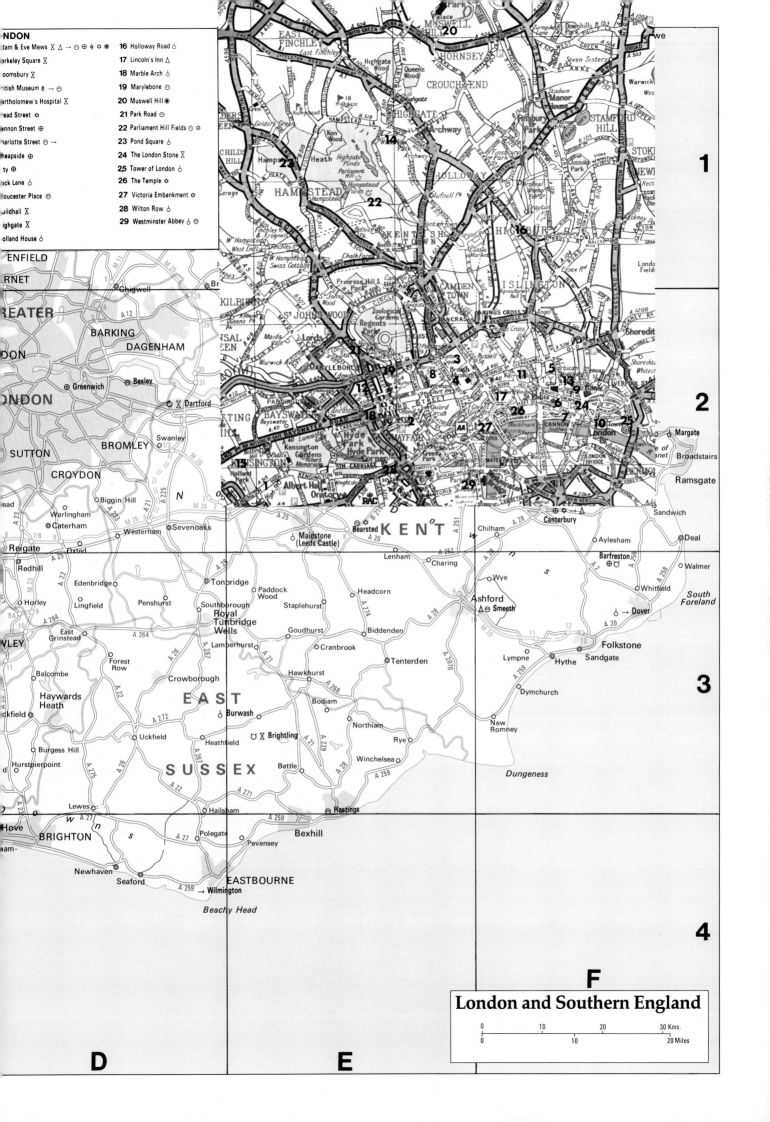

LONDON

dam & Eve Mews ✕ △ → ⊖ ⊕ ⊹ ☉ ◉
1 arkeley Square ✕
loomsbury ✕
ritish Museum ⊹ →
artholomew's Hospital ✕
read Street
annon Street ⊕
harlotte Street ⊖ →
heapside ⊕
ity ⊕
ock Lane ⊕
loucester Place
uildhall ✕
ighgate ✕
olland House ♂

16 Holloway Road ♂
17 Lincoln's Inn △
18 Marble Arch △
19 Marylebone ⊖
20 Muswell Hill ◉
21 Park Road ⊖
22 Parliament Hill Fields ⊖ ✿
23 Pond Square ♂
24 The London Stone ✕
25 Tower of London ♂
26 The Temple ✿
27 Victoria Embankment ✿
28 Wilton Row ♂
29 Westminster Abbey ♂ ⊖

London and Southern England

0   10   20   30 Kms.
0   10   20 Miles

Abingdon, Berkshire △

B1 SU 4997

In February 1579 four women were condemned at Abingdon for having committed murder by witchcraft. It seems that they had made small images (poppets) from red wax to resemble their victim and had then pierced these with briar thorns until their victim was dead.

■ *Abingdon is signposted to the east of the A34, south of Oxford.*

Barfreston, Kent ⊕ ☾

F3 TR 2660

The Norman carvings on the doorway of St Mary's Church are among the most interesting in the country, and several of them are of esoteric origin. There are over a hundred separate pieces of carving, the best of them in the two registers which curve around the door. Some are now mythological mysteries, as, for example, the one which depicts the wolf (or is it a dog?) playing a harp to a man who appears to be doing a somersault. The symbolism for others is perhaps a little less difficult to interpret: below the harp picture is a roundle which show a man or woman being tempted by demons, the message of which is obvious. On the other hand, the roundel which shows the monkey riding a goat with a rabbit thrown over his shoulder may have been derived from a misunderstanding of the constellation Centaurus depicted in some of the early medieval star books. The monkey would represent the man half of the centaur, the goat would be the horse part, and the rabbit would be the stellar *Bestia* ('beast') which in medieval times was often portrayed as a hare. Some of the carvings are of a more obvious astrological significance.

■ *Barfreston is east of Eythorne, signposted to the east of the A256, north of Dover.*

Basingstoke, Hampshire ⊚

B2/3 SU 6352

The remarkable writer, barrister and occultist Charles Carleton Massey was born at Hackwood Park, Basingstoke, in December 1838. He abandoned a promising legal career to study philosophy and psychology, and developed a keen interest in occultism and psychic phenomena, becoming one of the founder members of the Society for Psychical Research (see **London – Adam and Eve Mews**). He was also one of the chief organisers of the British Theosophical Society (see **London – Gloucester Place**). He must not be confused with Gerald Massey, his contemporary, who was one of the great occultists of the 19th-century, and whose theory of the origin of languages is seminal to the study of the history of magic.

■ *Basingstoke is signposted off junction 6 of the M3. Hackwood Park is one mile south of Basingstoke, the entrance is off Tunworth Road. It is open to the public.*

Bearsted, Kent ⊚ ✡

E2 TQ 7955

The great 17th-century Rosicrucian and occultist Robert Fludd was born in this village, at Milgate House, (which still has some of the original 16th-century features), though he passed much of his childhood in Berwick-on-Tweed, where his father worked. Few Englishmen have had the breadth and depth of occult and esoteric knowledge as Fludd. Something of his inner political power – and indeed, something of the ramifications of occult brotherhoods in England – may be sensed from a simple occult decoration used in one of his published books. This was virtually identical to that used in the first folio of Shakespeare's published works, which appeared in 1623, the same year as Fludd's book. Similar designs appear in early editions of Francis Bacon, Walter Raleigh and the poet Edmund Spenser – all individuals with an interest in occultism, and all (according to esoteric history) involved in a Rosicrucian

The portrait of Robert Fludd by Merian. Famous both as a Rosicrucian and an occultist, Fludd possessed a remarkable store of esoteric knowledge.

An example of an occult decoration, from Robert Fludd's Anatomiae Amphitheatareum. *This symbol is found in several Rosicrucian texts of the period.*

fraternity. The symbol, which is not quite what it first appears to be, is also found in the 1611 edition of the King James Bible, but we may be sure that James I of England was no Rosicrucian. For a further account of Fludd, see **Oxford – St Johns** (Central England). There is a commemorative plaque in Bearsted parish church, put there by Robert Fludd in memory of his father. A well-executed portrait of Fludd by Merian incorporates some interesting occult details. Note, for example, the different pattern of lace-work in the fifth ruff fold from Fludd's left. This is a symbolic form of the rose (usually drawn as a five-petalled flower), a clear reference to the Rose of the esoteric Rosy-Cross, the image of the redemptive force [Christ] on the cross (page 9).

■ *Bearsted is signposted to the south of the A20, east of Maidstone.*

Bexley, Kent ◎

D2 TQ 4775

The occultist and electrical engineer C.F. Varley died at Bexley, at Cromwell House, in September, 1883, and was buried at Christ Church in the same village. He seems to have been linked with a tradition of occultism, for he was a descendant of the famous painter, John Varley, author of a book on zodiacal physiognomy as well as a keen astrologer, who had cast the horoscope of his friend William Blake, and helped Blake during his seances, when he made drawings of apparitions. Additionally, C.F. Varley was a descendant of Oliver Cromwell (see **Worcester** – Wales and Western Counties). In the non-occult world he is remembered mainly for his work on the successful design of the first Atlantic cable. His interest in spiritualism began in the middle of the century, when he was invited to do experiments which determined that genuine table-rapping in spiritualistic seances was not due to any detectable electromagnetic force. Some of his devices to test mediumship and fraud were used in famous seances during the rest of the 19th century. In this connection he worked especially with the famous medium Florence Cook, studied by several other scientists, including Sir William Crookes: who took many

photographs of a materialised spirit 'Katie King' under test conditions devised by Varley. As a short official biography of Varley reports, 'He himself experienced numerous psychic manifestations in his own home, believed himself to be possessed of mesmeric healing power, and observed a number of apparitions.'

■ *Bexley is on the A2(T), in the eastern part of London. Cromwell House is on Bexley Heath.*

A photograph by Sir William Crookes of the materialisation of Katie King.

Brightling, East Sussex ♂ ♉

E3 TQ 6821

In the parish churchyard at Brightling is buried Mad Jack Fuller, a wealthy local eccentric who built, among other things, a mock church steeple, and the Brightling Needle or obelisk, as a land-marker on the highest spot in the area. He died in 1834, and a legend quickly grew up that anyone who ran backwards around his pyramid tomb for seven circuits would meet the Devil, or (as some say) the ghost of Mad Jack himself. The legend has it that Mad Jack requested that he be buried sitting upright, wearing a top hat, and with a bottle of claret in front of him.

■ *Brightling is signposted to the north of the B2096, to the east of Heathfield.*

Brighton *See* Hastings

Burley, Hampshire ☿

A4 SU 2103

The ancient earthworks on Burley Beacon are said to have been the nest of the Bisterne Dragon, which is supposed to have lived on a pail of milk a day. The saviour knight, who is reputed to have lost his dogs in the fight with the dragon, died of wounds after killing the beast. There are sculpted images of a dragon and what appear to be dogs on the facade of Bisterne Park.

■ *Burley is signposted south of the A31(T), east of Ringwood.*

Burwash, East Sussex ♀

E3 TQ 6724

The 17th-century house known as 'Bateman's' was once the home of the writer Rudyard Kipling, who was deeply interested in the paranormal. After his death in 1936 the house was to gain such a reputation for haunting that members of the Ghost Club visited it in 1975, and one of their number was rewarded by a first-hand encounter with the ghost of the famous author. In earlier decades Thurston Hopkins, also interested in ghost lore, organised a night-time ghost hunt in the nearby Glydwish Wood (a favourite walk of Kipling), and the group were confronted by a horrendous partly decomposed spectre, which lunged towards them moaning. Thurston Hopkins was so fascinated by this encounter that he investigated the matter thoroughly. Much to his surprise he discovered that in 1928 a man had been hanged for a murder committed in Glydwish Wood, and that after his execution new evidence emerged to show that he was completely innocent. According to the records, before being hanged he had insisted on his innocence and had told the chaplain who attended him that he would return to haunt those who had brought about his death in this manner.

■ *Burwash is on the A265, signposted to the west of the A21.*

Canterbury, Kent ⊕ ✡ → △

F2 TR 1557

The floor of the Trinity Chapel in the cathedral is one of the most remarkable in any English cathedral, as a rare survival from the days when astrological imagery was much used in church ornament. It is a complex marble inlay design into which have been woven the twelve images for the zodiacal signs, the corresponding 'monthly labours', and what were probably the corresponding 'virtues and vices' of the zodiacal signs. Unfortunately the majority of these images have been worn away over the centuries by pilgrims' feet,

and only one or two of the distinctive designs are now recognisable, for example the roundel of the sign of Scorpio. Some of the symbols are of the most esoteric kind however – one, which is associated with the sign Libra is said to be an ancient symbol for the quintessence, a term for what modern occultists call the etheric, the vital life-force of the cosmos. Also in Trinity Chapel is the magnificent effigy-tomb to Edward, the Black Prince, whose sobriquet is perhaps the most popular misunderstanding in English history. It is widely supposed that he was so called because he habitually wore black armour, or was in some way wicked although there is no evidence of this, and contemporary pictures show him in silver armour. The term appears to have been used towards the end of the 14th century, however, by which time the prince was dead. The name has suggested to some that he was involved with the darker side of black magic, which is far from the truth. However, his father, Edward III, was more than once the object of attacks from witchcraft, and the power which his lovely mistress, Alice Perrers had over the king was often attributed to witchcraft or necromancy. It was claimed in Parliament that, with the aids of a magician, she had cast spells by means of waxen magic to ensure the love of the king, and that she owned a magic ring of forgetfulness and memory, by which she forever kept the king mindful of her as his mistress.

■ *Canterbury is well signposted from the A2, between Faversham and Dover.*

The zodiacal symbol Scorpio from the marble floor of the Trinity Chapel, Canterbury.

Chichester, West Sussex →

C4 SU 8604

When the smuggler William Jackson was convicted of murder, and hanged at Chichester in 1649, it is recorded that there was found in a linen purse around his neck a magical spell, which appears to be entirely religious:

> Sancti tres reges
> Gaspar Melchior Balthazar
> Orate pro nobis nunc et in hora
> Mortis nostrae
> (Three holy Kings, Gaspar, Melchior
> and Balthasars, pray for us now and
> at the hour of our death.)

In fact, the three names in the second line are those of the three Kings or Magi, who followed the star when they visited the new-born Jesus, and so when viewed from a magical standpoint the entire prayer really carries an occult or magical notion. As we shall see in the analysis of another (partly related) amuletic inscription in **Middleham** (The North), it is quite usual for occult symbols to consist of hidden meanings or of 'double entendres', and the multi-layer use of symbols was a commonplace in the manufacture of hidden charms. Spells and charms of the kind worn by William Jackson were sold widely as protections for those taking a journey (on the basis that the Three Kings had taken a great journey to find Jesus). We may therefore be certain that the reason why he wore it on that day was because he knew that he was taking the last journey of all, and wished to be guided by his own star, to the Christ. In a sense, therefore, he wished to follow the direction taken by the Magi (whose name is actually linked with our word 'magic'), which is why their three names are petitioned in the spell. It is indeed a magi-cal spell in more senses than one.

■ *Chichester is to the north of the A27, east of Havant.*

Cobham, Surrey ♂

C2 TQ 1060

A frightening spectre of a huge man, radiating its own pale grey-yellowish light, and wearing something resembling a great-coat or shroud, has been seen gliding along a pavement in Cobham in the dark hours of the night. It has been observed by a variety of people, but the most notable sighting, discussed at length by Owen and Sims, is that recorded by four members of a pop group in November 1965. Some writers have suggested that it might be the ghost of Lord Ligonier, Commander-in-Chief of the British Army in the 18th century whose home used to be at Cobham Park, and whose tomb is in the church at Cobham, but the evidence for this is extremely slight.

■ *Cobham is signposted to the south of the A3(T), in south-west London.*

Crowborough *See* Hindhead

Dartford, Kent ♂ ⚔

E2 TQ 5474

One of the finest possessions of the 13th-century church is the fresco measuring 20 feet by 12 feet/6 metres by 3½ metres showing St George dealing admirably with the dragon. The 15th-century fresco was lost for many years until a wall was cleaned of whitewash and plaster in the 19th century. The green dragon advances from a pool of water, but already the knight's lance is in its gorge. Between the contesting pair stands the princess, intended as dragon fodder, but unchained, and walking out with her dog as on a summer morning. People in medieval dress watch from the turret of the nearby castle. It is without doubt the finest medieval dragon painting in any English church.

■ *Dartford is signposted to the west of the M25, south of the Thames.*

Dover, Kent ♂ ⚔

F3 TR 3141

The Roman lighthouse is said to be the oldest free-standing building in England; yet even the upper part of this structure (with its curious crenellations) is a medieval restoration. It

The Roman Pharos or lighthouse at Dover, the upper part of which is a mediaeval addition.

has witnessed much English history, and was almost a thousand years old when William the Conqueror came to devastate and then rebuild the country. Its antiquity and its strange proximity to the medieval church of St Mary's probably account for the stories of its hauntings – the ghost of a Roman soldier has been seen there, as well as the standard black monk in a cowled habit. The church appears to have been partly built from the remains of the pagan Roman buildings which once dominated the site, and is therefore an admirable illustration of the attempts made by the early Church to 'redeem' pagan beliefs by bringing them within the confines of the Christian faith.

■ *Dover is on the south-eastern end of the A2, well-signposted from the M2.*

Felpham, West Sussex ♀
C4 SZ 9699

The great poet, mystic and occultist William Blake lived in a thatched cottage in this village, rented from the manager of the Fox Inn, from 1801 to 1804. It was here, in his vegetable garden, that Blake saw fairies, and later had one of his deepest mystical experiences which lead to him writing his poem *Milton*.

He records his vision of the fairies: 'I was walking alone in my garden, there was great stillness among the branches and flowers and more common sweetness in the air; I heard a low and pleasant sound, and I knew not whence it came. At last I saw the broad leaf of a flower move, and underneath I saw a progression of creatures of the size and colour of green and gray grasshoppers, bearing a body laid out on a loose leaf, which they buried with songs, and then disappeared. It was a fairy funeral.'

His deep mystical vision is the great theme in his poem *Milton*, which he partly wrote in the Felpham cottage, at dawn. After experiencing the vision, the union of man with God, Blake fell to the garden path, unconscious, and recovered to find his wife kneeling beside him.

■ *Felpham is signposted to the south of the A259, a mile to the east of Bognor Regis – Blake's House is well indicated within the village.*

Guildford, Surrey △
C2/3 TQ 0049

In 1701 Sarah Morduck was tried at Guildford for bewitching a blacksmith's apprentice named Hathaway. This turned out to be one of exceedingly rare cases which resulted in the accused going free and those bringing the charge being marked out as impostors. It appears from the evidence that Sarah had been scratched several times by the apprentice, who was pretending to be possessed by a devil (for example, vomiting pins which he had hidden in his clothing for that purpose, and foaming at the mouth). The boy was found guilty of false witness and his unfortunate employers were prosecuted both for permitting the assault upon Sarah and for the riot of townspeople which was occasioned by the supposed bewitching.

■ *Guildford is on the A3(T) south west of London.*

Hastings, East Sussex ∞
E3/4 TQ 8109

The black magician and so-called 'Great Beast', Aleister Crowley, who wrote many influential books on the praxes of magic (most notably, *Magick in Theory and Practice* under his initiate-name The Master Therion), and greatly influenced certain notions about predicting the future with Tarot cards, spent the last few years of his life near Hastings, dying there in a small hotel at Netherwood. Crowley, who was born in 1875 in Leamington Spa, dissipated his father's fortune on a self-indulgent life-style, and then lived in an obscurity forced upon him by bankruptcy: after his death in 1947, his body was cremated at Brighton, and his ashes were sent to disciples in the USA. In his interesting autobiography James Laver (who was sufficiently acquainted with occult matters to write one of the most penetrating studies of the predictions of 16th-century savant Nostradamus), tells of a visit he made in March 1947 to Crowley, in his bankruptcy and obscurity in 'Netherwood'. Crowley asked Laver about his interest in occultism, and Laver replied that he thought that the essence of magic was to be summed up in Blake's words: 'Push imagination to the point of vision, and the trick is done.' 'Ah', replied Crowley, 'you realise that Magic is something we do to ourselves . . .'

■ *Hastings is on the south coast, east of Bexhill on the A259(T).*

Highclere, Hampshire ♉
B2 SU 4360

The ancient regional monster the Highclere Grampus is said to have been a demonic dolphin which nested in a yew tree in this village. It was eventually exorcised by the local priest, and, according to those who witnessed the exorcism, it was exiled to the Red Sea for a thousand years. The word Grampus is said to come from graundpose, which was a spouting, blunt-headed dolphin – but how a sea-creature found itself nesting in a tree has never been explained.

■ *Highclere is on the A343, south-west of Newbury.*

Hindhead, Surrey ∞
C3 SU 8835

Sir Arthur Conan Doyle, the well-known writer and authority on psychic matters lived at the house called 'Undershaw' in Hindhead from 1897 to 1907. He died at

'The Soul hovering over the Body reluctantly parting with life,' drawing by William Blake, 1805. Blake's occult vision permitted him to see into the realm of spirits and his writings, paintings and drawings often illustrate this ability. Here he depicts the female soul leaving the male body at death.

Crowborough in 1930, and was buried in the garden of his house there. Eventually (after 1945) his remains were moved to Minstead. In popular occultism Doyle is remembered for the part he played in publicising the **Cottingley** (The North) fairy photographs which fooled the public (and some of the specialists) for several decades.

■ *Hindhead is signposted off the A3(T), north-west of Haslemere.*

Leamington Spa *See* Hastings

London

Adam and Eve Mews ☿ ✡ ⊕ ∞ → ◉ △ ☓

In Adam and Eve Mews off High Street Kensington is the Society for Psychical Research, a centre for research into the paranormal, founded in 1882 as a result of work initiated round about 1873 by Myers at Cambridge, and linked with the names of some of the most prominent men of the late 19th century, such as Gurney, Lang, Barrett, James, Crookes, and so on. In the archives is a vast amount of material, case-histories, tapes and books relating to psychic phenomena, telepathy, mediumistic experiences, spiritualism, mesmerism, spiritualistic and mediumistic frauds and so on. Especially interesting is a small collection of psychic photographs, of which perhaps the most famous is one of the original prints of the **Combermere** ghost.

■ *The nearest tube station is High Street Kensington.*

Bartholomew's Hospital (St) ☓

In the 12th century the knight Rahere was returning home from a pilgrimage to Rome when he caught malaria. In fear for his life he vowed that if he reached England alive he would build a hospital for the poor. During his journey

Berkeley Square in the 19th century, said to be the most haunted square in London.

home he had a dream, or vision, in which he was carried high into the air by a vast eagle, which deposited him on the edge of a precipice ledge overhanging the bottomless pit. In the dream, he was rescued from this predicament by St Bartholomew.

Mindful of the cure and of the visionary dream, Rahere eventually built the hospital, alongside the Augustinian priory church, both of which were completed in 1127, and even within his lifetime the place became famous as a site of miraculous healings. It was said, indeed, that there were more cures in the adjacent church than in the hospital itself. The cures were reputed to take place most frequently on the feast of the saint, which is 24 August. The beautiful 12th-century tomb of Rahere, with its original effigy, is still in the church.

■ *The nearest tube stations to Bartholomew's are the Barbican and St Paul's.*

Berkeley Square

Several of the houses in this beautiful 18th-century London square are said to be haunted, but the 'Berkeley Square ghost', usually means the ghost of the house at number 50, which is now the rather chic house of an international bookseller. The house fell empty after 1859 when the tenant, Elizabeth Curzon, left and soon (like most empty houses) it began to gather a reputation for being populated by evil spirits. 'The house in Berkeley Square contains at least one room of which the atmosphere is supernaturally fatal to body and mind', as one account concluded, after various awful events before 1879. The author Lord Lytton (eventually the Viceroy of India) was one among many who admitted that the house was haunted: he left a graphic account of how he had tried to sleep in the troubled room for an entire night, armed with a couple of guns. In the candlelight he had seen something leap at him, and he had fired one of his guns at it – yet when he looked for the fallen creature, there was nothing to be seen! Other stories circulated – a young servant saw such horrors in the room that she went insane – a baronet, scorning the question of ghosts, passed the night in the room to pooh-pooh the spirits, but on the following morning he was found dead in the middle of the floor! In spite of its reputation for evil, the haunted house was eventually bought by the Earl of Selkirk in 1880, and he arranged for it to be completely restored and redecorated in order to exorcise the troublesome spirits. However, in the year before the earl moved in, when the house was at its worst point of dilapidation, another tragedy happened in one of the rooms. Two sailors, finding themselves without a bed for the night during their Christmas leave, broke into the house, which by now had all the appearance of being a derelict property. They fell asleep in one of the upper rooms, but were woken in the middle of the night by a ghastly intruder. One sailor escaped to the street, calling for the police.

A policeman happened to be in the square, and they both ran back towards the house. Even before they reached number 50, they heard the other sailor scream, then the breaking of glass, and a further terrible scream. The poor fellow had fallen from an upper window: he had died immediately, impaled on the ornate metal railings around the front of the house.

■ *A convenient tube station for Berkeley Square is Green Park. The square is part of the continuation of Berkeley Street, to the north of Piccadilly.*

Bloomsbury

The antiquary John Aubrey records that in 1693 he was walking on midsummer's day 'in the pasture behind Montague House', when he saw over twenty women, most of them well dressed, 'on their knees . . . as if they had been weeding'. Eventually someone explained to him that they were searching for a coal under the roots of a plantain, for if these were placed under their pillows on that night, they would have a visionary dream of their husband-to-be. This mysterious coal could only be found on that day, as near to midday as possible.

■ *Bloomsbury is no longer a pasture: Montague Street runs into Russell Square, which is best approached by the tube station of that name.*

Bread Street

Significantly, there is a huge department of the Bank of England in Bread Street, between Cannon Street and Cheapside. Many of the symbols which decorate the externals of the building, and the walls of the inner courtyard, are esoteric or occult, as for example the unicorn bearing a shield with the entwined basilisks of heraldic origin. One might write a whole book on the occult

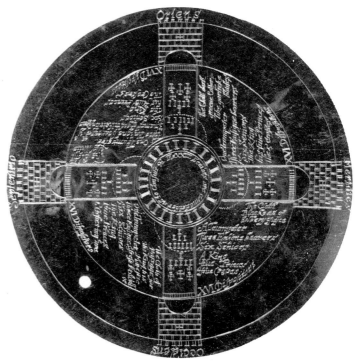

One of the plates which supported the legs of the table on which John Dee looked into the future on behalf of Elizabeth I. British Museum.

In forma arietis sut stelle. 13. ex quibs due sut de magnitudie tua ɛ̃ c̃

Above *Astrological image of the zodiacal sign Aries, from a 15th-century manuscript in the British Museum.*
Left *Images of the demons Apollyon and Belial, from an occult text by Barrett now in the British Museum.*

significance of both the unicorn and the basilisk, and indeed the 19th-century esotericist Browne did precisely that, writing an extraordinary study of the deeper meaning of the unicorn in relation to occult lore.

■ *The nearest tube stations are Mansion House and St Paul's.*

British Museum

There may be little doubt that the British Library, and the related manuscript departments of the British Museum in Bloomsbury, contain within their 15 million or so books the finest collection of occult books in the world. Almost all the great occult and esoteric scholars of the past hundred years have consulted the more arcane texts housed here, and there are few important works by occultists, esotericists, demonologists, magicians or rosicrucians which are not represented within the library or manuscript departments. The collection of alchemical, astrological and demon-ological texts in the British Library and in the various manuscript departments is quite extraordinary, and well beyond adequate catalogue: the representative pictures shown here are intended merely to symbolise the main streams of occultist lore covered within the titles. In the area of alchemy one might mention in passing the alchemical manuscripts the 'Splendor Solis' and the masterpiece called the Ripley Scroll; among the astrological texts the magnificent 16th-century manuscript catalogued as Additional 23770, of which the image of the zodiacal sign Aries is a sample. In the field of divination one of the most remarkable texts is a copy of the Chinese *I Ching*, printed as a block book in the 8th century; in the arcane realm of Rosicrucianism, the hand-coloured plates made for William Law's edition of the occultist-mystic Jacob Boehme.

In the collection of the museum itself are many occult items of popular interest, some of them on open display, ranging from Egyptian magical papyrii and statues of esoteric images and symbols, through Greek, Roman and Arabic amulets, to the 16th-century scrying glass used by the magician John Dee, beloved by the general visitor, to the 11th-century Lohan appreciated by esoteric specialists.

■ *The nearest tube station is Tottenham Court Road.*

A unicorn holding the ancient hermetic device of the entwined basilisks on the Bank of England in Bread Street. Many of the symbols which decorate the outside of the building are esoteric or occult.

Cannon Street ⊕

The main door of the London offices of the *Financial Times* in Bracken House, Cannon Street, is surmounted by a beautiful zodiacal clock, some 7 feet/2 metres square. The clock, installed in 1959, was made and designed by the engineers Thwaites and Reed. The external face has three rotating rings and two small indicator windows. The outer concentric, driven (like all the other mechanisms) by electric motors, revolves once an hour to indicate minutes, the middle ring marks out the passage of the hours, in a twelve-hour sequence, while the inner ring, containing the images of the zodiac, takes a complete year to turn. Astrologers will note that, for all the beauty of its design, the image for Pisces is technically inaccurate, since it does not include the 'silver cord' which normally joins together the mouths of the two fishes. Virgo and Gemini both betray 'Egyptian' elements in the design which have no real part in zodiacal imagery. The resemblance of the central sun-face to Winston Churchill is not accidental: this great statesman was a friend of Lord Bracken, after whom the building is named. The instrument is probably the most lovely large-scale zodiacal clock in Britain.

■ *The nearest tube station is Cannon Street.*

Modern zodiacal clock over the door of Bracken House, one of the 'Financial Times' buildings in Cannon Street.

Charlotte Street ⊙⊙ →

In an autobiographical note the Irish poet W.B. Yeats tells us that he was initiated in the Hermetic Order of the Golden Dawn in May or June, 1890 (it was in fact 7 March), in 'a Charlotte Street studio'. The G.D., as it was often called, was involved with a Christian form of the Jewish Cabbala, and was essentially rooted in a series of ritual designed to make contact with invisible and powerful spiritual beings.

Among the members of this curious Order (founded officially in 1888) were many occultists and pseudo-occultists, including the scholar A.E. Waite, and Pamela Coleman-Smith (who drew the familiar 'Waite' versions of the Tarot cards), Liddell Mathers (later known as MacGregor Mathers) and, later, the notorious Aleister Crowley (see **Hastings**). In a later account of these days Yeats wrote, 'I look back to it as a time when we were full of phantasy that has been handed down for generations . . . That phantasy did not explain the world to our intellects, which were after all very modern, but it recalled certain forgotten methods and chiefly how to so suspend the will that the mind became automatic and a possible vehicle for spiritual beings . . .' Yeats was certainly helped in the development of his mystical vision by his experiences in the Order. When in 1917 he married Georgie Hyde-Lees, however, they attempted a seance together on their honeymoon, and found that she was able to do automatic writing through the influence of a spirit-communicator. This took Yeats well beyond anything he learned through his initiation into the order, and actually provided him with the occult symbolism which gave rise to his poems 'A Vision' (1925). One wonders precisely which of the Charlotte Street studios it was where Yeats was initiated: could it have been that used in the late 18th century by John Constable, and later owned by the painter Augustus John? During his student days, the present author lived in that studio, and, by what is normally called 'chance', happened to be present when it was pulled down, round about 1963.

■ *The most convenient tube for Charlotte Street is Goodge Street. Constable's Studio was No. 72, though of course it has long disappeared. The numbers appear to have been changed in the early part of the present century.*

Cheapside

At number 107 Cheapside is the building leased to the Sun Alliance Insurance Group, which has twelve stone images of the zodiacal signs inset into the fabric of the huge doorway surround. One of the interesting symbolic details is that the symbol for Pisces is not portrayed with the traditional pair of fishes linked by the silver cord, but consists of three fishes, reminding one of certain of the 16th-century woodcuts which depicted the sign in this unusual way, as for example in the zodiacal print shown below.

■ *The nearest tube station is St Paul's.*

A curious image of Pisces from the twelve zodiacal images on the Sun Alliance Insurance building, Cheapside. One of the interesting details is that the symbol for Pisces is not portrayed with the traditional pair of fishes, linked by the silver cord. It consists of three fishes, reminiscent of some 16th-century woodcuts which depicted the sign in this unusual way.

The 'Fool Card' of the Tarot Pack, designed by Pamela Coleman Smith – one of the so-called 'Waite Pack' cards. (See Charlotte Street).

City ⊕

The city is ruled by the zodiacal sign Capricorn, but London itself is ruled by Gemini. The 17th-century astrologer William Lilly had this ruleship in mind when he published a 'hieroglyphic' showing two boys, arms interlinked, over a burning city. This figure was published without comment in 1665, and was taken by some as a prediction of a great fire. In the aftermath of the Great Fire of London in 1666, some recalled the predictive image, and Lilly was called to the House of Commons, with the feeling that he might well have been personally involved in bringing about the fire. After an amiable discussion, he was honourably discharged, however. The story is amusingly told in Lilly's *Autobiography*: there is a fluted Doric column, designed by Wren, erected as a memorial to the Great Fire in Fish Street Hill. The view from its 202-foot/62-metre height, over Geminian and Capricornian London, is well worth the climb. For more about Lilly, see *Westminster Abbey*.

■ *The nearest tube station to Fish Street Hill is Monument.*

The 'Hieroglyphic' printed to William Lilly's design in 1664, generally taken to predict the Great Fire. The two twins in the picture represent the zodiacal sign Gemini, and astrologers insist that this sign has rule over London.

Cock Lane ♂

The house which was number 20 Cock Lane, pulled down in 1979, was once the most famous haunted house in London. The ghost of Cock Lane started out in 1760, as what would nowadays be called a poltergeist, for the tenants heard scratchings and tappings for which they could give no reasonable account. Fanny, who was the mistress of the main tenant, Mr Kent, was convinced that the ghostly sounds were a portent that she would shortly die – which within a few weeks she did. The ghostly rappings continued some months afterwards, and eventually a simple form of communiction was established with the unknown agency, so that it became possible to answer questions put to it. By this means it was established that Fanny had been poisoned to death with arsenic administered by Mr Kent. Whatever the truth behind this ghostly message, by 1762 the Cock Lane ghost was widely famous in England, and many people, including the writer Samuel Johnson, visited Cock Lane in order to hear the mystery sounds, or to investigate. On very little evidence, Johnson came to the conclusion that the haunting was a fraud perpetrated by Elizabeth Parsons, but not before he had visited Fanny's coffin in the vault's of St. John's church in Clerkenwell, where it was said that similar ghostly rappings might be heard. Although Johnson did not make a systematic or thorough investigation of the hauntings, his view of the Cock Lane as a fraud or hoax has often been taken as the final word – however, those who believed in the reality of the agency did 'test' Elizabeth in the most extraordinary way, suspending her bed as though it were a hammock, and ensuring that her feet and hands were securely bound. When tied in this way, there were no more rappings, and the Parsons family, around which the haunting had centred, were sentenced to jail, protesting their innocence. In the following century, Fanny's coffin was found once again in the crypt of St. John's, and opened by those who remembered the story of her murder. Inside the coffin was the corpse of a young woman with a face still perfectly preserved – a sign, among other things, of arsenic poisoning.

■ *The house at Cock Lane has been pulled down, but St John's Church at Clerkenwell is still standing. The nearest tube station is Farringdon Street.*

Gloucester Place ⧗ ♀ → ✡ ☉

At 50 Gloucester Place is housed the library and membership rooms of the Theosophical Society of Great Britain. The society was founded in New York by the great occultist Madame Blavatsky and her friends Olcott and Judge in November 1875, the principal centre being established in 1879 at Adyar, Madras. The library at Gloucester Place, which was begun with the founding of the English section of the society in 1888, and which has since been built around the preserved original core of Blavatsky's own collection of books, is one of the finest occult libraries in Britain, covering a wide range of subjects, well beyond the theosophical context – such as alchemy, witchcraft, astrology, divination, psychic science, and so on. In the public membership rooms of the society building public seminars and lectures in astrology and related subjects are held. The occult device linked with the society incorporates oriental, middle-Eastern, western, Christian, Jewish and other symbols, as an indication of the society's expressed aim of transcending all personal faiths and beliefs. See also **Basingstoke**.

■ *A near tube station is Baker Street.*

Greenwich (on main map) ⊕

On the foundation of the Greenwich Observatory by Charles II John Flamstead became the first Astronomer Royal. Like his friend, and later enemy, Isaac Newton, he was a keen practical astrologer, and records indicate that he cast a horoscope to determine a satisfactory cosmic moment to lay down the foundation stone for the Observatory (August 1675). This horoscope is preserved at the Royal Observatory, and as the astrologer Alfred Pearce remarks, some 'learned astronomer hostile to astrology' has scrawled on the figure the Latin 'restrain your laughter, friends', in mockery. Pearce is quite correct in pointing out that Flamstead's judgement of the moment is amply vindicated in the 'just renown, stability, and usefulness of the Royal Observatory.'

■ *Greenwich is on the A206, in the eastern part of London. It can be reached by BR from Charing Cross Station.*

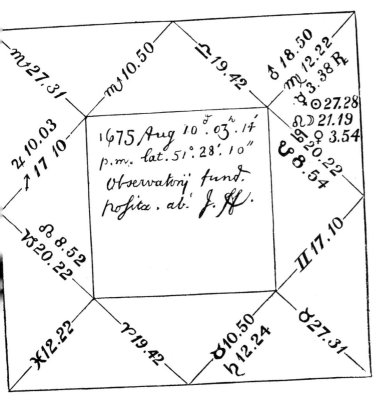

A Greenwich horoscope produced for the founding of the Royal Observatory, Greenwich in August 1675, cast by the first Astronomer Royal, Flamsteed. (From a facsimile reproduced by A.J. Pearce).

Guildhall ⚊

In English legend it is said that the daughters of the Emperor Diocletian, having murdered their own husbands, were set adrift on the seas. They were washed ashore in Britain, and fell into the company of a number of awful demons who took them as wives. From this demonic breeding sprang a race of giants, who were all killed in later wars, with the exception of the brothers Gog and Magog, the latter sometimes Goemot, as in the Geoffrey of Monmouth version of the tale. This pair of giants were brought to London as slaves, and put on duty as porters or guardians in the royal palace, the site of the modern Guildhall. Their effigies are said to have stood there as guardians ever since their deaths, but literary records of them go back only to the early 15th century, and these were certainly destroyed in the Great Fire of London in 1666. In Elizabethan times the figures were called Gogmagog and Corineus, and the original figures, which were eventually set up in the Guildhall in 1708, had been used in pagan parades and pageants during preceding centuries. The present statues, set up in 1952, high at the musician gallery end of the Guildhall, were the gift of a Lord Mayor, who had them carved in limewood by David Evans as replacements for those destroyed in the bombing in the Second World War. It is doubtful if there is any relationship between the gigantic or demonic Gog of English mythology and the Gog mentioned in the Bible (Ezekiel xxxviii), though such a relationship is often claimed. See also **Wandelbury** (Eastern Counties).

■ *The nearest tube stations to the Guildhall are Mansion House and St Paul's.*

Highgate ⚊

The name probably derives from the fact that this was the site of a toll gate, spanned by an arch, on this London hill. Alongside the arch was a little chapel, dedicated to St Michael (like so many chapels on hills and mounds).

■ *Highgate village is not well served by tube stations – it is probably best to take the tube to Archway, and to walk up Highgate Hill, passing on the left of the road the cat memorial to Dick Whittington, Lord Mayor of London, and character of Pantomime fame.*

Holland House ⚭

Of all the haunted buildings in London the 17th-century Holland House is the most interesting, if only because of the fame of those spirits who were reputed to live their half-lives within its walls. The ghost of Lord Holland, beheaded in March 1640 for his part in the civil war, was often seen in the gilt room of the house: it was said to issue 'forth at midnight from behind a secret door.' His daughter Lady Diana Rich is also believed to haunt one of the rooms, and the story is told that while she was still alive, she went for an evening stroll in the garden, and saw a ghostly image of herself walking towards her, 'as though in a looking glass'. Within the month she was dead of smallpox. Presumably, both ghosts, as well as that of her sister Lady Elisabeth Thynne, have now been laid, as Holland House was largely destroyed by bombs in the early part of the Second World War.

■ *The nearest tube station is Holland Park.*

Holloway Road

It is often said by historians of psychic phenomena that the first spirit-photographs made in London were taken in the garden studio of Mr Hudson at 177 Holloway Road, on 4 March 1872. Observers or clients were surprised to find that even while Mr Hudson took photographs of the spirits he could see, his photographic equipment behaved in a most extraordinary way: 'he has been moved from one part to another of his operating room; his camera and its stand have been moved about by unseen agency', writes one detached observer in the *Spiritual Magazine*, adding 'we have been told that Mr Hudson's house was uninhabited for above a year before he occupied it in consequence of its being reputed to be haunted'. In case one might consider the works of Hudson as being merely fakes, it is worth observing that several of his pictures survive, and (perhaps more important) a large number of testimonials to his having obtained recognisable portraits of people long-dead – in one case of someone who had died before ordinary portrait photography was a possibility. Hudson's work is of great interest, yet there are records of such spirit-pictures being made even earlier in other parts of Britain (as on the Continent), though it is fairly certain that the first spirit-pictures ever made were taken in Roxbury, in the United States of America, prior to 1861. The first important spirit-photographer was William Mumler, who worked in Boston (USA) from that year. One clairvoyant photographer of the period, Robert Boursnell, who also had a studio in London, claims to have made spirit pictures, or 'shadow pictures', as he sometimes called them, almost by accident as early as 1853, and it is true to say that Boursnell's later work is among the most fascinating of Victorian spirit-photographs. Among the work typical of Boursnell's studio is the one showing the (then living) W.T.Stead, an important pioneer-worker in psychic investigation, and then editor of the psychic magazine *Borderland*, with the spirit form of an old Boer called Piet Botha. Stead recalls, 'When I went to sit with Mr Boursnell I did not know that Piet Botha was dead. He appeared – much to Mr Boursnell's surprise – in the studio, (and) was photographed standing behind me. When asked by Mr Boursnell, at my suggestion, what was his name, he said it was Piet Botha . . . I kept the print until the end of the (Boer) war, and then submitted it to the Boer delegates who came to London after peace had been made. It was instantly recognised as a striking likeness of Commandant Pietrus Johannes Botha, who was the first Boer commandant killed at the siege of Kimberley.'

■ *Holloway Road is best approached from Holloway Road tube station: some of the records give No 177 as in Palmer Terrace, but the street numbering appears to have changed since 1872.*

The photograph of an unidentified sitter with a spirit 'extra', taken by Boursnell, circa 1896, at 177 Holloway Road.

The psychic worker W.T. Stead with the spirit form of Piet Botha, taken at 177 Holloway Road, around 1902.

Lincoln's Inn

When, in the late 16th century, a wax image of Queen Elizabeth I was found in Lincoln's Inn Fields, people were horrified to see that a pin had been stuck through its middle – a sure sign of treasonable witchcraft, designed to kill the Queen. The poppet was sent to **Mortlake** for the great occultist John Dee to examine, and he came to the surprising conclusion that it was intended only as a joke.

■ *The nearest tube station is Chancery Lane.*

Marble Arch

The Marble Arch now marks the site of the infamous Tyburn gallows. Many stories are told about the ghosts which inhabited the place, but the most remarkable tale is that of five men who were hanged for murder in 1447. As the law required, they were hanged, then cut down, and were being stripped for dismemberment, when their belated reprieve was announced. The story tells that the men came back to life, but the hangman refused to give them back their clothes (these being part of his pay), so the men returned down Oxford Street naked. Almost 300 years later a youth of seventeen who had been hanged for rape showed signs of life when laid out on the dissecting table. He had soon completely recovered, and was eventually deported for his crime. He is reported to have had extraordinary postmortem experiences, finding himself in the company of the long-dead.

■ *The nearest tube station is Marble Arch.*

Marylebone

Francis Barrett, one of the best-known occultists of the early 19th century, lived in Marylebone, which was then a quiet suburb of London. His most famous book is *The Magus, or celestial intelligencer*, which appeared in 1801, and which is now often used in modern occult texts because of its excellent colour plates of demons, sigils, and so on. The text is in no way original, as almost all the occult lore with which Barrett was familiar was derived from standard works on occultism, witchcraft and demonology. This did not prevent him from opening up a school devoted to the study of esoteric matters.

■ *Marylebone is best explored from Regent's Park tube station, or Baker Street: the house in which Barrett lived has long been pulled down, however.*

Muswell Hill

Muswell Hill was once the site of a shrine, linked with the friars of St John of Jerusalem. The shrine was alongside a sacred well, from which poured miraculous waters that healed those sick who drank from it.

■ *Muswell Hill is served by the Muswell Hill tube station.*

Park Road

In the Steiner House building at 35 Park Road, a few hundred yards or metres north of Baker Street tube station, is housed the main part of the library of the Anthroposophical Society of Great Britain. While organised mainly around the extraordinary writings and lectures of the great esotericist Rudolf Steiner, and his followers, the titles within the library cover a wide range of occult, philosophical and allied spiritual-scientific subjects. The library is open to the public.

■ *The nearest tube station is Baker Street.*

Parliament Hill Fields

On these fields to the north of London, which offer extensive views over the City, the occultist C.W. Leadbeater set up an intriguing programme designed to portray for the first time what clairvoyants saw on the astral plane. Working towards the end of the 19th century, he described in great detail what he himself saw clairvoyantly on the astral plane (invisible to normal vision) to a small group of artists, so that they might make pictures of the forms and colours which he described, and thereby obtain an approximation to his inner vision. The astral forms he described were later called 'thought forms', an extensive literature developed around them and very many paintings were made of the curious formations which are said to be created on the astral plane whenever a person thinks or feels about anything. Leadbeater often described the astral visions in the most curious circumstances – for example, at a funeral, or during a shipwreck, but perhaps the most interesting theme was the 'appearance' of music on the astral plane.

One of the most important of the artists working in this curious way was John Varley, a direct descendant of another John Varley who, at the beginning of the 19th century, had worked in a similar way with the mystic poet William Blake, in drawing creatures which Blake saw on the astral plane. The 19th century drawings were almost all abstract, and have been described by the art historian Sixten Ringbom as being indeed the first truly abstract paintings. It is no accident that the book in which the body of this strange artistic work was published should have fallen into the possession of Wassily Kandinsky (an active occultist), who is generally supposed to have painted the first abstract pictures in the first decade of our own century. Abstract art was born of occultism, and this birth was witnessed on Parliament Hill Fields.

■ *Parliament Hill Fields lie to the east of Hampstead, to the north of Camden Town, and are most conveniently approached from Hampstead Heath station (Broad Street line).*

'Thoughtform of Music' seen in the astral plane hovering above a church, 1895.
Taken from the first edition of Besant and Leadbeater's 'Thought-forms'. (See Parliament Hill Fields)

Pond Square ☿

The ghost of Pond Square, which no longer exists, is nothing more than the disconsolate spirit of a hen. It is said to be the hen which was the object of Sir Francis Bacon's famous experiment, in 1626, when it occured to him that snow might be used to preserve a dead body. He bought a hen, had its innards removed, and then stuffed it with snow to see how long it would be preserved. It is said that it was a result of this first experiment in refrigeration that Sir Francis caught the chill from which he soon died.

■ *The nearest tube station is Hampstead.*

The London Stone ☒

The stone set into the wall between the London Stone pub and St Swithin's Lane is said to be an altar stone erected by the legendary Brutus of Troy, who is supposed to have founded London. Most archaeologists dismiss it as an ordinary Roman milestone, however. It has not always been placed in the St Swithin wall, for the antiquary John Stow records that it was set in the ground opposite the modern Cannon Street station, from where it was removed in 1742, first to a wall in St Swithin's church (demolished 1962), then to its present position.

■ *The nearest tube station is Cannon Street.*

The Tower of London △ → ☒ ⊕ ☿

According to the large number of ghost stories which have been woven around the Tower of London, one would expect every room and corridor to be haunted. The most famous ghosts are those of Sir Walter Raleigh, whose spirit still roams the passages of the Beauchamp Tower, and (of course) Anne Boleyn, the one-time wife of Henry VIII, who haunts the Queen's House, and who, ignoring the challenge of a sentry in 1864, so terrified the unfortunate man as to send him into a swoon, as a result of which he was court-martialled. Fortunately, his encounter with the ghost had been witnessed by two other soldiers, who testified on his behalf, thus leading to his acquittal. In 1817 the Keeper of the Crown Jewels, Edmund Swifte, witnessed an extraordinary happening which seemed to be a sort of presage of a coming disaster. One evening in October he and his family were entertaining guests to supper in their house at the Tower. Just as Swifte handed his wife a goblet of wine she began to tremble and then shouted out in alarm. She was pointing to a strange vision of light which floated above the table. Swifte's own words tells the tale: he could see 'a cylindrical figure like a glass tube, something about the thickness of an arm' hovering a couple of feet over the table. Its contents 'appeared to be a dense fluid, white and pale blue, like the gathering of a summer cloud and incessantly rolling and mingling within the cylinder'. This vision hung over in the air for about two minutes, and then began to float slowly towards one of the female guests, passing

directly in front of Swifte. As it hovered over the back of his wife, she fell down in terror, for the vision 'siezed' her in some curious way, and hurt her shoulder. Swifte grabbed at a chair, and hit out powerfully at the vision, but the solid wood went through it harmlessly and crashed against the wainscot behind. The vision floated across the head of the table once more, over to the recess of the window at the end of the room, and disappeared.

The Tower.

Salt Tower △ ⊕

In the Salt Tower of the Tower of London is what is often called Draper's astronomical clock, which is not so much an astronomical clock as an astrological machine. It was constructed by the prisoner Hugh Draper of Bristol, in May 1561. It seems that Draper was in the tower because he had been accused of witchcraft against Sir William St Loe and his wife. Draper calls his design a 'sphere', and it is of interest to astrologers that he uses some rather personal symbols in the carving. It is instructive to compare the twelve sigils for the zodiacal signs which Draper has carved into the concentric circles within the large circle (the 'sphere') with those given in Table 1, page 15. The sigil for Capricorn appears to be entirely personal. One wonders why Draper insisted so much on recording the exact date? There is nothing untoward in the heavens on the 30 May of that year, though the moon did go into Pisces, the sign generally associated with 'prisons and confinements'. Perhaps the 'sphere' and the date were somehow connected with his own natal horoscope? The Tower guide says that the carving may be used to cast horoscopes, which is

Hugh Draper's 'astronomical sphere' in the Salt Tower of the Tower of London, dated 30th May, 1561.

nonsense. The tables to the left of the sphere list the sigils for the twelve planetary hours of the day. As there are seven columns, we may take it that this plots the sequence of planetary hours for a whole week.

The Tower Jewel House

In the early 19th century one of the night guards on duty outside the Jewel House saw a cloud of grey smoke emerge from beneath the door of the tower, and form itself into a fearsome image rather like a huge bear. In a panic the sentry lunged at it with his bayonet, but the blade passed through the creature, and stuck fast in the wood of the door. The sentry fainted away on the floor, and remained there until discovered by the other sentries. The keeper Edmund Swifte, on being informed of the guard's story, visited him, and records how shocked he was to note the physical change in the soldier, who was clearly terrified by his experience, and swore that he had neither dreamed the vision nor seen it in a drunken state. A couple of days later, the man died, insisting to the very end that his story was true!

White Tower

The White Tower stands on a mound called The White Mound by mythologisers. It is said that when Bran, the Blessed Raven (Bendigeidfran) of Welsh mythology, died, he commanded his seven followers to bury his head within the White Mound. The mythology of this Bran is complex, however, and the buried head of Bran, known as The Wonderful Head (*Uther Ben* in Gaelic) was said to have been dug up by King Arthur, a deed which was called by some 'one of the three wicked uncoverings of Britain'. Bran appears to have been the leader of a tribe which had adopted a crow or raven as its magical totem, and he is sometimes figured or symbolised as a black raven. This was also one of the symbols in the mystery wisdom of the ancients – especially of the Persian Mithraic cults, which were carried to Britain by the Roman armies. The ravens which live within the Tower, and feed on the lawns, are the 'birds of Bran', and it is said that when they fly away, London will be destroyed.

It is also claimed that Brutus (see **London – The London Stone**) is also buried in the White Mound.

The White Tower is vastly haunted with the spirits of people tortured or imprisoned there, from Guy Fawkes and Walter Raleigh to the Lady Jane Grey, who seems to haunt so many places in Britain.

■ *The nearest tube station is Tower Hill.*

symbolised in terms of the chalice or the Holy Grail. It is said that the secret lore of the Templars was passed on to the charge of the Masonic lodges when the order was dissolved in the 14th century. On the wall opposite the western entrance to the Temple are two enormous bell strikers, representing the giants Gog and Magog (see **Guildhall**).

■ *The nearest tube station is Temple.*

Victoria Embankment

The Egyptian obelisk called Cleopatra's Needle (which has nothing to do with Cleopatra) was originally erected at the Egyptian esoteric centre of Heliopolis, where Jesus and his parents were said to have lived after the flight from Herod. The obelisk was brought to London by boat, encased in a specially constructed metal cylinder, in 1878. The copies of Egyptian sphinxes to the east and west of the obelisk add a strange quality of the occult to this most light-filled part of the London panorama.

■ *The nearest tube station is Embankment.*

Westminster Abbey

The astrologer William Lilly records a strange treasure-hunt which took place in the cloisters of Westminster Abbey during the mid-17th century. Lilly was one of the party, which also included David Ramsay, Charles I's clock-maker, and John Scott, who was adept in the use of the divining rod. Ramsay had been convinced that a huge treasure was buried in the abbey, and employed Lilly and Scott to locate it by means of horoscopes and the divining rod, which was sensitive to metals and hidden wealth. Scott's rods clearly indicated that they should dig on the west side, and at the place indicated, about 6 feet/2 metres down, they came across a coffin. Curiously, because the coffin was lightweight, they did not open it. When they moved back into the abbey church, however, a terrible and quite unnatural storm arose, and the winds blew so fiercely that they began to believe that the walls would cave in. Lilly, who knew something about demonology, tells us that he 'gave directions and command to dismiss the demons', and immediately all was quiet once more. He blamed the failure of their occult treasure hunt on the great company of people who were watching the operation, and concludes, 'secrecy and intelligent operators, with a strong confidence and knowledge of what they are doing, are best for this work'.

The Stone of Scone under the Coronation Chair in Westminster Abbey is regarded as being the sacred stone of England. With the exception of Mary I, every English monarch has been crowned sitting above it. Records indicate that thirty-four Scottish kings were also crowned over the stone, before it was moved from Scotland to Westminster in 1296, on the orders of Edward I. Tradition insists that it is the biblical stone on which Jacob rested his head, but the occultist Blavatsky regards it as one of the surviving magical stones with the power of 'inner speech'. She writes: 'It is also known that the famous stone at

The Tower ravens are linked in mythology with ancient stories which may be traced back to the Mystery Lore.

The Temple

The Temple church, hidden away in the maze of Inner Temple inn of court, is, like most of the ancient Templar churches, built on a circular ground plan. It was founded in the late 12th century by the Knights Templars, and (it is often claimed) many of the 12th- and 13th-century effigies in the floor of the church commemorate these remarkable men who were exoterically concerned with the defence of the pilgrimage routes to Jerusalem, and, esoterically, the guardians of the mediaeval occult Christian lore, often

Effigy of a crusader in the Temple.

Westminster was called 'liafail' – 'the speaking stone,' – which raised its voice only to name the king that had to be chosen.'

■ *The nearest tube station is Westminster.*

Wilton Row ☿

The Grenadier pub in Wilton Row has a reputation for being haunted by poltergeists, and by the appearance at times of unexplained wisps of smoke (which have even been photographed). The psychic investigators Owen and Sims point out that the inn has strong historical connections with the Duke of Wellington and his officers, and record a tradition that in the last century an officer was flogged to death for cheating in one of the rooms in the pub. However, no evidence has been raised to connect this event with the haunting.

■ *The nearest tube station is Hyde Park Corner.*

Maidstone (Leeds Castle), Kent ☿
E2 TQ 7656

People accustomed to the number of houses and castles in Britain reputedly haunted by the ghost of Anne Boleyn may well be surprised to find that Leeds Castle near Maidstone has no such reputation, despite the fact that a pair of the lady's shoes are still preserved here. The ghost of Leeds Castle is a phantom hound, which will appear from nowhere and disappear with the same disturbing ease. Some of the previous inhabitants of the castle have claimed that the vision of the spectral dog bodes evil for those who see it, but others dispute this. Leeds Castle is almost entirely rebuilt, but in former times the infamous Eleanor of Gloucester was imprisoned here for the crime of witchcraft (officially for 'witchcraft, necromancy and treason'). Inevitably, some claim that the spirit dog was one of her hounds, which was really a witch-imp.

■ *Maidstone is signposted off junctions 5, 6 and 7 of the M20, south-east of London.*

Margate, Kent ☿
F2 TR 3571

The old Theatre Royal in Margate is one of the many haunted theatres in Britain, though in recent years it has been the focus of the attention of more than the usual number of ghost-hunters. Archer, in his *Ghost Writer*, has said that the place has witnessed 'the most diverse psychic happenings', which include as the star attraction an orange-coloured ball of light, with a paranormal repertoire of strange noises, screams, ghostly footsteps, ghastly smells, curtain manipulations by poltergeist agencies, and so on. The regular appearance of a ghost has been linked with an actor who committed suicide in the theatre in the 19th century. In his own book on hauntings Joseph Braddock refers to the actor-ghost, and maintains that it was seen so frequently during the first decades of the present century that the management completely curtained off the offending box, and finally had it bricked up. Unfortunately, at the time of writing, this historic theatre is in a state of disrepair, and is boarded up, with a somewhat uncertain future.

■ *Margate is at the eastern termination of the A28, north-east of Canterbury. The theatre, recently used as a bingo hall, is in Addington Street.*

Minstead *See* Hindhead

Mortlake, London ⊕ → ◉
C2 TQ 2075

One of the most versatile of men – a magician, scholar, mathematician, astrologer and learned courtier – of the Elizabethan period was Dr John Dee, who in the early 17th century owned a house at Mortlake. It was here that Queen Elizabeth I would come in progress to consult Dee on important matters of state, as well as on questions of futurity. Among many other predictions, Dee is reputed to have told of the accession of Elizabeth I to the throne, the coming (and destruction) of the Spanish Armada, and (perhaps unwisely, while Mary was still alive) of the execution of Mary Queen of Scots, and so on. It was while living in this Mortlake estate (which was eventually pillaged and burned by the mob, suspicious of his ways) that Dee wrote his esoteric work, *Monas Hieroglyphica*, a profound

John Dee's Monad symbol from his book Monas Hieroglyphica. *The symbol, in the shield, contains the 'powers' and virtues of the first six signs of the zodiac. Images for these are hidden in the decorative motives around the shield.*

and influential study of occult symbolism in the guise of an analysis of a single occult sigil. He died at Mortlake in 1608 in the house which had the most magnificent collection of occult and scientific books of the 17th century. One of the tablets Dee used for raising demons, now called the Seal of Aemeth, is preserved in the **British Museum** (see under **London**): for further information on Dee, see **Walton-le-Dale** (The North) and **London – Lincoln's Inn**.

The astrologer and almanac maker John Partridge, who was made famous by the satire of Jonathan Swift, also lived in Mortlake, and during that time he wrote his most important book on astrology.

The extraordinary linguist, traveller and savant Sir Richard Francis Burton lived in Mortlake, and though he died abroad, in 1890, his body was brought back for burial to the village (1890): his sarcophagus, an exotic tomb in the shape of an Arab tent was designed by his wife Isabel as a suitable memorial among the less ambitious tombs in the Roman Catholic cemetery at Mortlake. Besides being interested in all occult matters (especially in oriental magic) Burton was also a proficient astrologer.

■ *Dee's Mortlake estate gave way to urban spread many years ago.*

Newbury, Berkshire △

B2 SU 4666

The case of the 'Newbury Witch' is part-historical, part-fiction. In 1643 some soldiers serving in Cromwell's army under the Earl of Essex seized a woman they took to be a witch and decided to shoot her. The legend runs that she merely laughed at their bullets, catching them in her hands as they sped towards her and chewing them. Eventually a soldier slashed her forehead, a dramatic form of witch pricking, no doubt (see GLOSSARY), to render her evil magic ineffective, and then shot her dead with a bullet beneath the ear. As the historian of witchcraft, R.H. Robbins, points out, the execution of a witch by shooting is most unusual. It appears also to have been a form of military lynch law, since there was no trial and no proof whatsoever that the woman was a witch.

■ *Newbury is at the junction of the A4 and the A34.*

Smeeth, Kent △ ◉

F3 TR 0739

Here in Scots-Hall, as it was once called, Reginald Scot, who was to become one of the best and most sane demonologist of the 16th century, was born. According to his own account, his critical view of the witchcraft delusion resulted from his personal experiences at the trial of about eighteen people accused of witchcraft at the **St Osyth** hearings when sixteen were found guilty and hanged. It is said that it was the shock of these mass executions of 1582 which persuaded Scot into writing his influential denunciation of witchcraft, *The Discovery of Witches* (1584), the

first published book in English to deny the reality of witchcraft, and to condemn it as an illusion. So influential was this book that when the witch-fearing Scottish King James came to the English throne in 1603, he ordered all copies to be destroyed.

■ *Smeeth is signposted to the north of the A20(T), off junction 10, going east.*

Steyning, West Sussex ♂

C3 TQ 1711

Bramber Castle in Steyning is little more than a perilous ruin of upright walls, but these are still said to be haunted by the three starved children of William de Braose, whose family was imprisoned and done to death (though probably in Windsor Castle) on the orders of King John in the early years of the 13th century. In fact the castle is said to have two separate groups of ghosts, Lady Maud, wife of Sir Hubert de Hurst, was killed there by her husband for infidelity with William de Lindfield, who was in turn walled up by Hubert in a tiny oubliette set within the walls of the castle. The skeleton, said to have been discovered by the victorious Parliamentarians in the 17th century during an attack on Bramber Castle, was long believed to have been the remains of de Lindfield.

■ *Steyning is signposted to the south of the A283, to the west of Brighton.*

Tedworth *See* Tidworth

Tidworth, Hampshire ♂

A3 SU 2349

The most famous haunting in England during the 17th century was that of the Tedworth Drummer, which reached such fame that Charles II appointed a committee to look into the matter. (The name Tedworth has changed since those days, and there are now two villages, North Tidworth and South Tidworth). This drummer was not a ghost in the ordinary sense of the word – in modern times we would almost certainly call it a poltergeist. An early engraving made to illustrate the book *Saducismus Triumphatus* by the 17th-century student of psychic phenomena, the Reverend Joseph Glanvill, pictured it as a devil. The story opens normally enough in March 1662, with the arrest of a conjurer named William Drury, who had once been a regimental drummer, but who now earned his living as a wandering entertainer. He was arrested for fraud, and brought before the magistrate, Mr Mompesson. Drury was discharged, but had his drum confiscated. Within hours all hell had been let loose – eyewitnesses spoke of the drum rising in the air inside Mompesson's home, and, thus, suspended, being beaten by invisible hands. After a few days of ceaseless drumming, which virtually drove Mompesson insane, he managed to have the drum destroyed – but this did not bring to an end the awful sound of constant drumming. Other strange things began to occur in the house – people were lifted into the air, objects would fly around, thrown by invisible agencies, and so on. Naturally, people began to suspect that it was just the fraudulent Drury up to his tricks. Drury was arrested on another charge, and was transported for his crimes. With the physical drummer himself gone, even the committee appointed by the king to investigate the Tedworth hauntings was unable to give a rational explanation for the disturbance. At the end of exactly one year, in 1663, the demons (or whatever they were) left the village for good.

■ *North Tidworth and South Tidworth straddle the A338, to the west of Andover.*

The Tedworth Drummer, here represented as a demon, though it was never actually seen. From the frontispiece of Joseph Glanvill's Saducismus Triumphatus, 1683.

Walton-on-Thames *See* Diseworth (Central England)

Wherwell, Hampshire   ☿ ✗ ♂
A3 SU 3840

The terrible Wherwell Cockatrice is said to have been hatched by a toad from a duck's egg in a crypt of Wherwell Priory, whence it proceeded to crawl forth to feed on human beings. In mediaeval lore, the cockatrice could kill merely by the power of its glance, but by the 16th century it was confused with the crocodile, and so this Wherwell monster was probably a saurian demon. Whatever its form, the legend tells that many good knights met their deaths in attempting to kill the creature, but eventually it was despatched by the guile of a local man, who leapt into the crypt carrying a mirror which he held up to the face of the cockatrice. As in the classical story of the confrontation of the Gorgon Medusa by Perseus, the monster was struck dead by the reflection of the dark power which streamed from its own eyes.

The priory was said to have been built for magical reasons, for its founder Queen Elfrida (wife of King Edgar, who died in 975, and mother of Ethelred the Unready) wished to expiate the murder of her stepson, and accordingly made this foundation as a sort of 'blood-money'. Only fragments of the original 10th-century priory may be seen, however: the so-called 'Priory' is now a private house, of the 19th century. The church is a late rebuilding of the mid-19th century, but quite fantastic grotesques from the original church have been incorporated into a mausoleum in the churchyard.

■ *Wherwell is about 3 miles/5 km south-east of Andover, on the B3048.*

Wilmington, East Sussex   →
D4 TQ 5405

The chalk figure of a man or god over 230 feet/70 metres high, holding a staff in each hand, cut on the downland grass on Windover Hill is probably 2,000 years old. It was mentioned in antiquary literature in 1779, but its origin or purpose is unknown: it certainly is not meant to represent Harold, King of the Saxons, as a few writers suggest. Some occultists say that the figure is that of the pagan god Helith. The Long Man, as he is called, was restored in the late 19th century, the outline reworked and the innards of the lines filled with bricks, so it is difficult to know precisely what it looked like in earlier times. Like most of the hill-figures, it is not seen to advantage from any of the surrounding viewpoints, for the man is seemingly designed to be seen from the air.

■ *The Long Man of Wilmington is to the south-east of the village, signposted in the direction of Westdean, between the A27 and the A259.*

Winchester, Hampshire   ⌂ ✗
B3 SU 4729

St Catherine's Hill in Winchester is part of an ancient fort system. On the top of the hill is a turf maze of distinctive loop and whorl patterns, the age of which is unknown.

The so-called Round Table on a wall in Winchester Castle is a vast circle of painted wood, some 18 feet/5.5 metres in diameter. It is said, on little historical authority, to be a representation of King Arthur's original round table: but see also **Caerleon**. The circle is divided up into 25 painted segments, alternating in yellows and greens, with a central floral design made from two superimposed roses (one red, the other white), which suggests that the panel was painted in the 15th century: indeed, it first appears in historical records in 1450. Some historians have suggested that it might have been made for a masque connected with the Arthurian stories.

■ *Winchester is at the southern termination of the M3. The maze is just off the A33, on top of the hill. The round table hangs in the Great Hall of the castle.*

Eastern Counties

Borley, Suffolk

B3 TL 8442

Borley Rectory was once described as being the most haunted house in England, for within its walls were encountered the most diversified of psychic manifestations and poltergeist activities. The hauntings were made famous (perhaps infamous) by the 'researches' of the psychic investigator Harry Price, who, it later appeared, had a vested interest in bringing about the supposed hauntings which he pretended to study. Specialist historians of psychic phenomena, such as Trevor Hall, have been aware for a very long time that Price was a charlatan and liar, and that he himself perpetrated many of the 'diabolic' happenings for which the house was later infamous, yet in spite of this it is still popularly believed that Borley Rectory was haunted, and that in 1939 it was burned down by poltergeists or some unknown agencies. Harry Price appears to have been a congenital liar, and even went to the extent of forging a coat of arms for certain bookplates, in order to 'prove' some of his lies: his choice of emblem for his genuine coat of arms is some indication of his rather histrionic view of psychic phenomena, for it is an entirely imaginative image derived from witchcraft, and has nothing whatsoever to do with the phenomena Price was supposed to investigate 'objectively'. It is certain that not one of the claims he made in connection with supposed psychic phenomena at Borley – or indeed in any of the places he was supposed to investigate – was genuine. The barrister Sir William Crocker, who investigated the fire-damage claim for Borley, records that the insurance company concerned refused to recompense the owner, pleading that he had started the fire himself. Almost as a balance to the many lies which Price built into the (now destroyed) Borley Rectory, it has recently emerged that the nearby church of Borley is genuinely haunted, by a variety of ghosts, from a spirit nun to a phantom coach. A recent article on the haunting of the 12th-century church maintains with some truth that 'Price may have missed his real chance to confront the paranormal'.

■ *Borley is signposted off the B1064, to the north-west of Sudbury.*

Bourn, Cambridgeshire

A3 TL 3256

Inside the village church, set in the red and black tiling of the floor beneath the bell tower, is a maze – sometimes said to be the only internal maze in a British parish church. It is evident that the font, which is at present central to the maze, was put there long after the maze had been designed, for it to some extent now cuts into the formal pattern, and prevents anyone from following the entire geometric sequence of the 'dance'.

■ *Bourn is signposted on the B1046 to the east of the junction with the A14.*

Brantham, Suffolk

C3 TL 1034

The cellar of The Bull inn is said to be haunted by the ghost of a child.

■ *Brantham is north-east of Manningtree, on the B1080.*

An 18th-century print of witches preparing for a sabbath. This was chosen by Harry Price as the motif for his personal bookplate: the drama and imaginative element within such a plate reflects Price's own histrionic view of the nature of the psychic phenomena he was supposed to investigate.

The much haunted 'Bull' pub in Brantham.

Bungay, Suffolk

C3 TM 3389

In the churchyard of St Mary's in Bungay is a rounded boulder called the Druid Stone, which is supposed to give access to the Devil. Anyone who knocks on the stone twelve (some say seven) times will be rewarded by the sudden appearance of the Dark Majesty.

■ *Bungay is on the A143 west of Lowestoft. The church of St Mary is in the centre of the town.*

Bury St Edmunds, Suffolk

B3 TL 8564

Of particular interest to occultists is the Moyse's Hall Museum's display of witchcraft paraphernalia. There are witch-bottles, and related bellarmine bottles, numerous charms against witchcraft, including such grisly things as the mummified corpses of puppies, found stuffed in a chimney alongside many other specifics against evil working. The pride of the collection is a genuine witch poppet, a doll made by witches to be used for casting evil spells.

■ *Bury St Edmunds is on the A45(T), junction with A143. Moyse's Hall Museum is in the Cornhill.*

Cambridge, Cambridgeshire

B3 TL 4558

King's Chapel

The architectural gem of King's College Chapel has gained a certain notoriety among those interested in what they call geomancy because it is widely believed that Henry VII left instructions in his will for the chapel to be built according to 'geomantic measurements'. Not only was there no such phrase in the 15th century, but there is no record of such instructions being left. Additionally, what are taken for 'dragon symbols' – the four on the western gate, and the 'dragon-saints' of St Catherine and St Margaret on the south door of the choir – are quite conventional Christian symbols which figure in many great works of art.

Queen's College

Above the archway in the first court of the college is a curious zodiacal sun-dial, dated 1733, with inset images of the twelve signs of the zodiac. For further note of the college see **Warboys**.

■ *King's Chapel is best approached from King's Parade. Queen's College is best approached from Queen's Lane, off Silver Street.*

A demonic figure on mock-Tudor facade in the central square of Bury St Edmunds.

A witch poppet, probably 18th century, in the Moyse's Museum, Bury St Edmunds.

The Chelmsford witches hanged in 1589. From a contemporaneous pamphlet in Lambeth Palace Library.

Chelmsford, Essex △

B4 TL 7007

It was here, in 1566, that the first hanging for witchcraft is supposed to have taken place in England (see **Hatfield Peverell**). A second series of witchcraft trials was held in Chelmsford in 1579, when Elizabeth Francis and Ellen Smith were also hanged as witches. The third of the most important trials was held in 1589, when nine women and one man were charged with murder by witchcraft, four of them being convicted and hanged, largely on the evidence of children who claimed that the adults had familiar imps. The famous woodcut which shows Joan Prentice, Joan Cony and Joan Upney on the gallows with their familiar on the ground is from a popular pamphlet of the time: each of these supposed witches was hanged within an hour or so of the completion of the trial. The fourth trial was held at the instigation of Witch-finder Hopkins, when nineteen out of thirty-two accused were hanged for witchcraft, in 1645 (see **Manningtree**). Another famous Chelmsford trial is recorded under **St Osyth**.

■ *Chelmsford is on the A12(T), signposted at the roundabout junction with the A414, going north-east.*

Coggeshall, Essex △ ✧

B4 TL 8523

Paycock House in Coggeshall has a long wooden frieze on its street facade which points to esoteric symbolism. The left of the frieze begins with a curious dragon, while the extreme right finishes with the image of a man wearing a phrygian cap, one of the standard mediaeval images of initiation. This cap is almost the same as the one shown in many occult images of the Mithraic cult, and like the one which has survived in the remarkable statue of the alchemist, high on the tower above the facade of Notre Dame in Paris. The French occultist Fulcanelli writes of it as being one of the most consistent symbols of initiation in the west. In view of this contrast between the 'lower' demonic to the left, and the 'initiation' symbol to the right, the symbolism of this long and narrow Paycock frieze may be read as the story of the progress from the demonic levels which beset man, through life's experiences, to the spiritual awareness and clarity of thought of initiation.

In 1699 an old woman was lynched as a witch in Coggeshall. She was called Old Widow Colman, and the local vicar persuaded her to confess to him that she had indulged in witchcraft to the extent of making a pact with the Devil, practising black magic with poppets, and (quite naturally) refusing to go to church. It appears that having confessed to all this, Old Mother Colman was not prepared to recant, or return to the way of life which pleased the vicar. No doubt urged on by this man, the mob took the law into its own hands. She was dragged off and 'swum' in the local pond: as she floated on the surface of the waters, this was regarded as proof that she was indeed a witch. In fact, the old woman died as a result of this manhandling and wetting, but the vicar was not content to let the dead rest in peace. He had her corpse examined by a midwife, who reported that the 'witch' had supernumerary teats such as demons and imps were believed to suck from.

■ *Coggeshall is to the west of the junction of the A120 and the A12(T).*

Colchester, Essex △ ✡ ⊕

C4 TM 0025

Only a handful of the 17th- and 18th-century houses of old Colchester have survived the recent urban refurbishing and expansion, but until recently the town used to boast of itself as 'Britain's oldest recorded town', as it is said to be the first city to have been built by the Romans (later to be destroyed by Boudicca). In the 16th century it was an important witchcraft centre, and though most of the old buildings have gone, the town is still said to contain over a hundred building fragments from its glorious past, including the massive but ruined fortress, built on the base of the Roman Temple of Claudius (now a museum). Inevitably one finds among its ruins, and on display in its several museums, a number of interesting occult devices and symbols. The famous 1582 **St Osyth** witch trials were held here, and caused ripples of witchcraft hunting throughout England, yet this is one of the few towns in East Anglia to ignore its witchcraft past.

Some of the most interesting survivals of hermetic symbols in the town are the stonework vases and lilies on the facade of St John's Gateway to the old priory. These are linked with the Trinity (the three lilies), with the waters of life and baptism (the vase), and with the idea of incarnation in the physical body: the lily is derived from an occult symbolism which holds that when the Milky Way of stars was made in the skies, so the lily was made on earth. The belief is that what is enacted in the heavens must be reflected on the earth: the stars were made at the same time as the spirit of man descended to live on the earth plane. It is this esoteric view of the lily which accounts for its appearing so often in images of the Annunciation (announcing the birth of a God to the earth), and why it should appear on a building linked with St John, whose Gospel deals in its first fourteen verses with the incarnation of the Logos or Word, into the earth plane.

During the siege of Colchester by the Cromwellians in 1648 the astrologers William Lilly and John Booker were called to the camp to encourage the soldiers with predictions that the city would soon fall. Meanwhile behind the beleagured walls the astrologer John Humphrey was casting horoscopes for the governor, Sir Charles Lucas, to show that a relief column would soon arrive, and the city would be saved! It was claimed that if King Charles had hired Lilly, he would have been more value to his cause than half a dozen fighting regiments.

■ *Colchester is to the east of the A12(T), at the roundabout junction with the A604.*

Crowland, Lincolnshire ✠

A2 TF 2410

The aptly named Three-Ways-to-Nowhere Bridge now stands waterless over tarmac walks, but when the monks of Crowland Abbey built it in the 13th century the triple bridge almost certainly spanned the junction of two streams. What nature has withdrawn, local imagination has invented: it is said that beneath the intersection of the three arches there is a bottomless pit with an ever-swirling whirlpool just below. Many people press their ears to the ground to listen to the turbulence of this deadly pool, but the most they hear is the noise of drains and the vibration of the traffic!

■ *Crowland is on the A1073, north-east of Peterborough.*

Elmswell, Suffolk ✡

C3 TL 9863

The church of St John the Baptist in Elmswell is justly famous for the quality of flint and stone symbols on its tower and on the south facade. These have been restored in recent times, yet there is still sufficient indication that the designs are virtually a numerologist's paradise, if less complex than the example at **Rushton**. The designs include every significant numerological grade from one to forty, and also contain many esoteric symbols, such as the pentagram, chalices and the vased lily.

Inside the church is a most remarkable sculpture of a rhinoceros on the monument to Sir Robert Gardener (died 1619): strictly speaking there is nothing 'occult' about this monstrous figure, as it is derived from Gardener's heraldic crest. However, the notes on the influence of heraldic devices in the Introduction may be worth recalling in this context.

■ *Elmswell is north-east of Woolpit, at the junction of the A45(T) and the A1088.*

Arcane symbols on the exterior of Elmswell parish church.

Ely, Cambridgeshire

B3 TL 5380

The most outstanding occult symbol in Ely cathedral is the geometric 'maze' which is set in its floor tiles immediately below the west tower. Since there is no possibility of being 'lost' within this formal pattern, it is not really a maze in the accepted sense of the word, but more a formal dance. One arrives at a centre where there are four slabs, set into a square – so deceptively simple is this occult symbol that most people fail to recognise its true significance. It is in fact the quartered lozenge, an old symbol for the magical quintessence. Just as the greatest power on earth is the quintessence (here symbolised at the centre of the earth-bound maze), so are the two greatest ranks of the spiritual hierarchies symbolised in the skies above us.

On the painted ceiling in the tower immediately above the maze we see Christ in glory, with the two highest ranks of the seraphim and cherubim on either side. It is no accident that the quintessence symbol (the fifth element) of alchemy and astrology really portrays each of the four elements of earth, air, fire and water in union and harmony, holding together the material structure of the world. The seraphim and the cherubim were the sources for the ancient images of the four zodiacal elements of earth as bull, air as human, fire as lion and water as eagle. Just as the occult nature of the fourfold elements of the physical world are held together in union by the powerful quintessence, so in the heavens the four spiritual archetypes of the four elements are held together by the power of Christ.

Of particular interest to occultists are the images contained in the space between the vesica piscis (which contains Christ in Judgement) and the vast circle which circumscribes this vesica – these are symbols of the stars, and the sun and moon wrongly orientated to each other, the crescent of the moon pointed away from the sun. This latter device is derived from alchemical symbolism, and is intended to portray the male and female elements in the created world in a state of tension – the tension which the Healer Christ is resolving. This panel is an example of mediaeval occult symbolism at its best.

The Ely Imps are sometimes mentioned by those interested in occultism and demonology. These are two demonic grotesques, one with a leonine head above a more demonic head. The pair may be seen from the north side of the choir (facing south), below the point where the first and second arches join, above the stalls of the choir. Much more interesting, however, are the numerous demons and demonic scenes to be found among the misericords in the choir stalls: note especially the delicate carving of the devil leading the two clerics, as though they were old friends.

■ *Ely is signposted off the A10(T) at the junction with the A142. The cathedral dominates the town.*

The maze in the marble floor of the west tower of Ely Cathedral.

Erwarton, Suffolk

C3 TM 2134

The late mediaeval effigies in the church (among which is that of a crusader, buried in the church in 1287) witnessed the enactment of a curious prophecy. It had been said that the heart of Anne Boleyn had been buried in this ancient church, and would one day reveal itself again. Records indicate that in 1836 masons restoring the south wall came on a leaden box, which was opened, to reveal only a heap of dust. The box was closed once more, and placed in a coffin in the vault of the Lady Chapel. One of the workmen, however, had remembered the old prophecy told to him by his grandparents, and knew that this leaden box contained the heart of that sad Ann Boleyn who had been beheaded in 1536 on the whim of Henry VIII. There is still something strangely disturbing in the atmosphere of this church.

■ *Erwarton is on the Shotley Peninsula, signposted off the B1456, south of Ipswich.*

Hadstock, Essex

B3 TL 5544

The gravestone of the artist Michael Ayrton (who died in 1975) in the burial grounds of St Botolph's church is decorated with a curious copper labyrinth. In his sculpture, drawing and paintings, Ayrton had often showed an intelligent interest in Daedalus, the Athenian craftsman who is reputed to have designed the Cretan maze where the Minotaur was incarcerated: we should therefore not be surprised to find Ayrton interested in mazes. Daedalus is said to have made himself wings from the feathers of birds, and to have flown over the Aegean Sea, and Ayrton was interested in such notions of flight. A maze which Ayrton built at Arkville in the USA contained two bronzes also made by him – one represented the Minotaur, and the other Daedalus and his son Icarus. One wonders if the curious form of the Hadstock maze is intended to pull together the notion of the genuine maze with the idea of flight, for the outline is not circular, as with most mazes, but suggests the shape of a butterfly's wing.

The maze on the gravestone of Michael Ayrton at Hadstock, in the graveyard at St Botolph's church.

In the western part of the churchyard are the remains of St Botolph's well, the waters of which were once used as a cure for scrofula.

■ *Hadstock is on the B1052, south of Linton, which is to the south-east of Cambridge.*

Harkstead, Suffolk

C3 TM 1834

On the late mediaeval font of St Mary's church there are four wodewose figures, grouped between four lions and the four symbols for the evangelists. The woodwose, or wildeman, is one of the mythical wildmen of Suffolk mythology. The restorations of 1875 revealed in the splay of one of the north windows traces of a mediaeval fresco of a devil with yellow wings. He appears to be holding the apple, or 'malum' by which demonic evil was brought into the world. The magnificent coloured marble intarsia work on the pulpit depicts the four symbols of the evangelists.

■ *Harkstead is on the Shotley Peninsula, signposted off the B1080 between Manningtree and Ipswich.*

A woodwose or wildeman on the font in the village church, Harkstead.

Hatfield Peverel, Essex

B4 TL 5215

In 1563 Elizabeth I passed a new witchcraft law, which indirectly led to one of the most notable trials of that period, at **Chelmsford**. The three accused were called Elizabeth Francis, Agnes Waterhouse and her daughter Joan, all of whom came from the village of Hatfield Peverel. The first, said to have a familiar cat called Sathan, which would turn itself into a toad, was charged with betwitching a child, so as to turn it into an old man. She was imprisoned. A second charge at a later point (this time for betwitching an adult) led to another year in jail, and four spells in the public pillory. Finally, in 1579, she was charged with bewitching Alice Poole to death. She was convicted and hanged. The witch Agnes Waterhouse was charged with bewitching to death William Fynee, but while denying this, she confessed to attempting the murder of someone else. She also 'confessed that falling out with one widow Gooday she willed Sathan (the familiar she had taken from Elizabeth Francis) to drown her cow . . . Also, falling out with another of her neighbours, she killed her three geese.' She was hanged on 29 July, 1566, and is sometimes said to be the first woman hanged for witchcraft in modern England. Her daughter Joan, who was then only eighteen, was charged with bewitching a young girl, but was found not guilty.

■ *Hatfield Peverel strings out along the A12T, signposted north-east of Chelmsford.*

Hilton, Cambridgeshire

A3 TL 2966

The turf maze at Hilton leads to a decorative (18th-century?) upright stone which bears an inscription to the effect that it was cut by one William Sparrow in 1660.

■ *Hilton is on the B1040, south-east of Huntingdon. The maze is on the village green.*

Kimbolton, Cambridgeshire

A3 TL 0967

Kimbolton Castle is really a fortified mansion, built in Tudor times, and now one of the most beautiful private schools in England. It is said to be haunted by the ghost of Catherine of Aragon, one of the divorcees of Henry VIII, who lived there (in what was called the Queen's Room) for the last few months of her life, until 1536.

■ *Kimbolton is on the A45, east of Wellingborough.*

Kimbolton Castle in modern times a school, once said to be haunted.

King's Lynn, Norfolk

B2 TF 6119

St Margaret's Place

On the western facade of the priory church of St Margaret facing the square is a rare 17th-century lunar clock, sometimes called the Moon Clock. The moving pointer is in the form of a dragon, said to be the dragon which attacked St Margaret – and therefore symbol of the Devil himself. The dragon-hand points to the time of high-tide, according to the 24-hour clock. The central disc, surrounded by the astrological symbols for the planetary aspects (relationships of planets as viewed from the earth) of trine, opposition, conjunction and square, revolves to reveal the phases of the moon in the circular opening.

In the square itself (St Margaret's Place) is an interesting sundial, on the facade of a 15th-century hall of the Guild of the Holy and Individual Trinity. The regalia room of this guildhall contains what is said to be the oldest paper book in the world – though it is probably only the oldest western paper book, for there is a Chinese charm-book printed on paper which is almost a thousand years older.

Tuesday Market Street

On one of the high window ledges of the house at number 15 there is an unusual symbol of a heart contained within a lozenge. This is said to mark a curious event in the history of witchcraft. In June 1616 the wife of a glovemaker was hanged as a witch in Tuesday Market Square, which then contained the market cross, and was used for such public executions. It seems that she had been convicted merely because she had roundly cursed a sailor who had hit her son. The curse appears to have been effective, however, and the woman was charged, tried and found guilty of witchcraft. She died still protesting her innocence of any diabolic pact or intention, and shortly before she was hanged she predicted that when she expired her heart would fly out from her body and perch on the window of the magistrate who had condemned her. Contemporaneous accounts insist that her heart, in the form of a bird, did fly from her body, and settled on the window.

Clifton House

The beautiful merchant's house at 17 Queen Street has a mediaeval crypt which is said to be haunted.

■ *King's Lynn is at the junction of the A17(T) and the A10.*

A witchcraft symbol on the window lintel of a house in Tuesday Market Square, King's Lynn associated with a legend of witch burning.

Knebworth, Hertfordshire

A4 TL 2420

Knebworth House was the family seat of the Lytton family from the 15th century, and the house (remodelled in 1843 to a romantic Victorian's castle-dream) was the birthplace and home of Sir Edward Bulwer Lytton, famous among occultists for his book on Rosicrucianism, *Zanoni*, his life of the adept Paracelsus, and certain curious words which he introduced into occult lore, mainly through the writings of the theosophists who followed the teachings of the occultist Madame Blavatsky. One of these words was 'vril' (which he introduced in his book *The Coming Race*, 1871), concerning which Blavatsky herself said: 'The name vril may be a fiction; the Force itself is a fact doubted as little in India as the existence itself of their Rishis (Holy Teachers), since it is mentioned in all the secret works. It is this vibratory Force, which, when aimed at an army from an Agni Rath fixed on a flying vessel, a balloon . . . reduces to ashes 100,000 men and elephants, as easily as it would a dead rat.' The vril is a destructive agency which could 'reduce Europe in a few days to its primitive chaotic state with no man left alive to tell the tale'. The most remarkable thing is that Blavatsky wrote these words in 1888, long before man had tampered with the forces hidden within the atom.

■ *Knebworth House is in Old Knebworth, to the west of Knebworth, which is signposted to the west of the A602, south of Stevenage.*

Lincoln, Lincolnshire

A1 SK 9771

In 1406 Henry VI was informed that the diocese of Lincoln was 'infested by sorcerers, wizards, magicians, necromancers, diviners, and soothsayers of every sort'. As a result he commanded the Bishop of Lincoln to search out all those guilty of such practices, and commit them to jail. In modern times there is no sign of such diabolic practices in this quiet, historic and charming old town, dominated by its exquisite cathedral.

The demonic grotesques on the west facade were there in the time of Henry IV, for they were part of the rebuilding programme after the 1185 earthquake which destroyed the earlier building – these grotesques are among the finest in Britain.

Inside the cathedral there is one famous demonic grotesque known as the Lincoln Imp, high on a pillar in the Angel Choir: it is more like a nature sprite than anything demonic, and in any case, all such infernal power in the fabric is adequately overcome by the power of the surrounding exquisitely carved angels. The story tells that the Lincoln Imp was once a real elemental creature, a troublesome demon which caused much difficulty for those building the cathedral: he was turned into stone when the priests exorcised him, to become what is probably the only petrified demon in England.

Anyone interested in arcane symbolism cannot fail to be impressed by the mediaeval misericords in the 14th-century choir stalls.

■ *Lincoln is on the junction of the old Roman roads of the Foss Way (A46) and Ermine Street (A15).*

Demonic grotesques from the west facade (around the portal) of Lincoln Cathedral.

Long Marston, Hertfordshire

A4 SP 8915

Long Marston has been modernised during the past century or so – the village pond has been filled in to make room for a small green and war memorial, while the old church has been almost destroyed and a new one built to replace it, yet there are still old houses which witnessed a painful event which many of the modern villagers still speak about with a sense of shame. When a local innkeeper named Butterfield fell ill in 1750, he suspected that he had been bewitched by an old couple whom he had once met. These were the Osbornes, who lived at Long Marston. The couple were arrested, but a riotous mob decided to take the law into their own hands, and news got around that the couple would be ducked for witches on 22 April. The mob forced their way into the local prison and the couple were dragged through the streets of nearby Tring, where they had been imprisoned, stripped naked, had their hands tied behind their backs and were then taken to a nearby river. The locals, who know the story well, insist that this mishandling and ducking took place at the village pond in Long Marston. For a footnote to the story see **Tring**.

■ *Long Marston is signposted off the B489, itself to the left of the A4146 to Leighton Buzzard.*

Lowestoft, Suffolk △

C3 TM 5493

The witch Amy Duny and her accomplice Rose Cullender (both from Lowestoft) were executed at **Bury St Edmunds** on the 17 March 1665, having 'confessed nothing'. They had been tried in Lowestoft in 1664 for casting an evil spell on Deborah Pacy, a nine-year-old girl, and her sister Elizabeth. Immediately after being cursed Deborah had 'the most violent fits, feeling most extream pain in her stomach, like the pricking of pins, and shrieking out in a most dreadful manner.' As the 20th-century witchcraft historian Montague Summers recorded, there 'were strange stories of spectral mice, a toad, and poultry that haunted the house, running hither and thither.' Records of the trial indicate that six women stripped and searched Rose Cullender, and found the Devil's Mark, a teat by which she was supposed to give suck to the devils who gave her the power to do black magic.

■ *Lowestoft is on the East Coast, on the A146 from Beccles.*

Manningtree, Essex △

C3 TM 1031

It was in this village that the notorious witch-finder General Matthew Hopkins lived, and where his attention was first drawn to the scourge of witchcraft. In the 17th-century Hopkins set himself up as a witch-finder: he had no particular qualifications for this, having read only a handful of books on the subject (most notably the demonology of King James I), but his Puritanical background made him a man of conviction – additionally, the money received for revealing witches, and bringing them to trial, was good. It seems that by 1644 he was persuaded that a whole coven of witches lived in Manningtree, meeting near his house: these, 'with divers other adjacent Witches of other towns, who every six weeks in the night (being always in the Friday night) . . . had severall solemn sacrifices there offered to the Devill.' Hopkins took it on himself to root out these witches, and the result is that twenty-nine women were hanged. Hopkins obtained evidence against them (often the evidence being mainly his own word against their own) on the flimsiest of pretexts. His favourite method of discovery was to show that they had a 'familiar' – a witches' pet, such as a cat, a dog, a hen, and so on, which was really a devil in disguise – that would suck milk or blood from them. The famous picture of familiars from Hopkins' own book shows the witch-finder standing between two of his victims: on the left is Elizabeth Clarke, the first witch that Hopkins caught in Manningtree, and had hanged after a trial in July 1645. Hopkins himself died a couple of years later, in the comfort of his bed, though local legends still current in Manningtree, insist that Hopkins was seized by the villagers who were thoroughly fed up with his nonsense, and was drowned as a result of being swum in the river.

■ *Manningtree is signposted on the A137, north-east of Colchester.*

A portrait of Matthew Hopkins, the so-called 'Witch Finder General', between two of his victims. From Hopkin's Discovery of Witches, *1647. (See Manningtree.)*

Merton, Norfolk ○

B2 TL 9098

Writing in 1927, the historian of witchcraft, Montague Summers, tells the true story of someone who said she regularly saw the ghost of Edward Fitzgerald in Merton Rectory (now called the Old Merton Rectory, and a private dwelling). Fitzgerald had started his free 'translation' from the Persian of the *Rubaiyat of Omar Khayyam* in the rectory, and although he had died in 1883, the cook often saw the poet in spirit, and was quite nonchalant about her experiences. 'I have the gift of second sight,' she said. 'I saw my grandfather long after he was dead . . . I dropped the pennies I had in my hand and ran home all of a tremble with fright. I never saw granddad but once. But this Fitzgerald, I have often seen.' The incumbent reverend asked her to describe the ghost, which she did very precisely, in a way which left no doubt that what she saw resembled closely the dead poet.

■ *Merton Rectory is about a mile/1¼ km east of Merton village. It is best approached down the third turning to the right (a narrow road with inadequate passing points) from Watton on the A1075 south. The house is on the left in a well-wooded garden.*

Norwich, Norfolk
C2 TG 2308

Among the many symbols of interest to occultists in Norwich cathedral are the series of ceiling bosses in the ambulatory of the huge cloisters. These include a number of Green Men and demonic figures, but the most interesting boss in the ambulatory is that which depicts Christ in Hell – the entrance to which is symbolised in the gaping jaws of a multi-toothed demon. The esoteric connection between such a mediaeval image of Hell and Christ is that the latter works through the power of his word (He being the Logos): the image of the Word passing into hell is a reversal of what happens when humans speak, for then words pass out into the world. Hell is therefore seen as a perversion of the holy Word or Logos. In occult terms, Hell is a place of spiritual inversions and mirror-images.

■ *Norwich is at the northern termination of the A11(T).*

The mouth of hell, Christ, the damned and devils. A mediaeval roof boss in the ambulatory of the cloisters of Norwich Cathedral.

Peterborough, Cambridgeshire
A2 TL 1998

It was in the air above Peterborough that one of the earliest illustrated sightings of a UFO (an unidentified flying object) was made in 1909. The two policemen who saw it, early in the morning, thought at first that it was a mysterious airship, but they described it as being 'oblong and narrow in shape, carrying a powerful light'. An engraving of the UFO, its light shining on Peterborough cathedral, was printed in the magazine *Lo!*, published by the extraordinary American collector of occult and mythological lore, Charles Fort.

■ *Peterborough is to the east of the A1(T).*

Royston Hertfordshire
B3 TL 3540

In Royston is a unique cave, some 30 feet/9 metres below ground, the walls of which are covered in extraordinary petroglyphs of unknown origin or purpose. One or two of the symbols are distinctly occult, and appear to be involved with the darker side of magic. The suggestion that it was used by the Knights Templars appears to be unfounded, for they were not involved with satanic worship, as they are often popularly represented.

■ *Royston is on the A10(T), south-west of Cambridge. The entrance to the tunnel is in Baldock Street.*

St Albans, Hertfordshire
A4 TL 1407

In one of the gorges of the hills above St Albans there was a cave in which dwelled the Wormenhert Dragon, which is said to have been bricked in by an 11th-century priest, using the stones of the ruinous Roman city of Verulamium. The story, which may be seen in symbolic terms as pointing to the demise of the pagan cults, was first told by the historian Matthew Paris in the 13th century: perhaps Paris was aware that the name could be interpreted as meaning 'dragon-heart', in reference to the darker beast in every man and woman?

■ *St Albans is approached by the M10, from junction 7 of the M1, north-west of London.*

St Osyth, Essex
C4 TM 1215

In 1582 there was a witchcraft trial in **Chelmsford** which the historian Summers describes as 'the most remarkable of all Elizabethan cases'. The trial is generally called that of The St Osyth Witches, although only six of the women involved came from this tiny village, others being from nearby Little Oakley, Walton Ashes and Thorpe le Soken. It seems that Ursley Kemp of St Osyth, who earned her living as a nurse, midwife, and so on, also eked out her living by 'unwitching', or healing, the sick. Davy, the son of Grace Thurlow fell ill, and was cured by Kemp, but the old woman was not allowed to nurse a newly-born baby. Shortly afterwards the baby fell out of her cradle and broke her neck. Eventually Ursley Kemp was arrested, and on the evidence of an eight-year-old boy (the 'base son' of Ursley) was said to possess a number of evil spirits in the form of cats, a lamb and a toad. As a result of this initial trial, a local coven of old witches was uncovered and brought to trial, all blamed with causing a variety of different rustic accidents. Annys Herd, for example, was according to the records charged with the murder by witchcraft of a man and two women, and for bewitching animals, and turning milk and cream sour. The documents claim that she was possessed of six 'impes or spirites, like avises and black byrdes, and vi other like kine, of the bygnes of rats, with short hornes.' For the outcome of the trial, see **Smeeth** (London and Southern England).

■ *St Osyth is on the B1027, south-east of Colchester.*

Saffron Walden, Essex ✡ ⌘
B3 TL 5338

The pargeting on the houses to the south of Church Street probably dates back to the 16th century when most of the houses were part of the Sun Inn. There are a number of esoteric symbols in this plasterwork, but most interesting of all are the images of the two 'giants' above the coach door. These are said by locals to represent Gog and Magog (for legend, see **London – Guildhall**), but this is unlikely. The giant to the left is definitely a sun hero, with his sword pointing up to the heavens (here represented as a heart, which in mediaeval symbolism was linked with the sun). The giant to the right is probably a lunar being, with his staff pointing down to the earth. This view of the symbolism is reinforced by the actual magic woven by the direct sunlight as it falls on these figures, for towards evening the sun lights up the solar giant, working up from his feet, and picking out his form completely before it even touches the lunar giant. An interesting occult detail is that in the course of this magical weaving of sunlight the buckler in the hand of the solar giant is picked out as a circle with a central dot (formed from the fingers of the giant in the middle of the buckler). This occult symbol of an encircled dot was adopted in the late 15th century as a symbol for the sun, and this may be the earliest use of such a symbol within the framework of sunlit magic.

The so-called 'Gog and Magog' figures in the pargetting of the old 'Sun Inn', Saffron Walden.

The Common ⌘
To the eastern side of the common is preserved the largest turf-cut maze in England. It is 115 feet/35 metres in diameter, and the convolutions of the maze-like pathway are 1,650 yards/1,500 metres long. The date of the original cutting is unknown, but records show that in 1699 payment was made for redefining its extent and re-cutting its formal pattern. In 1911, subsequent to several other re-cuttings, the chalk underbase was laid with red bricks in an attempt to preserve it.

The turf maze at Saffron Walden.

St Mary's Church ✡
Inside St Mary's church is a beautifully coloured tapestry kneeler in crewel wool depicting the Saffron Walden maze.

Outside in the southern part of the churchyard is an emblematic gravestone designed to commemorate the mason Jonathan Parker. Most of the symbols at the head of this stone are esoteric.

■ *Saffron Walden is signposted to the east of the B1383, off junction 9 of the M11.*

Sible Hedingham, Essex △
B3 TL 7834

The Swan Inn in this village was the scene of one of the last fatal witch swimmings. On 3 August 1865 an old Frenchman who had a reputation as a witch, and who made his living telling fortunes and giving advice (in spite of being deaf and dumb) to the locals, was attacked by one Emma Smith of Ridgwell. A crowd soon gathered, and at last they dragged the unfortunate man down to the river by the side of what is now Aberford Street, down to Rawlinson's Mill, and pushed him in to swim him as a witch. The next day the man died of exposure, and though Emma Smith continued to insist that she had been bewitched by the old man, she and one of her accomplices, were tried for murder.

■ *Sible Hedingham is at the junction of the A604 and B1058.*

Sible Hedingham, now serene, was once the site of a fatal witch-swimming in 1865.

Stow Longa, Cambridgeshire ♉

A3 TL 1070

The charming priest's door in the south wall of St Botolph's church has a Norman tympanum with the image of a mermaid with monstrous beasts on either side of her. Looking down from the nave wall is a magnificent demonic gargoyle.

■ *Stow Longa is on the minor road between Spaldwick (A604) and Kimbolton (A45).*

Swaffham, Norfolk ✡

B2 TF 8109

In the churchyard, to the north of the church, is a red-brick house which once was part of the (now removed) priory properties. On the western side of the house are a number of partly Christian, partly esoteric symbols picked out in the brickwork. The basic configuration of symbols is built from groups of triangles.

Inside the church is a magnificent wooden ceiling, with exquisitely wrought angels. The poppyheads are among the most beautiful in the country, and include such rare symbols as the 'pedlar' (the mythical pedlar of Swaffham, who figures in many symbols in the town), the pedlar's dog, the four evangelist symbols and two beautiful pelicans feeding their young with blood. The most interesting symbolism, however, is connected with the rosary on two of the

poppyheads, for the rosary is arranged with the arms of those who hold them to form a figure 8, the esoteric lemniscate, one of the most profound of all occult symbols. One half of the figure is made from hands and arms, and is therefore the human half, the other half is made from rosary beads, and therefore represents the spiritual, or God-like. The mystic centre of the figure is where man and God meet.

■ *Swaffham is just south of the junction of the A47(T) and the A1065.*

Thaxted, Essex ⊕

B3 TL 6130

The great composer Gustav Holst, who was born at Cheltenham in 1874, lived for many years in this village, first in Monk Street Cottages, which were burned down, and later, from 1917 to 1925, in the manse. While in Thaxted he played the organ in the north transept in the parish church (the choir organ in the tower being a later addition), and composed the famous suite *The Planets*, in which he gave musical equivalents for the traditional pictures of the planetary virtues and influences, and indicated his deep knowledge of astrology.

■ *Thaxted is on the B184, north of Great Dunmow. There is a plaque in commemoration of Holst on the front of the manse.*

Thriplow, Cambridgeshire ♉ ♍ →

B3 TL 4346

The parish church is sited on a hill above the village, and is a good example of the tradition which insists that church building was interfered with by the Devil. The story runs that the intention was to build the church at the bottom of the village, near the Townsend Springs, but that the stones were miraculously transported to the top of the hill – naturally enough, the locals took it as a sign that they should build the church there, even though they suspected that the Devil had a hand in the business. In fact, the church was built near an ancient burial mound (a few traces of which may be seen, though it was levelled in the 1800s), perhaps indeed the burial place of an ancient chief named 'Trippa', from which the name for the village evolved: in the middle ages such mounds were regarded with suspicion as being pagan and therefore devilish.

The church and churchyard were once regarded as places of sanctuary, at a time when theft was as much a capital offence as murder. One seeking such sanctuary could stay untouched in the churchyard, but would be given no food, and had to choose between trial or exile. The earliest record of someone seeking sanctuary in Thriplow is 1260.

On a south-west pillar in the church is inscribed a Holy Hand, perhaps derived from the magical amulet tradition. It was scratched there by Mathias Prime in 1691.

■ *Thriplow is signposted to the north of the A505, south of Cambridge.*

Tring, Hertfordshire △

A4 SP 9211

It is said by the historians that the Osborne couple suspected of witchcraft in the village of **Long Marston** in the 1750s were imprisoned here, and were taken from this jail by a mob who wished to see 'justice' done the rough and illegal way. We may now only be sure that they were thrown into a nearby river or pond either here or in Long Marston, however. Wherever these waters are, the court records indicate that the woman did not sink, and so a chimney sweep called Colley forced her down with a pole, and then, after dragging her out of the water beat her until she died. Her husband was killed later. Colley was eventually hanged for murder, and certain of the others were punished. The event was the most notorious witch-swimming in English records.

■ *Tring is on the A41(T) to the east of Aylesbury.*

Wandelbury, Cambridgeshire ⊣

B3 TL 4953

On Wandelbury Hill a huge chalk figure was discovered by Lethebridge, which has been linked with the Gog Magog legends (see **London – Guildhall**). The figure has the appearance of a goggle-eyed giant with a horse or dragon, but the real significance of the vast chalk image, and what it actually depicts, is lost. It is known that names similar to Gog and Magog were respectively lunar and solar gods (some say 'mother' and 'son') of the British Iron Age, and it is remotely possible that the figure represents one (or both) mounted on horseback. Some associate Gog with Og, the giant King of Bashan, from whom the word ogre is said to have been derived by the French fable-writer Perrault. Others associate Gog with the Celtic god Ogma, who is reputed to have constructed the pseudo-magical Ogham lapidary alphabet.

■ *The site of the hill figure, the Gog Magog Hills, is to the north of the A1307, south-east of Cambridge, but the figures are now once more covered over.*

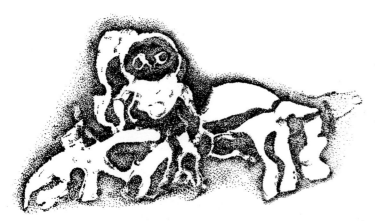

Gog-Magog figures on Wandlebury Hill, discovered by the archaeologist T.C. Lethbridge, who described it as a goggle-eyed goddess with chariot and horses. Later interpreters see it as a god (or goddess) with a dragon.

Warboys, Cambridgeshire △

A3 TL 3080

Warboys was the scene of one of the most unusual cases of witchcraft in the 16th century, when it was believed that the eldest daughter of Sir Robert Throckmorton was bewitched by a woman called Gammer Alice Samuel. It would appear that the child was a hysteric, and perhaps a little insane, for she complained that Alice was trying to suffocate her with frogs, toads and cats. Eventually the other daughters of Throckmorton were similarly afflicted, and Alice was taken before one of their uncles, who immediately 'scratched' her as a witch – that is to say, he drew blood from her in the belief that this would relieve the sufferings of those she had enchanted. A little later it was asserted (on virtually no evidence) that Alice had killed a lady with her witchcraft, and the poor woman was then so persecuted by those around that she eventually confessed before the Bishop of Lincoln to bewitching the children and killing the woman. She was condemned to death, and although she was well over eighty years old, she set up a plea of pregnancy, which convulsed the court with laughter, at which she eventually joined in. She, and her family, were hanged on the 7 April 1593. The witchcraft historian Montague Summers, records that the husband of the lady allegedly bewitched to death by Alice Samuel left an annuity to Queen's College, Cambridge to finance an annual sermon at Huntingdon, to be delivered by one of the divines of the College, on the horrors of witchcraft. The anti-witchcraft sermons appear to have been continued until well into the 19th century.

■ *Warboys is on the A141 north-east of Huntingdon.*

Welbourn, Lincolnshire ♉

A2 SK 9654

The exterior of the parish church has some of the most interesting gargoyles in the county, among which are initiation-figures in the form of mermaid-like creatures.

■ *Welbourn is to the west of the A607, south of Lincoln.*

Gargoyles and grotesques on the south wall of the church at Welbourn.

West Walton, Norfolk ☿

B2 TF 4713

The Devil is said to have made an attempt to fly off with the church tower, but dropped it about 20 yards or metres from the main body of the church, where it still stands, none the worse for its flight.

■ *West Walton is signposted to the west of the A47(T), north of Wisbech.*

The church tower at West Walton is said to have been moved by the Devil.

Withersfield, Suffolk ☿

B3 TL 6547

Among the many interesting mediaeval poppyheads in the parish church is a striking image which is probably intended to portray St George and the dragon. Another poppyhead appears to symbolise an initiation of two humans, who emerge from a floral pattern.

■ *Withersfield is signposted to the north of the A604, to the north of Haverhill.*

Woolpit, Suffolk ◉ ☿ ✡

B2/3 TL 9762

The name of this village has been explained as relating to either wolves or wool, but the word 'Wlpet' had nothing to do with either, this being the name of its original landowner in pre-Norman times. The place was once a centre of pilgrimage to the sacred Lady Well which was reputed to heal eyesight. The desolate remains of the well are to the east of the village, in a moat-like bog-land fed by the flow of its own waters: the last recorded use was in the first decade of the present century, and only the older locals appeared to know that it was once supposed to be sacred. In the mediaeval period, however, the Lady Well was a flourishing healing centre, served by at least one attendant, and probably with a small chantry: there is a possibility that Elizabeth I visited the well, when she stopped at Woolpit while on progress.

The wooden 15th-century angel-roof of St Mary's is one of the finest in the country, and the demonic grotesque poppyheads are a delight to any collector of demon-lore: it is interesting that the official guide to the church should pass them off as images 'mainly of dogs'. It seems to have been commonplace symbolism in mediaeval churches to have demonic images below (on the human level) and angelic images above, in the space symbolic of heaven. With such demonic images surviving, one wonders what the nature of the eighty 'superstitious' pictures and images must have been which were removed from the church in 1644 by the puritans?

Adjacent to the western wall of the churchyard is a mediaeval house, into the walls of which are inset symbolic images of flowers, clearly of magical origin: this stone-work has been restored in modern times, however.

The mediaeval story of the Green-Children of Woolpit, a legend which is now over-used for tourist purposes, is preserved in a useful translation (from the Latin) inside the church.

■ *Woolpit is signposted off the roundabout intersection of the A45(T) with the A1088. The well is within the dense undergrowth of the clump of trees on the further side of the road, about a quarter of a mile/400 metres to the east of the church: access is difficult, and the flow is now marked only by a trap-door of rotting wood.*

A 16th-century demon poppyhead on a pew in St Mary's Church, Woolpit.

Central England

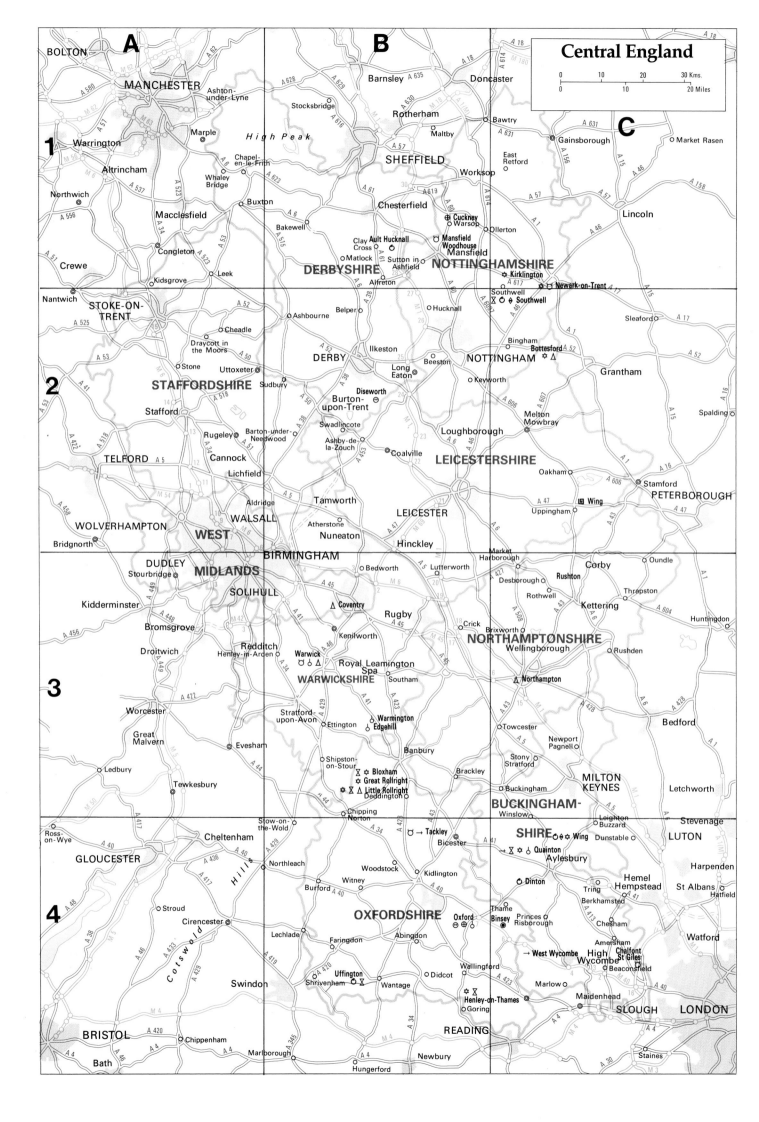

Central England

0 10 20 30 Kms.
0   10   20 Miles

A

BOLTON
MANCHESTER
Ashton-under-Lyne
A 62
A 628
A 580
M 62
Warrington
Marple
A 57
M 63
Altrincham
Chapel-en-le-Frith
A 6
M 56
Whaley Bridge
A 523
Northwich
A 537
Macclesfield
Buxton
A 556
A 34
A 623
Crewe
A 51
Congleton
A 523
A 6
Kidsgrove
Leek
A 53

High Peak

B

Barnsley A 635 Doncaster
A 628 A 629 A 18
Stocksbridge A 616 Rotherham Maltby
A 630 A 61 Bawtry
A 57 A 619 SHEFFIELD
Worksop
Chesterfield A 60 Cuckney Warsop Ollerton
Clay Cross Ault Hucknall Mansfield Woodhouse
Matlock A 61 Mansfield
Alfreton Sutton in Ashfield

C

A 18
A 614
A 180
A 631
Gainsborough Market Rasen
A 156 A 115 A 46
A 631 A 57 A 158
East Retford
A 57 Lincoln
A 46
A 1

Nantwich
STOKE-ON-TRENT
A 525
A 52
Ashbourne
Belper
A 38
Hucknall
Cheadle
Draycott in the Moors
DERBYSHIRE
Ilkeston
DERBY
Beeston
NOTTINGHAM
A 52
A 53
Stone
A 50
Uttoxeter
A 50
Long Eaton
Keyworth
A 41
STAFFORDSHIRE
Sudbury
A 518
Diseworth
Burton-upon-Trent
A 42
Swadlincote
Barton-under-Needwood
Ashby-de-la-Zouch
A 453
Coalville
LEICESTERSHIRE
Loughborough
A 6 A 46
Melton Mowbray
A 607 A 606
A 1
Uppingham
A 47 Wing
Oakham
A 606
Stamford
PETERBOROUGH
A 16
Sleaford A 17
Bingham
Bottesford A 52
Grantham
A 1
Spalding
A 16
A 15
A 52
Kirklington
Newark-on-Trent
Southwell
A 617 A 46
A 607

Stafford
A 41
Rugeley
A 51
Cannock
Lichfield
A 5
TELFORD A 5
Aldridge
WALSALL
Tamworth
Atherstone
Nuneaton
LEICESTER
Hinckley
A 47
A 6
WOLVERHAMPTON
WEST
Bridgnorth
DUDLEY
MIDLANDS
BIRMINGHAM
Bedworth
Lutterworth
Market Harborough
Corby
Oundle
Stourbridge
A 449
SOLIHULL
A 45
M 6
Desborough
Rushton
Thrapston
Kidderminster
A 448
Coventry
Rugby
A 45
Rothwell
Kettering
A 604
Huntingdon
Bromsgrove
A 456
A 41
Kenilworth
Crick
Brixworth
NORTHAMPTONSHIRE
Droitwich
A 449
Redditch
Henley-in-Arden
Warwick
Royal Leamington Spa
Southam
WARWICKSHIRE
A 429
A 41
A 423
Wellingborough
Rushden
Northampton
A 6
A 428
Bedford
Worcester
A 422
Stratford-upon-Avon
Warmington
Edgehill
Banbury
Towcester
A 5
Newport Pagnell
Great Malvern
Evesham
Ettington
Shipston-on-Stour
Bloxham
Great Rollright
Little Rollright
Deddington
Brackley
Stony Stratford
Buckingham
MILTON KEYNES
Letchworth
Ledbury
Tewkesbury
A 44
Chipping Norton
A 44
A 43
BUCKINGHAM-
Winslow
Ross-on-Wye
A 40
A 417
Cheltenham
Stow-on-the-Wold
Leighton Buzzard
Stevenage
A 40
Tackley
Bicester
SHIRE
Wing
Dunstable
LUTON
GLOUCESTER
A 436
Northleach
Woodstock
Kidlington
Quainton
Aylesbury
Harpenden
Stroud
Burford
Witney
Dinton
Tring
Hemel Hempstead
St Albans
Cirencester
A 40
Berkhamsted
Hatfield
Lechlade
OXFORDSHIRE
Oxford
Thame
Binsey
Princes Risborough
Chesham
Amersham
Watford
Faringdon
Abingdon
Wallingford
West Wycombe
High Wycombe
Chalfont St Giles
BRISTOL
Stroud
Uffington
Shrivenham
Wantage
Didcot
Marlow
Maidenhead
Bath
Swindon
Henley-on-Thames
Goring
Beaconsfield
SLOUGH
LONDON
Chippenham
Marlborough
READING
Newbury
Staines
Hungerford

Cotswold Hills

Ault Hucknall, Derbyshire

B1 SK 4765

An 11th-century Norman tympanum has been built into the west front of the village church here: at least one of these stonework symbols is esoteric. The lower register of the lintel depicts a man (St George, perhaps) confronting a curious dragon, which has only two feet, a curled tail and an arrow-ended tongue. Above, on the tympanum itself, is a strange centaur-like creature which evades classification. The architectural specialist Nicholas Pevsner thought that it might be an image of St Margaret emerging from the body of the Devil (see **Bretforton** – Wales and Western Counties in this connection), and that the odd-looking creature opposite it is the Lamb of God: however, the centaur had an esoteric meaning much the same as the mermaid (and for much the same reasons of dualism) in mediaeval art, and we may therefore take it as an initiation symbol.

Inside the church, which the historian Thorold evocatively describes as 'primitive and full of mystery', is a memorial slab to the philosopher Thomas Hobbes, who died in the nearby Hardwick Hall in 1679. Perhaps he had in mind the leviathan-like dragon on the tympanum when he entitled his politico-philosophical study *Leviathan*?

■ *Ault Hucknall is off junction 29 of the M1, to the south of the A617, close to the signposted Hardwick Hall.*

Binsey, Oxfordshire

B/C4 SP 4821

The Binsey wishing well was in former times a healing well, said to have been founded by a St Frideswide. Its magical waters were drunk to cure eye-troubles and to aid fertility, and records indicate that Henry VIII took its waters.

■ *Binsey is to the north-west of Oxford, at the end of a lane north of the A420 at Osney.*

Bloxham, Oxfordshire

B3 SP 4235

The church of Our Lady of Bloxham is said to have been built partly with the aid of the Devil, who worked as a skilled stonemason. Some of the gargoyles at Bloxham are of excellent quality, and one of the west windows contains a stone pattern image of the Seal of Solomon so frequently linked with the Devil and with devilish practices. This device, in such a context as a church, is entirely wholesome however, and is derived from an ancient tradition that it represents the magical quintessence. The six rays of the Seal of Solomon are said to be built from the interpenetration of the four triangles which represent the four elements, and the empty space within the star is believed to represent the invisible fifth element (the quintessence) which lies as the secret force behind all matter. The identical symbol is also found on one of the upright gravestones to the east of the church.

■ *Bloxham is on the A361, south of Banbury. The church is to the east of the road.*

Bottesford, Leicestershire

C2 SK 8039

On the exterior of the south wall of the church of St Mary the Virgin there is a gargoyle called the Bell-man, a semi-human, who carries a bell in either hand. It is said that this is one of the symbols linked with the prevalent fear of witchcraft in the Belvoir Valley, for it was believed in late mediaeval times that witches could not fly when church bells were ringing. For this reason church bells were often rung at the time when it was supposed that sabbats were being held in the neighbourhood. The idea probably goes back to the notion of the power of sound in the Word, the Logos, who is Christ.

Inside the church is a unique memorial, called the witchcraft tomb, with effigies of two young children, who are reported (in an inscription on the tomb, above effigies of

A gargoyle on the south wall of the parish church, Bottesford.

their parents) to have died 'by wicked practice and sorcerye'. They were the sons of the sixth Earl of Rutland: the effigy of the elder boy holds a skull, while the younger one holds in his right hand a flower – possibly a symbol of innocence, but perhaps also a reference to Flower being the family name of the women who were supposed to have killed him. Three members of the family were arrested for the supposed witchcraft: the eldest died in prison, and her two daughters were hanged. As the official historian of nearby Belvoir Castle points out, 'The principal charge against them . . . was, their having a cat called Rutterkin; the supposed diabolical agent of their machinations.'

■ *Bottesford is on the A52 to the west of Grantham. The church is to the north of the village, its magnificent steeple visible at almost every point for miles around.*

Chalfont St Giles, Buckinghamshire ☿

C4 SU 9893

The charming red-brick timber-frame house in this village was once the home of the blind John Milton, who had been driven here from London by the plague of 1665, when the place where he lived had been turned into a huge burial pit. It was at Chalfont St Giles that he completed his great occult poem *Paradise Lost*, and it was here that he received inspiration for his *Paradise Regained*. The demonology of Milton was something entirely new in the realm of occultism – he took the names (and some of the attributes) of his major demons from biblical lore, from classical sources, and from early Christian writings (such as the commentaries of Jerome), but unlike anyone before him, Milton made his demons tragic figures, caught up in entirely human emotions and vices, rather than the hideous theriomorphic parodies so frequently encountered in the earlier demonological tradition. Through Milton's approach to demonology we can almost understand the thinking, and feel the tragedy, of the angels who fell, rather than merely condemn them out of hand, as is so often the case with the earlier poems and plays in which demons are important figures.

■ *Chalfont St Giles is signposted to the west of the B4442, south-east of Amersham.*

Milton's House at Chalfont St Giles, where Paradise Lost *was finished, and* Paradise Regained *conceived.*

An illustration from Milton's Paradise Lost *(Book VI, line 874), Hell receiving the fallen angels, by Gustave Doré.*

Coventry, West Midlands △

B3 SP 3379

One of the 'most important cases of Witchcraft' in England took place in Coventry, in 1324. A group of witches tried to murder King Edward II by hiring a well-known wizard, John of Nottingham, to make magical wax image poppets of the king, and some of his important followers, with a view to killing them by sympathetic magic. This dark work was done at Shorteley Park, and the story is worth telling with the help of quotations from the trial records in the official 'Parliamentary Writs' of that period. One of the evil workers was Robert Marshall, from the city of Leicester, assistant to John of Nottingham – it was this man who later confessed. As the records put it, the wizard John 'gave the said Robert a curious pin wrought of sharp lead, and bade him thrust it two inches deep into the forehead of the image made in the likeness of Richad de Sowe'. The next day, they sent for news of how this unfortunate Richard had reacted to the black magic, and found him 'writhing on his bed in agony, uttering piercing cries, with burning pains in his head'. Later the wizard John 'drew the said leaden pin out of the forehead of the said image made in the likeness of the said Richard, and thrust it into the heart. And so the said pin remained . . . until the Wednesday following, upon which day the said Richard died.' The plotters were arrested, and while John died in prison even before being brought to trial, Robert Marshall was jailed: all the other plotters denied the charges and were set free.

In 1802 a magical ring was found in a park in Coventry, and is now safely lodged in the British Museum. On this ring are depicted images of the wounds of Christ, each one named a 'well' – that is a hole in the body from which pours forth healing blood. The five wounds are then referred to in five words: 'Iasper Melchior Baltasar ananyzapta tetragrammaton'. The first three words refer to the supposed names of the Three Magi, who followed the star to visit the new born Jesus: these three names are often used on magical stones and amulets – see for example **Chichester** (London and Southern England). The last two words, the ananyzapta and the tetragrammaton are standard magical words which are touched upon in more detail under **Middleham** (The North). If we bear in mind the magical significance of these two, and imagine them alongside the triad of the three kings, then we shall see that besides the five words referring mystically to the five wounds of Christ, there is also the numerological significance:

$$3 \quad + \quad 10 \quad + \quad 4 \quad + \quad 5$$

| Three Kings | Ten of Ananyzapta | Tetragrammaton | Five wounds |

which gives a total of 22

By numerical reduction, this gives $2 + 2 = 4$

which means that numerologically speaking the whole five letter inscription is to be seen as a four, linked with a single Tetragrammaton. This mystical way of viewing letters, words and numbers is rather foreign to modern thought, but it was part and parcel of the ancient magic upon which charms and spells depended.

Cuckney, Nottinghamshire ⊕

B1 SK 5671

On the 12th-century tympanum of the parish church of St Mary at Norton-Cuckney is a stone Norman demon, on the head of which is incised an image of the cross within a circle of twelve dots. In ordinary terms this probably symbolises Christ standing within the ring of twelve disciples, but it may be regarded by occultists as an early example of the symbolic form which was later adopted as the basis for the horoscope figure.

■ *Cuckney is at the junction of the A60 and the A616.*

Dinton, Buckinghamshire ♻

C4 SP 7611

The Norman tympanum of the church of St Peter and St Paul in Dinton depicts two forked tailed dragons devouring fruit from a tree, supported by a lintel which has a winged dragon with an enormous tongue, being attacked (not very convincingly) by a diminutive St George.

■ *Dinton is signposted to the south of the A418, south of Aylesbury.*

Diseworth, Derbyshire ⊚

B2 SK 4524

The great English astrologer William Lilly was born in this village on 1 May 1602. He died at Walton-on-Thames, and was buried in the parish church there, in 1681. See **Colchester** (Eastern Counties), **London – City**. Lilly's book *Christian Astrology* is still used by astrologers in modern times.

■ *Diseworth is signposted on the A453, west of junction 24 of the M1. Lilly's house is privately owned.*

Edgehill, Warwickshire ♂

B3 SP 3847

The first important battle of the civil war was fought on 23 October 1642 at Edgehill, and resulted in the deaths of 2,000 men. The struggle must have been terrible, for it seems to have left some sort of 'imprint' on the astral plane. Shortly after the battle people reported seeing ghostly enactments of the battle, hearing the crash of gunfire, the sound of cavalry, and so on. So insistent were the stories of this phantom battle that eventually the king ordered their investigation. The reporting officer, Colonel Sir Lewis Kirk, was not only convinced of the accuracy of the reports made by the Edgehill locals, but on two occasions actually saw the spirit battle himself, recognising among those who fought both the living and the dead.

■ *The battlefield of Edgehill lies to the north-west of Kineton, and is best viewed from the highest point of the hamlet of Ratley, just off the B4086, north-west of Banbury.*

The castle on top of Edgehill overlooking the haunted fields where the battle of the Civil War took place.

The fields on the top of Edgehill, said to be haunted by soldiers killed during the Civil War.

Great Rollright, Oxfordshire ✧

B3 SP 3231

The fascinating Norman arch over the south door of St Andrew's church in the village is rightly regarded as one of the best in England, yet it contains several esoteric symbols, including the initiation image of the man being devoured by a serpent (wrongly linked by some ecclesiastical texts with Jonah and the whale), as well as a whole bevy of tongue-devils, which remind one of the more sophisticated versions at **Lincoln**. The wall to the north of this porch has a most interesting mediaeval carving of a Green Man.

■ *Great Rollright is signposted off the A34, north of Chipping Norton.*

Hardwick *See* Ault Hucknall

Henley-on-Thames, Oxfordshire ✧ ⌛

B/C4 SU 7682

The beautiful five-arch bridge at Henley has two surprising keystone decorations, one of the Egyptian goddess Isis, and the other of a bearded 'god' said by some to be 'Tamesis', though she was in fact a Celtic goddess. These heads were carved by a remarkable woman, Anne Damer, daughter of General Conway of Park Place. She did not design the bridge, but obtained permission to use her carvings when the designer of the bridge (William Hayward) died during its construction, begun in 1786. 'Tamesis' is said to have been a Celtic river goddess, and it is this name which has been perpetuated in the word Thames: one presumes that Anne Damer was not aware of the deeper significance of the Celtic connection, and merely carved a male mask to represent what she took to be 'Father Thames'. The mask of Isis on the Henley bridge faces up-stream, towards Oxford, reminding us that the Oxford part of the Thames is locally called Isis, from above the point where the Thames is joined by the River Thame, near Dorchester. In fact, this word Isis, used in connection with the Thames, has little or nothing to do with the Egyptian goddess, for the river was originally the 'Isa', and the word now used may well have come from the Latin name for the river 'Tamesis'. Isis has less to do with water than Tamesis, as she was an Egyptian goddess, wife of the sun-god Osiris, and regarded by some as the prototype of the various Black Virgins (black statuettes of a woman, sometimes holding the child Horus) which are found in certain sacred sites in Europe – most notably in the crypt of Chartres Cathedral. However, certain of the temples of Isis did have sacred streams and wells, for Romans would bring back the sacred waters from the temple of Isis at Philae to use for healing purposes. In the later Roman world, Isis was identified with the Virgin Mary, and pictures of her holding her child Horus are almost indistinguishable from the early images of the Mother and Child. Ean Begg has written a useful account of the 'Black Virgins', which proves of interest to occultists.

■ *Henley-on-Thames is on the A423, west of Maidenhead.*

Details of Norman symbols on the tympanum of the village church at Great Rollright.

Detail of the mask of Isis on the five-arch bridge over the Thames at Henley.

Kirklington, Nottinghamshire ✡

C1 SK 6757

On the south wall of St Swithin's church is a 12th-century sundial (the gnomen now missing). This large stone is worked with occult symbols, from four- and five-pointed stars, to a nine-squared grid reminiscent of the magic squares used in occult texts which relate numbers to planets. The nine-squared grid is that linked with the planet Saturn, for which the numerical equivalent is forty-five. That such a correspondence is intended in this sundial is confirmed by the fact that there is to the left of the figure a four-pointed star and to the right of the figure a five-pointed star, both stars reading together forty-five. The association with the planet Saturn is fairly reasonable within a mediaeval occult context, as Saturn had rule over time and was indeed sometimes called Chronos, the god of Time. The symbolism is therefore an occult play with the notion of the passage of time which finds its expression in the daily working of a sundial. An extra nuance of occult symbolism is found in the mediaeval notion that stone itself was ruled by Saturn.

■ *Kirklington is on the A617, north-west of Southwell.*

Norman symbols on a stone formerly used as a sundial in Kirklington Church. The symbols of stars and squares were involved originally with a complex magical numerology.

Little Rollright, Oxfordshire ✿ ✗ △

B3 SP 3231

The so-called King's Men, or Rollright Stones, consists of an almost perfect circle of megalithic uprights. It is said of this circle – as of many others – that the number of the stones in it may not be accurately determined. The stones are supposed to walk at midnight, and, like wild animals, will troop to the spring in Little Rollright Spinney to drink.

The nearby Whispering Knights, a short distance to the south, and visible from the road, are the upright remains of a burial chamber, around which an entire mythology has been developed, woven into the story of an encounter between a king (who would conquer all England) and his companion knights being turned to stone by a witch. The witch turned herself into an elder tree. Modern folklore studies reveal that the stones are still regarded as 'whispering oracles' by countryfolk and children: if one listens at the crevices of the stones, they will whisper of futurity. The notion of whispering stones used to be more widespread than now, and there was a class of small stones, called betyles (others being serpent stones and star stones) used precisely because they were believed to be animated by some force which could whisper the secrets of nature. The physician Eusebius kept a serpent stone which would give oracles in a small whisper. A distinctive outlying marker stone is called the King Stone, but in recent times it has been railed in, and now stands like an rearing petrified beast.

■ *The stones are about half a mile/1 km above the hamlet of Little Rollright, signposted to the north-east of the A44, between Chipping Norton and Moreton-in-Marsh. The circle and whispering stones are to the west of the road, the former hidden in a thick clump of trees: the King Stone to the east.*

The Rollright Stones at Little Rollright, perhaps the most famous of the smaller megalithic circles.

Mansfield Woodhouse, Nottinghamshire ☿

B1 SK 5463

The gargoyles on the outside of the parish church of St Edmund, King and Martyr are among the best in the country. There is a particularly humorous demonic gargoyle on the corner of the north-east walls.

■ *Mansfield Woodhouse is on the A60, immediately north of Mansfield.*

A demonic gargoyle on the north wall of the parish church at Mansfield Woodhouse.

Newark-on-Trent, Nottinghamshire ✡ ☿

C1 SK 7953

The beautiful 'Old English' style Ossington Hotel in Beastmarket Hill was designed by the Victorian architect Sir Ernest George in 1882, following the structure and symbolism of a famous Tudor house. Among the stucco reliefs and wooden carvings are a whole bevy of occult images relating to initiation and esoteric lore, from solar deities, basilisks and dragons, to men-fish and mermaids. The building was intended by Viscountess Ossington to serve as a temperance tavern (that is, as a coffee house), and one wonders to what extent the amulets on the facade were intended to drive back the 'demons' and 'spirits' of drink?

The Ossington Hotel, Newark, its exterior covered in esoteric symbols.

St Mary Magdalene

Inside the church the Markham tomb is interesting for its fresco, dated circa 1520, of a skeleton, which is almost certainly from a Dance of Death theme. Its esoteric significance lies in the fact that behind the panel is a squint, through which anyone in the tiny chapel-memorial might watch the elevation of the host during Mass. This symbolism is of a very deep order: within the chapel, there is (so to speak) the experience of life, but on its outer form there is death. This is an analogy for the Christian (and the occult) notion that the physical body is involved with death, while the soul within the body is deathless. One may be sure that this symbolism was intentional.

The copper and brass masonic memorial to Frederick Vernon Bussell, situated in the north-west of the nave, is replete with esoteric and hermetic symbols, and is well worth a close scrutiny.

On the outer fabric of the west end is a rare demonic gargoyle in the form of a spider.

■ *Newark is on the A1(T) and the A46(T).*

Northampton, Northamptonshire △

C3 SP 7560

In the 17th century Northampton was infamous for its witches and witch trials. The witch-finder Matthew Hopkins brought entire batches of his discovered covens for trial and hanging in this city (see **Manningtree**), and so far as records go, it was, in 1612, the first place to subject a suspected witch to the ordeal of swimming. Ann Foster was hanged 'at the place of Execution' in Northampton in 1674 for witchcraft. It is recorded that she had been upset in some way by a local farmer, and punished him by killing (through evil spells) thirty or so of his sheep, which were found with their 'leggs broke in pices and their Bones all shattered in their Skins'. She later confessed (probably under duress, however) to this crime, and to having burned his house, barns and corn. Whatever the farmer had done to upset Ann Foster, this piece of witchcraft must surely belong to an early example of evil over-kill.

■ *Northampton is to the north-east of the M1, off junction 15 north-bound, junction 16 south-bound.*

Oxford, Oxfordshire ♂ ⊕ ◉

B4 SP 5106

Cathedral ♂

In July 1923 the image of the famous scholar Dean Liddell (the father of Alice Liddell, the 'Alice' of Lewis Carroll's *Alice in Wonderland*) appeared on the wall of Christ Church Cathedral. The face, in profile, developed something like a ghostly fresco portrait, close to the Burne-Jones window which Liddell himself had placed in the cathedral in memory of his daughter. A photograph of this 'spirit-painting' was reproduced in *The Oxford Journal* of 1923. Dean had died in 1898, but the portrait had only 'developed' slowly on the wall in the preceding two years, until by 1923 it so clearly resembled the Dean that people flocked to the cathedral merely to study the picture.

A ghostly portrait of Dean Liddell on the wall of the south aisle of Oxford Cathedral.

Merton College ⊕

In the underarch of the Fitzjames Arch in Merton College there are twelve sculptures of the signs of the zodiac. The date of the arch is 1497, and some have attempted to show that the arrangement of the signs is designed to figure a horoscope cast for 12 March of that year. However, there is no indication in the arrangement of the twelve carvings that they signify a 'horoscope' of any kind, for there is no ascendant, and no meaningful orientation.

St John's College ⊕ ☺

The 17th-century occultist and Rosicrucian Robert Fludd was a student here, and an anecdote recounted of his time before his graduation in 1596 tells us how well he was versed in astrology, even at the age of twenty-two. One day he discovered that his valuable scabbard and sword-belt had been stolen. Immediately, he sat down and cast a horoscope (in fact, what is called a horary chart), for the moment he had discovered the theft. From this chart he was able to identify and apprehend the thief, who eventually returned the stolen goods. His university friend, who had witnessed this event, begged him to give up astrology, as he could not see how such a thing could have been done without the aid of demons. For a further account of Fludd, see **Bearstead**.

■ *St John's College is to the north of the town, to the east of St Giles. Directions to the arch in Merton College and permission to visit it, must be obtained from the porter at the main entrance to the college.*

Quainton, Buckinghamshire → ⋈ ✡ ♁

C4 SP 7420

Brudenell House → ⋈ ✡

Until 1962 Brudenell House was the rectory (though largely in disuse) for the parish church, and the site had been so used since the 13th century. Until comparatively recently a thorn tree grew in the garden, between the house and the church, which was linked with the **Glastonbury** thorn (The West

Country). These were said to have been taken by a pilgrim in the Holy Land from the hawthorn which grew from the staff of Joseph of Arimathea. Both bushes were said to flower on Christmas day. In the 18th century there was an account of people gathering to watch the flowering of the bloom on Christmas day. 'The day is very cold, but nothing will keep us from our watching and waiting. There is food and a plentiful supply of warmed ale, but even without this we would not turn away from our vigil . . . The hour of midnight is drawing near. Our limbs are stiff from the cold. A few of us decide to take a walk to thaw them, when suddenly there is a great shout. "The thorn, The thorn, look at the wonderful flowers. Thanks be to God." The bells ring out into the night. There is a great burst of singing . . .'

Inside the house is a beautifully refurbished mediaeval screen near the top of which is a rebus for George Brudenell, the name of one of the 16th-century rectors. The G is a carved floriate capital with a finial in a dragon-head, while the BRU is represented by a bird which is the curlew or 'bru', followed by DENELL.

Lower Road ✡

One of the houses to the north of Lower Road has a door almost covered with amulets, mainly of the horseshoe variety, and the result is probably the most interesting example of occult over-kill in the British Isles. The door itself appears to have been protected by no fewer than fifteen amulets, though only nine now remain. There is a simple horseshoe amulet above the door (as indeed above some of the other houses in the same block). The amulets on number 8's door were put there over a period of time by a previous owner, a Mr Smith. Perhaps he was fearful of the local hauntings of Grange Hill.

Grange Hill ♁

The hill to the north west of Quainton is said to be haunted by a headless huntsman who rides with his pack of hounds down the hill, over to Mill Hill. Some locals insist that it is nothing more than the ghost of a previous owner of The Grange, whose practice it was to ride at night over to Denham Lodge.

■ *Quainton is signposted off the A4(T) north of Waddesdon. Brudenell House is to the north-west of the parish church. Grange Hill is the most westerly of several hills which lie to the north of Quainton village, approached by a signposted pathway to the west of the Mill.*

Brudenell House, Quainton, in the garden of which was a sacred thorn tree.

Rushton, Northamptonshire ✡

C3 SP 8482

The Triangular Lodge of Rushton is probably the most occult building in Britain, and not quite what it seems to be on the surface. Most of the guidebooks will tell you that it was built in the 16th century as an exercise in the magic of three, to satisfy the folly-taste of Sir Thomas Tresham, a Roman Catholic who is generally believed to have had an obsession with the Trinity, but whose connections with one occult stream of thought might suggest an interest in esoteric matters – his grandfather, whose altar tomb is between the chapel and the chancel in Rushton Church, was the Grand Prior of the Knights Hospitallers. Sir Thomas was more subtle than his interpreters would have us believe, for the 'triangular' building is much more than a complex play on the theme of the Trinity – it is really an essay in numerology, as well as a hyperbole on the first three letters of Tresham's own name (*Tres* in Latin means three). On superficial acquaintance, the lodge does appear to be entirely trinitarian in form: it has three sides each 33 feet 3 inches/ 10.13 m long, and three floors, either three or six-sided rooms. Each of the three sides is roofed by three triangular gables, topped by triple finials. There are Latin inscriptions on each of the three faces, each of thirty-three letters. Even the decorative inlay of brickwork windows is designed to reflect the trinity, but when you begin to look at the structure more carefully, you see that it is in fact a lapidary praise of all numbers. For example, one trefoil contains what has been called by occultists the tetractys, built from inverted triangles.

This mystic figure is linked with the magical 'secret number' of seventy-two in Hebrew mysticism, a number derived from the numerical equivalents for each of the four letters in the name Jehovah: in modern times, the significance of this figure, and its related seventy-two has been touched on by Fred Gettings. The tetractys may appear to consist of a pile of six triangles, but in fact there are ten such triangles within its various permutations. In addition, in the stonework tetractys, this figure gives ten triangular shapes, with fifteen shapes between (set in the trefoil), and it is therefore magically connected with all numbers up to twenty-five, for the ten and the fifteen may be added together. Thus, this 'tetractys' form alone gives the numerical permutations of six, ten, fifteen, twenty-five and seventy-two. Another trefoil on the same register gives four basic shapes, with seven spaces between them. The lower register contains a block with three times three roundels, which of course gives

the number twelve: within the roundels is a cross, which therefore gives four. The dates and numbers on each of the three faces are also of considerable numerological import: for example, it is interesting that the groups of seven dates yield every number except seven (though the Lodge itself was finished in 1597), and that the date over the doorway is linked with the ancient notion of the creation of the world having taken place in 3,962 BC, which permits all the other six dates on the stonework to be related to major Biblical events, such as the date of the Passion, the Deluge, and so on. Every number below seventy-two may be discovered within this remarkable building by means of numerological multiplication, reduction and extension. It is said that Sir Thomas designed the Lodge during one of his long incarcerations in prison, during which time he also decorated the surface of his cell with secret devices and texts, avoiding all those more obviously 'Papist' symbols which would have raised the anger of his gaolers. Fortunately, the useful handbook published Her Majesty's Stationery Office indicates that the author, Sir Gyles Ishan, is aware of some of the deeper implications of the building, and is well worth studying while walking around and inside the Lodge.

■ *Rushton is signposted to the north-west of the A6(T) at Desborough. The Triangular House is in the grounds of Rushton House, its location well signposted.*

The Triangular Lodge built by Sir Thomas Tresham in 1597 at Rushton.

Shorteley Park *See* Coventry

Southwell, Nottinghamshire ⚥ ☉ ☿

C1/2 SK 7053

In the chapter house of Southwell Minster there are several pagan Green Men, in some cases with floriations and tendrils issuing from the mouth, in some cases with the head set among a surround of leaves. Perhaps the most remarkable of these images are those which portray a Green Man with birds one either side of his head.

Over the doorway in the west wall of the minster itself there is a wonderful 11th-century low relief representing Michael fighting a dragon, seemingly caught up in its own convolutions. The figures to the left are said to depict David rescuing the lamb from the lion. Of many interesting grotesques and gargoyles, on the external fabric of the minster, the most impressive are the series of a bull, boar, ram and fishes, which almost certainly represent the animal equivalent of the four elements. These four, taken with the three gargoyles higher on the same buttress pinnacle, may well originally have represented images of the seven deadly sins. They are recent restorations of older images, but still convey much of the esoteric symbolism – the double fishes, representative of water, link directly with the astrological image of Pisces.

■ *Southwell is on the A612, north-east of Nottingham.*

Green Man symbols in the Chapter House of Southwell Minster – probably from the 13th century.

Tackley, Oxfordshire ♉ →

B4 SP 4720

There are stories that Tackley church was one of those whose site was determined by the Devil, who interfered with the building when it was being sited near the top of the hill. As a result it was placed half way down the slope, though still raised slightly above the village.

There is a curious cat-like (or demonic) face set in the stone high on the northern face of the tower, which some have claimed was intended as an amulet against the evil eye.

■ *Tackley is signposted to the east of the A423, between Banbury and Oxford.*

Uffington, Oxfordshire ☉ ⚥

B4 SU 3089

The landscape around the White Horse of Uffington is dotted with prehistoric remains, such as Wayland's Smithy (a megalithic burial chamber), the ramparts of the so-called Uffington Castle, and the prehistoric Ridgeway. G.K. Chesterton mused that the horse was cut into the chalk hill even 'Before the gods that made the gods Had seen their sunrise pass . . .'. Few of the white horses in the British landscape have gathered so many legends as the one at Uffington. It is probably not a horse at all, and certainly it was not cut by Hengist in the 5th-century as some maintain and does not represent the monster killed by Saint George – though the strangely formed knoll below the scarp of the Vale is associated with this saint, and is still called Dragon Hill. This Dragon Hill's top has been worn bare by innumerable hikers' feet, perhaps adding to the dragon-lore legend the story that the blood of the dragon was spilled here, which is why nothing will grow on the hill.

Whatever reasons the forgotten ancients had for placing this horse in this wonderful hillside, recent imaginations have certainly gone too far in claiming that because the horse may only be seen clearly from the air it was designed to be seen from ancient flying machines. From this notion it has been all too easy to slide into stories of prehistoric spacecraft.

Popular occult notions apart, it is likely that the archaeologists are right, and the 360-foot/110-metre long, 130-foot/40-metre high, dragon-horse was once a sort of tribal totem, an identification symbol – but of course the use of symbols in past times was less obviously divorced from magic as in our own day of instant imagery.

For all its age, the horse appears to have been mentioned in literature only as late as the 12th century, but it is distinctively Celtic in form (indeed, it reminds one of similar horse-forms on Celtic coinage), and it has been argued by some that it is not a horse at all, but a dragon (though not St George's dragon), which may have been turned into a horse by the numerous restorations of the past centuries. The cleaning of the horse, the periodic seven-year 'scouring' which was designed to ensure that the turf did not overgrow the exposed chalk, goes back at least to 1677, but this appears to have been a ritual something akin to a religious festival, and has long since been discontinued.

■ *The White Horse may be seen from many parts of the Vale of the White Horse, to the south of Uffington, and is best seen from the B4507.*

An aerial view of the Uffington white horse, probably the oldest chalk-cut figure in Britain. Archaeologists date it to the 1st century, but it may be a reworking of an even older figure. The hill-fort known as Uffington Castle is about a quarter of a mile south-east of the horse, over the hill.

Warmington, Warwickshire

B3 SP 4147

The village church at Warmington is one of the numerous churches in this area which is said to be haunted by the cavalry and soldiers that died in the battle of Edgehill. A number of those slain in the battle were certainly buried here, and the churchyard, for all its great beauty, has a curious feeling of desolation and mystery in its atmosphere.

■ *Warmington church is at the side of A41T, just north of the junction with the B4086 to Kineton.*

Warwick, Warwickshire

B3 SP 2865

There is a story that whenever a member of the family of the Earl of Warwick was on the point of dying, the ghost of the Dun Cow would appear as a portent. The legend proceeds that this cow when alive had been a vast creature, which gave enough milk to feed the whole of the region, but one day it was 'overlooked' by a local witch, and became a monster. Eventually the transformed cow was slain by Guy of Warwick, but it is said that the ghost of the monster still haunts the old castle.

In the Beauchamp Chapel of St Mary's church in Warwick is the beautiful Purbeck marble tomb to Richard Beauchamp, Earl of Warwick, who appears to have been partly responsible for obtaining the death of Joan of Arc, for witchcraft and heresy in 1431.

■ *Warwick is on the A41(T), south-west of Coventry. The castle is to the south of the city.*

West Wycombe, Buckinghamshire

C4 SU 8294

The strange oriental-like gold-encased finial on the church of St Lawrence, is said to have been designed by Sir Francis Dashwood, who founded the infamous Hell-Fire Club, the Monks of Medmenham. It is said that the bulb had sufficient seats for nine men in a modicum of comfort, and the space within was approached by a ladder. There are stories that the church was used by magic circles for various rites, and that the black magician Aleister Crowley held his black masses there. These stories are almost certainly based on misunderstandings, however: Dashwood certainly built the striking mausoleum to the south-east of the church, with its pseudo-classical facade shaping an hexagonal ground plan, and it is rumoured that black magical circles and witch-covens have met inside this protective magical shape, so it is possible that the stories have overspilled from the hexagonal into the globe finial. In his useful book on curiosities, Raymond Lea points out that the lectern in the globe (is it a lectern?) is a slim pedestal with three claws. Around the platform are four doves, and just below is another dove, being attacked by a snake which is coiled around the shaft. The snake attacking a dove is one of the symbols derived from alchemical imagery (as in the basilisk and dove), and we must presume that the 'lectern' was used for dark magical purposes: even within the Christian imagery, the notion of a snake (the Devil) attacking a dove (the Holy Ghost) is heretical.

■ *West Wycombe is to the west of High Wycombe, signposted to the north of the A40(T). The church is visible on the hill, from miles around.*

Wing, Buckinghamshire

C4 SP 8822

Some of the houses in Church Street have symbols picked out in the brickwork, the most interesting esoteric symbol being that derived from alchemy and intended to portray the nature of the quintessence.

The southern wall of the parish church bears a number of reinforcing irons with decorative finials. The central group picks out the date 1649, which we presume to be a date of the church reconstruction. To the right of these figures, are a couple of iron symbols which are a mystery because while their individual significance is known, the reasons for their being so displayed are unknown. The one to the left is an ancient form for Venus, while the one to the right is a symbol for Saturn.

It has been suggested that the Venus symbol may relate to spring (each of the four seasons was allocated to planetary and alchemical symbols, and the form was sometimes used in alchemical literature to denote the spring). If the second (Saturn) image is read as figure two, rather than as a sigil for Saturn, then the pair might possibly be interpreted as denoting the second month of spring – namely, under the old calendar, April. The entire metal work might therefore be interpreted as the 17 of April 1649. There are, however, a number of other ways of interpreting these curious symbols. In the churchyard is a magnificent cross, with a crucifixion on one side and an image of a dragon-slaying on the other side.

■ *Wing is signposted to the north of A418, south-west of Leighton Buzzard.*

Wing, Leicestershire

C2 SK 8903

The turf maze in this village is really a dancing pattern. Occultists often point out its proximity to an ancient tumulus as evidence of its age, but it would seem that most of the British mazes are late mediaeval in design and conception, this one included. One possible exception was the so-called Troy Town (formerly at Pimperne in Dorset) whose strange tri-form linear pattern was unlike any other known maze. This latter turf maze was removed to make way for farming in the early 18th century, and we owe our knowledge of its form to the antiquary John Aubrey.

■ *Wing is signposted to the east of the A6003, south-east of Melton Mowbray.*

Wales and
Western Counties

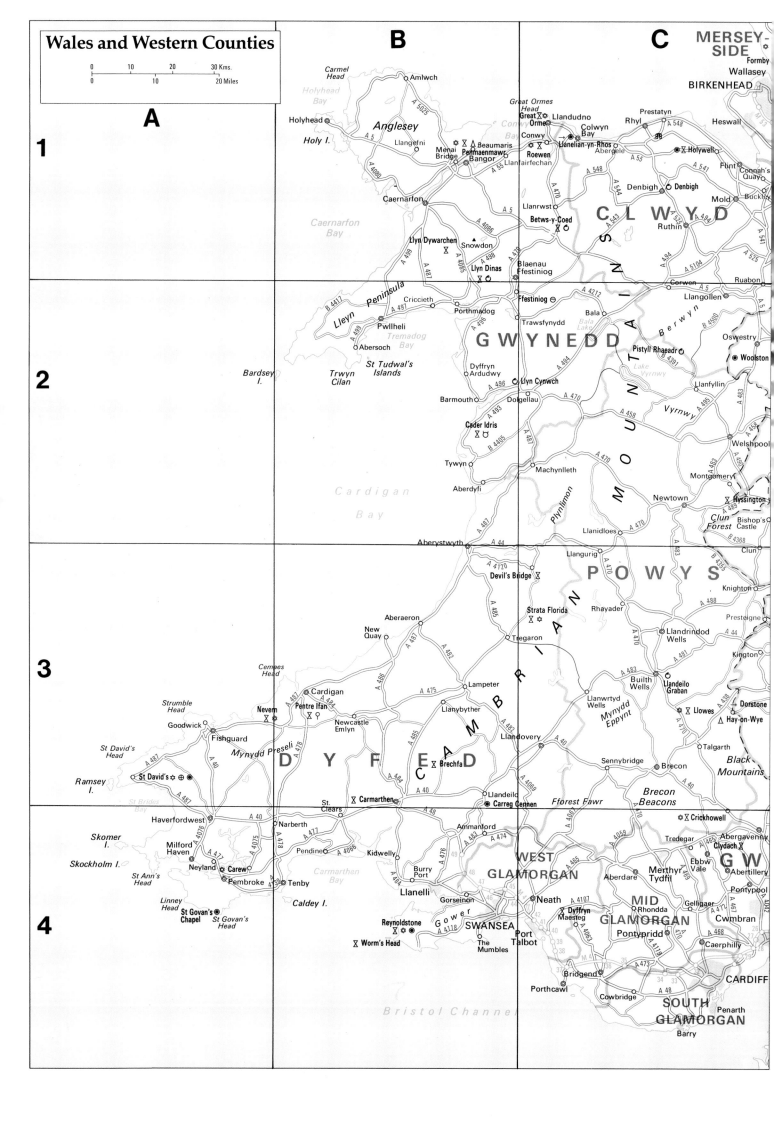

Wales and Western Counties

A

B

C

MERSEY-SIDE

Formby
Wallasey
BIRKENHEAD
Heswall

1

Carmel Head
Holyhead Bay
Amlwch
A 5025
Anglesey
Holyhead
A 5
Llangefni
Holy I.
Menai Bridge
Beaumaris
Penmaenmawr
Bangor
Roewen
Llanfairfechan
Great Ormes Head
Great Orme
Conwy Bay
Llandudno
Colwyn Bay
Conwy
Llanelian-yn-Rhos
Abergele
Prestatyn
Rhyl
A 548
Heswall
Holywell
Flint
Connah's Quay
A 541
A 55
A 548
Denbigh
Denbigh
A 525
Mold
Buckley
A 494

Caernarfon
Caernarfon Bay
A 4086
A 5
Llanrwst
Betws-y-Coed
A 543
CLWYD
Ruthin
A 494
A 5104
A 525
A 541

Llyn Dywarchen
A 499
A 498
A 4085
Snowdon
Llyn Dinas
A 487
Blaenau Ffestiniog
A 470

2

Lleyn Peninsula
B 4417
A 497
Criccieth
Porthmadog
A 496
Ffestiniog
A 4212
A 4500
Corwen
A 5
Llangollen
Ruabon

Pwllheli
A 499
Abersoch
Tremadog Bay
Trawsfynydd
Bala Lake
Bala
Berwyn
Oswestry
Woolston

Bardsey I.
Trwyn Cilan
St Tudwal's Islands
GWYNEDD
Dyffryn Ardudwy
A 496
Llyn Cynwch
A 494
Lake Vyrnwy
Pistyll Rhaeadr
A 4391
Llanfyllin
A 483

Barmouth
Dolgellau
A 493
A 470
A 458
Vyrnwy
A 495
Welshpool
A 458

Cader Idris
B 4405
A 487
Machynlleth
A 470
Montgomery
A 483
A 490

Tywyn
Aberdyfi
Plynlimon
Newtown
Myssington
A 489
Clun Forest
Bishop's Castle

3

Cardigan Bay
Aberystwyth
A 44
A 4120
Devil's Bridge
Llanidloes
A 470
Llangurig
A 470
POWYS
A 483
Knighton
B 4368
Clun
A 488
B 4355
Presteigne
A 44

Aberaeron
New Quay
A 487
A 482
Tregaron
A 485
Strata Florida
Rhayader
Llandrindod Wells
A 481
Kington

Cemaes Head
A 487
Cardigan
A 484
Nevern
Pentre Ifan
Newcastle Emlyn
A 475
Lampeter
Llanybyther
A 482
A 485
Builth Wells
A 483
Llanwrtyd Wells
Llandeilo Graban
Llowes
Dorstone
A 438

Strumble Head
Goodwick
Fishguard
A 487
A 40
Mynydd Preseli
A 478
DYFED
A 484
CAMBRIAN
Brechfa
Llandovery
A 40
Mynydd Eppynt
Talgarth
Hay-on-Wye

St David's Head
Ramsey I.
St David's
St Brides Bay
A 487
Sennybridge
Brecon
A 40
Black Mountains

St. Clears
Carmarthen
A 40
Llandeilo
Carreg Cennen
A 4069
Fforest Fawr
Brecon Beacons

4

Skomer I.
Skockholm I.
St Ann's Head
Haverfordwest
A 40
A 4076
Narberth
A 477
Pendine
A 4066
St. Clears
A 478
A 4075
Kidwelly
A 476
Ammanford
A 483
A 474
Crickhowell
A 4059
Tredegar
Abergavenny
Clydach
GW
Abertillery

Milford Haven
Neyland
Carew
Pembroke
A 477
A 4075
Tenby
Burry Port
Llanelli
Gorseinon
WEST GLAMORGAN
A 465
Aberdare
Merthyr Tydfil
Ebbw Vale
Pontypool
Gelligaer
A 467
A 4042

Linney Head
St Govan's Chapel
St Govan's Head
Caldey I.
Carmarthen Bay
Reynoldstone
Gower
A 4118
Worm's Head
The Mumbles
SWANSEA
Port Talbot
Neath
A 4107
Dyffryn
Maesteg
A 4063
MID GLAMORGAN
Rhondda
Pontypridd
A 473
Cwmbran
A 468
Caerphilly

Bridgend
Porthcawl
A 48
Cowbridge
SOUTH GLAMORGAN
CARDIFF
Penarth
Barry

Bristol Channel

Scale
0 10 20 30 Kms.
0 10 20 Miles

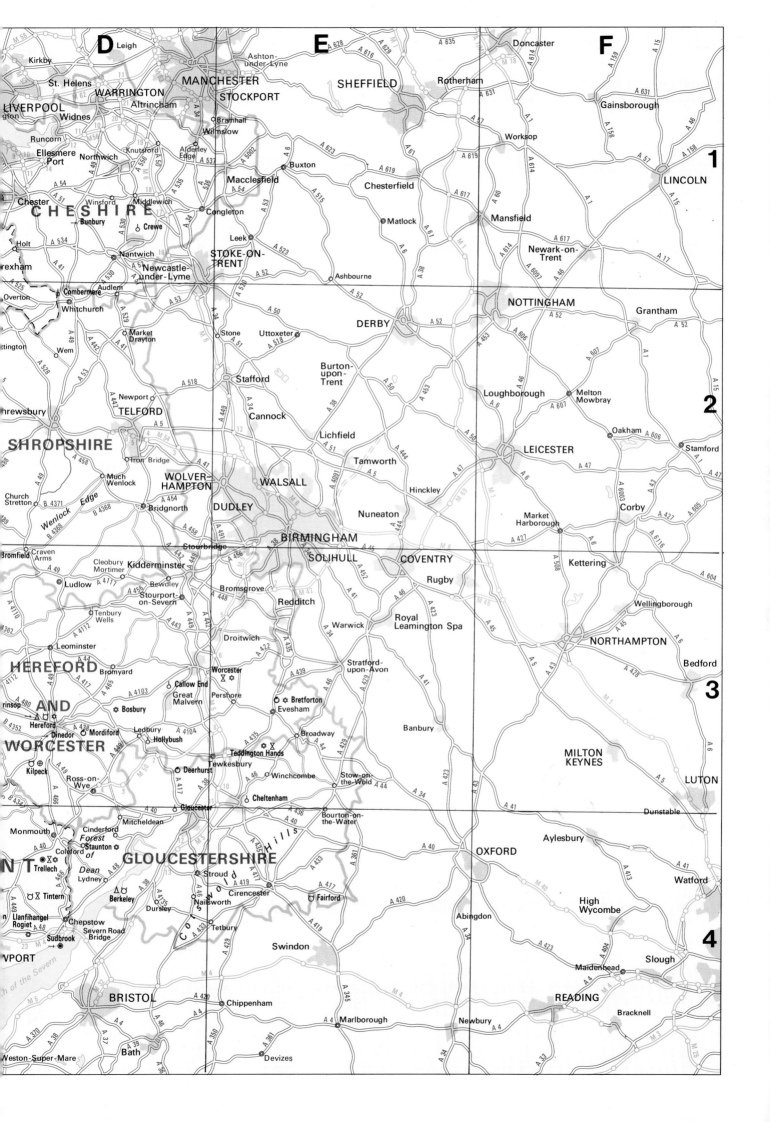

Alltwalis *See* Brechfa

Berkeley, Gloucestershire ☿ △
D4 ST 6899

The witch of Berkeley probably lived in the 9th century, and is remembered nowadays because she figured in a ballad by the poet laureate Robert Southey (1774–1843). An early account of the witch tells how in the year 852, realising that death was drawing near, she called to her a monk and a nun, and asked them to practise a curious burial in order to preserve her from her master, the Devil. 'When I am dead, sew my body in the hide of a stag, place it in a sarcophagus of stone, which make fast with iron and molten lead, binding around the stone three iron chains of the stoutest forge. Let fifty chantry priests sing a dirge for my soul . . . and if I lie for three nights in peace unharmed, on the fourth day ye shall bury me in the ground.' On the second day of the chantry signing, a host of demons burst into the church where her body lay and broke two of the three chains which bound her coffin. On the third night, a 'hideous spectre, a devil of gigantic form and baleful countenance shivered the church doors into fragments with a violent blow'. The Devil approached the sarcophagus, and, calling the woman by name, broke the third chain, caught up the wretched woman, flung her on to his coal-black steed, and galloped off. They say that her shrieks of agony could be heard for four miles.

■ *Berkeley is signposted off junction 14 of the M5.*

Betws-y-Coed, Gwynedd ⚔ ☿
C1 SH 7956

The Welsh-looking name 'Betws' points to the place originally being a religious centre, for it is a corruption of the English 'bead-house', a name for a prayer-cell. It is said that there was a hermit cell on the site of the present church of St Michael. Tourism seems to have corrupted the appropriate name of the falls, originally the Rhaiadr Ewynol (Foaming Falls) into Rhaiadr-y-Wennol (Swallow Falls), and a strange story persists that the waters are haunted by the soul of an evil man.

More interesting than such recently invented stories, however, are the ancient myths, among which that of the Wybrant Viper is the most complex and redolent with symbolism. From its size, the viper appears to have been a dragon, which brought great fear into the hearts of the inhabitants of Betws-y-Coed and local villages. The Hiraethog bandit who decided to kill this dragon, for suitable reward, first wisely consulted a wizard and learned that he would die of the bite of a viper. This restrained him, but later he saw the wizard again, now to be told that he would die by cutting his own throat. To a third question about this fate the reply was 'You will die by drowning' 'How may a man die three times?', he asked scornfully, and went off to kill the viper. As he climbed the rocks to Wybrant, the bandit encountered the viper, which promptly bit him: he fell from the cliff, tearing his throat on a jagged rock as he plunged into the river, and was drowned.

■ *Betws-y-Coed lies on the A5(T).*

The Swallow Falls at Betws-y-Coed, said to be haunted by the ghost of a wicked man.

Black Rock *See* Llanfilhangel Rogiet

Bosbury, Hereford and Worcester ░
D3 SO 6943

A striking example of a pagan mark-stone which had a cross raised over it was in Bosbury church, for when the churchyard cross was moved from its ancient site in 1796, the villagers found beneath it a huge boulder of stone, which was, in the opinion of the specialist Alfred Watkins, an old mark-stone. The stone was held to be sacred, and placed under the church tower, where it may still be seen to this day.

■ *Bosbury is on the B4220, north of Ledbury.*

Brechfa, Dyfed ⚔
B3 SN 5230

Behind a waterfall on the hills to the north-west of Brechfa (east of Alltwalis) is the entrance to the Ogof Myrddin or Cave of Merlin (in the upper reaches of the Afon Pib). Local tradition has it that the wizard lived in this cave, but it is likely that the poet Edmund Spenser confused it as that 'dreadfull place . . . a hideous hollow cave', where the magician was imprisoned. The cave itself, and the setting around, is beautiful, and carries none of the romantic frisson which Spenser hoped to raise in the emotions of his readers, their being no 'gastly noyse of iron chaines', nor does one sense any devilish sprites in the area. Further south-west is Merlin's Hill, with the chair-shaped rock on which Merlin (Myrddin) is said to have sat while making his prophecies.

■ *The cave is in the upper reaches of the Afon Pib, best approached by way of the Ordnance Survey map to GR 486320.*

Bredwardine *See* Dorstone

Bretforton, Hereford and Worcester
E3 SP 0944

In St Leonard's church is a mediaeval capital carved with a strange picture of a dragon devouring St Margaret. According to the Christian legends St Margaret was a martyr who was confronted by a dragon while in prison. The monster swallowed her whole, and while she was in its belly she made the sign of the cross: this cross grew until it eventually burst a hole in the dragon's stomach, and St Margaret was able to escape. This story accounts for St Margaret being the patron saint of pregnant women, but many occultists see it as a thinly disguised initiation myth. The Bretforton carving is particularly interesting as its shows St Margaret both being swallowed (only her feet and the hem of her skirt were outside the dragon's mouth), as well as bursting from the exploded stomach of the dragon.

■ *Bretforton is on the B4035, east of Evesham.*

Brinsop, Hereford and Worcester
D3 SO 4444

It is said the dragon image on the Norman tympanum in the village church is that of the Brinsop Dragon. This dragon is portrayed as a snake, for according to local mythology it was a water monster which had its nest in the innocent-sounding Duck's Pool Meadow in the village. The heroic fight with the dragon is said to have taken place in a water-meadow called Lower Stanks (from the Old English for pond). One wonders if the legend of the Brinsop Dragon grew from the Norman tympanum imagery, for it is very unusual for Norman ecclesiastical imagery to concern itself with local legends.

■ *Brinsop is signposted to the north of the A480, north-west of Hereford.*

Bromfield, Shropshire
D3 SO 4877

Records made in the 14th century refer to a dragon which had made its nest in the village of Bromfield, and was causing great bloodshed and damage on the lands of the Earl Warren. It seems that in 1344 the dragon was killed by the magical incantations of an Arabian physician. However, before it died, the dragon accidentally revealed that a great treasure lay hidden in its nest, as a result of which the Earl Warren became a very wealthy man.

■ *Bromfield is on the A49(T) north of Ludlow.*

Bunbury, Cheshire
D1 SJ 5658

On the walls of the appropriately named Images House at Bunbury, are a number of 17th- or 18th-century amuletic carvings set into the brickwork or used as grotesque supports. The story tells how a poacher was sentenced to deportation by the squire at Bunbury, and on his return made three rough images to represent the squire and two men who had aided him. The poacher then treated these figures as a witch might treat a waxen doll, or poppet, though instead of sticking pins into them, he cursed them each day. The story appears to have developed with Beatrice Tonshow's novel *Shiney Night*, but one may not doubt that the carvings were intended for magical purposes.

■ *The Images House fronts directly on to the west side of the A49, just before the turn to Bunbury, from Northwich.*

Detail of inset amuletic man on the so-called 'Images House' in Bunbury.

Caerleon, Gwent ⚔

D4 SS 9107

The ancient amphitheatre at Caerleon was once believed to be the Round Table of King Arthur: when it was excavated under the direction of Sir Mortimer Wheeler in 1926, the site proved to be a Roman construction.

■ *Caerleon is signposted to the north of the M4, at junctions 24 and 25.*

Caider Idris, Gwynedd ⚔ ☿

B2 SH 7013

Few mountains have been swathed in as many legends as Caider Idris, and the Llyn Cau which they surround. Some say that the name means Chair of Idris, and suppose that Idris was a giant, but it is more etymologically correct to think of Caider as meaning 'a settled place'. The notion that anyone who sleeps on the summit of the mountain (that is, on the Craig Lwyd) will be dead, a madman or a poet by morning, was probably invented by a Mrs Hemans, a romantic fiction-writer of the 19th century. The widely held idea that this is a place of fairies appears to stretch back beyond recorded history. The Llyn Cau near the summit of the Cader is said to be the haunt of a sea monster, living in the bottomless depths, emerging only to devour those who swim in its sacred waters. To the south of the Cader is a crag called The Rock of the Evil One, where the Devil danced wildly in celebration of the evil ways of those who lived in Llanfihangel-y-pennant to the south of the Caider.

■ *Caider Idris is to the south of Dolgellau, and is encircled to the east by the A487. The approach to Llyn Cau is most easily made from Minffordd, off the A487.*

Callow End, Hereford and Worcester ☿

D3 SO 8349

The Tudor (or Jacobean) Prior Court at Callow End appears to be haunted by several ghosts, all of them benign. The history of the house, set out by the historians Owen and Sims, is fascinating within the context of haunting, for it is said that at one time a box containing a book on black magic, and what might well have been an invocator's ritual knife, were found in a hole in the rafters, and that a skeleton in the dress of a 17th-century cavalier was found lodged in one of the great chimneys of a bedroom. The apparitions do not appear to have any connection with a royalist cavalier, however: the ghost which has been seen most clearly is taken to be that of a young Victorian girl, wearing a straw hat, and with her hair gathered up in a bun. During the early part of the present century the house was exorcised; yet in October 1964 one of the inhabitants of the house saw an incomplete and transparent human figure, bathed in its own light, wearing what appeared to be an old-fashioned night-dress.

■ *Callow End is on the B424, south of Worcester.*

Caider Idris, the Llyn Cau on the Caider.

Carew, Dyfed

A4 SN 0403

The Carew Cross, raised on a specially constructed stone platform beside the A4075, opposite the ruinous Carew Castle, is said to be the finest 6th-century Celtic cross in Britain. An ancient lapidary inscription on the back of the stone indicates that it was used (long after it had been carved) to commemorate King Mariteut, who ruled over south-western Wales in the 11th century.

■ *Carew is to the north of the A477, east of Pembroke. The cross is to the north of the A4075, near the entrance to the castle.*

The Carew cross, said to be the finest 6th-century Celtic cross in Britain.

Carmarthen, Dyfed

B3 SN 4120

The sacred tree at Carmarthen is linked with the romantic legends of Arthur – it is said that the city itself will last only as long as the tree.

Three miles/5 km east of Carmarthen is Merlin's Hill, the summit of which is said (by the imaginative) to resemble a chair. According to legend it is from this chair that the wizard Merlin delivered his prophecies, and some say that he is buried within the hill, while others say that he is sleeping, awaiting the call for his services which his nation will surely make in future times – one of the oldest legends in the mythological books, and told of many heroes and kings.

■ *Carmarthen is on the A40(T), north-west of Swansea.*

Carreg Cennen, Dyfed

B3 SN 6619

Carreg Cennen castle is a most romantic ruinous pile, overlooking the Cennen Valley from a cliff over 200 feet/60 metres high. A wishing well is at the end of an underground gallery and flight of stairs. It is said that in ancient times people would throw pieces of metal into the waters and make wishes.

■ *The castle is to the east of Trapp, signposted off the A483, south-east of Ffairfach.*

Cefyn Bryn *See* Reynoldstone

Charston Rock *See* Llanfilhangel Rogiet

Cheltenham, Gloucestershire

E3 SO 9422

Like most cities, Cheltenham has its own bevy of spirits, hauntings and ghost stories. A particularly famous one called the Cheltenham Ghost had its dwelling in one of the houses in Pittville Circus Road. The haunting started in 1882 as a fairly ordinary poltergeist activity, mainly expressed in the form of strange noises, footsteps, thrown objects, and so on. Eventually, however, a ghost began to appear in the shape of a tall woman dressed in black. She was seen so frequently by the inmates of the house that they began to take her for granted, though one did try tying a thread across the ghost's accustomed passageway to prove that she could pass with ease through matter – which of course she did. For some reason which is not quite clear, it was decided that the Cheltenham Ghost was that of a Mrs Swinhoe, who had died in the house in 1878.

Clydach, Gwent

C4 SN 6901

The Lonely Shepherd near Clydach is an upright pillar of limestone on the edge of the Llangattock escarpment, overlooking the Glydach Gorge. Local legend says that it is the petrified remains of a shepherd, whose cruelty caused the suicide of his wife. As in so many standing stones legends, the pillar is supposed to come to life on midsummer eve, and walk down to the river, returning only at cock-crow. In this case, the animated pillar is searching for the wife he harmed.

■ *Clydach is signposted to the north-east of the A465, west of Abergavenny.*

Coetan Arthur *See* Pentre Ifan

Combermere, Shropshire ♂
D2 SJ 5844

One of the most famous of all spirit photographs was taken in the library of Combermere Abbey, in 1891 by Sybell Corbet, an amateur photographer. No-one was in the room when the picture was taken (in those days, a long exposure was required), but when the plate was developed there was the image of an old man, seated in the high-back chair to the left of the room. While the picture was being taken the body of Lord Combermere was being buried at Wrenbury, a few miles away. Later, when the authenticity of the picture was being discussed, a relative of the deceased Lord pointed out that the ghost had no visible legs, and that Lord Combermere had died in a street accident which meant that (had he lived) he would never have been able to use his legs again.

■ *Combermere is north-west of Whitchurch, signposted to the north of the A525.*

The original photographic print of the Combermere Ghost.

Craig Lywd *See* Caider Idris

Crewe, Cheshire ♂
D1 SJ 7055

In the early part of this century Crewe was a centre of pilgrimage for those who were interested in psychic photography, or who wished to have pictures made of their deceased friends or relatives. It was in Crewe, in a street which has long since been removed, that the clairvoyants Mr Hope and Mrs Buxton held their most bizarre photographic seances in which they would take pictures of the living and frequently find alongside them images which were called 'extras', and which were very often identified as portraits of deceased people. The Crewe Circle became famous among the psychic investigators of the time, and their spirit-photographs were undoubtedly among the most impressive ever taken.

The story attached to the picture shown above right is told by the lady in the bottom left, a Mrs Leverson, who was travelling south from Scotland, and decided to call on the Crewe Circle (who were then staying at the vicarage in Weston) to see what they might obtain on the marked photographic plates which she carried with her. Hope photographed Mrs Leverson, who took the plates away and had them developed herself: she was astonished to find an 'extra' in the shape of a Scotsman called Brock, well-known to the Weston vicarage, and upside down above his head an image of a chow dog which had belonged to his first wife, who had died seventeen years previously. Very many other testimonials of the fidelity of the likenesses obtained by the Crewe Circle exist in psychic literature, and some of them throw an interesting light on how these photographic seances were conducted in Crewe.

■ *Crewe is signposted to the west of the M6, off junction 17.*

A spirit-photograph taken around 1931 in Crewe, of Mrs Leverson with an 'extra' reputed to be a Mr Brock and his pet dog.

Crickhowell, Powys ⧗ ⚬
C3/4 SO 2118

On the bank of the river Usk is an 18-foot/5.5-metre high standing stone, the curious shape of which resembles a fish balancing upright on its tail. Inevitably, the local mythology has the stone leaping from the earth and swimming in the river Usk on midsummer eve.

■ *Crickhowell is on the north bank of the Usk, on the A40. The stone is at Grid Reference SO 183198, and must not be confused with the other standing stones in the vicinity of Crickhowell, within a short distance of the A40.*

Croesfeilig *See* Llowes

Deerhurst, Gloucestershire ⏾

D3 SO 8729

It is said that this village was once haunted, in antiquity, by a serpent of great size, which stole the local cattle for food, and poisoned the inhabitants with its breath. Eventually a royal proclamation determined that whoever could kill the dragon should receive one of the crown estates in the parish. A man named Smith succeeded in drugging the monster with milk, and while it slept he beheaded it. His descendants still lived on the reward-estate well into the last century.

■ *Deerhurst is to the west of the A38, itself to the west of the M5, junctions 9 or 10.*

Denbigh, Clwyd ⏾

C1 SJ 0566

The old castle of Denbigh was said to be the haunt of a terrible dragon, which lived on the flesh of humans, and drove most of the inhabitants from the town. It was eventually killed by one Sir John of the Thumbs, who carried its severed head through the streets of the town to the relieved shouts of 'Dim Bych', which means 'no more Dragon'. It is said fancifully that such is the origin of the name Denbigh.

■ *Denbigh is on the A525, south of Prestatyn. The castle is to the south of the town.*

Devil's Bridge, Dyfed ✕

C3 SN 7376

The triple bridge over the waterfall gorge of the Mynach is linked with one of the most international of all legends – the story of how the Devil is tricked into building a bridge with the hope of gaining a human soul as reward. In this Dyfed story it is an old woman who agreed that the Satanic Majesty should own the first soul to cross after he had completed it: however, when the bridge was finished, the woman threw a stick across for her dog, whose soul was then impounded by the Devil, in place of that of the old woman.

History is perhaps more romantic than fiction, however, for the first of the bridges (the lowest one of the triple span) was almost certainly built by the Cistercian monks of the **Strata Florida** Abbey sometime during the 11th century – the name Mynach is Welsh for a monk, so perhaps rather than being called the Devil's Bridge, it should be known as the Monk's Bridge. The topmost bridge was constructed in 1901. Below the bridge is the dizzy gorge of the Mynach, which swirls through the black rock swirlhole of the Devil's Punch-bowl.

■ *The bridge stands over the gorge which marks the capture of the Mynach by the Rheidol, at the junction of the A120, the B4343 and the B4574, to the east of Aberystwyth.*

The Devil's Bridge. The triple bridge over the rock gorge through which runs the river Mynach: the lowest bridge is said to have been built by the Devil.

Dinas Emrys *See* Llyn Dinas

Dinedor, Hereford and Worcester →

D3 SO 5376

The ancient earthwork encampment above this small village has become famous among those who concern themselves with ley-lines because it is part of an all-too-rare series of alignments which are visible to the naked eye, rather than merely derived from consideration of maps. The alignment from the eastern end of the encampment is such as to give a view of the tower of Hereford Cathedral centred directly on the spire of All Saints' Church. The alignment, which was first pointed out by Alfred Watkins in 1925, is perfectly visible from the eastern corner of the camp, though in summer thick foliage requires the viewer to stand below the earthworks for a clear sight line. The photograph of the alignment used by Watkins to illustrate his important book on ley-lines was taken with a telephoto lens at a distance of 4 miles/6 km, from the further side of Hereford. In the picture All Saints' is in front of the cathedral tower, and on the horizon is the silhouette of the tree-lined camp of Dinedor. All Saints' is connected with another important ley-line, noted under **Hereford**.

■ *Dinedor is signposted to the west of the B4399, south of Hereford. The camp towers above the village, and is approached by the track to the south of the village.*

Dorstone, Hereford and Worcester →
C3 SO 3141

Arthur's Stone is the name given now to the whole megalithic burial on the summit of the hill to the north of Dorstone, but at one time it was used only for the huge lozenge-shaped capstone (now split). It was one of the ancient monuments which first led the ley-line expert Alfred Watkins towards formulating his principle of the ley: he noted in his classic book on the subject *The Old Straight Track* that it is involved with three ley-lines, one of which is still reflected in the present approach road from the east. The most conspicuous ley is that which aligns with Dorstone church a mile/2 km away, and a similar distance to the north, towards the Knapp, an elevation point above Bredwardine.

■ *Arthur's Stone is signposted up a narrow road to the north of the A4348, to the east of Hay-on-Wye.*

Arthur's Stone, the remains of a megalithic tomb (a cromlech) at Dorstone.

Druids' Moor *See* Reynoldstone

Dyffryn, West Glamorgan ✕
C4 ST 0971

Near Dyffryn in St Lythan's parish is a remarkable cromlech of three uprights and a capstone 14 by 10 feet/ 4.3 × 3 metres. There is a tradition that this vast capstone spins three times on its centre at midsummer eve. It is sometimes said that the hole in the side stone was put there to enable the spirit of the dead to 'escape' the tomb, but there is no evidence of this belief among those who built such structures. In his book *Mysterious Wales*, Chris Barber records that the land in which the cromlech is found is known as the 'Accursed Field', and mentions the belief that nothing will grow in it.

■ *Dyffyn is to the west of the A4063, east of Neath. The cromlech is about half a mile/1 km south-east of Dyffryn House.*

Fairford, Gloucestershire ♉
E4 SP 3791

In the roof of the chancel of St Mary's church there are carvings of eight of the nine orders of the angels, with only the rank of seraphim missing. The lower right-hand registers of the central west window show the traditional mediaeval demons involved in taking and punishing the souls of the damned. Note in particular the humour of the blue demon who is carting off the soul of a woman in a wheelbarrow. The windows were made circa 1490. The outer fabric (especially the south wall) displays several fascinating gargoyles and non-demonic figures.

■ *Fairford is on the A417, west of Lechlade, and the church lies to the north of the town.*

Demons from the 'Judgement' scenes on the west windows in St Mary's church, Fairford.

Ffestiniog, Gwynedd ◎
B/C2 GR 701413

Rising from the waters of the Cynfal in the valley below Ffestiniog is a column of rock closely resembling a pulpit, and called by the locals Huw Lloyd's Pulpit Stone. Tradition has it that the stone was used in the 17th century by a prophet of that name for sciomancy – the calling up from the lower world of shades of the dead. Huw Lloyd is a folklore figure, partly a poet, partly a demonomancer, partly a preacher of hell-fire, and mainly a wizard, who would roundly curse all who crossed him. It is said that shortly before he died he insisted that all his magical, astrological and demonological books be thrown into Llyn Pont Rhydden: however, just before they hit the water, a mystery hand rose from the surface and took the books, in much the same way as a fairy hand received the thrown sword of Arthur after he had died.

■ *The pulpit forms a grotesquely shaped island in the waters of the Cynfal. It is approached by a signposted trackway to the left of the chapel just south of Ffestiniog.*

Huw Lloyd's Pulpit Stone at Ffestiniog. This is a natural stone, the highest part of which is about 20 feet (6m) above the water surface, set in the middle of the Cynfal, in the valley below Ffestiniog, by the Rhaeder Cynfal.

Formby, Merseyside

C1 SO 2907

In the churchyard of St Luke's there is an unevenly shaped stone on which has been carved a most curious symbol – half a calvary cross and half an Egyptian ankh (a symbol usually regarded as being a life-bestowing amulet). The locals calls it the Godstone. In an amusing collection of Lancashire tales Kathleen Eyre records the ancient custom of carrying a newly deceased corpse around such stones to persuade the spirit to go on its journey without haunting the place. One wonders, however, if this Godstone is just another one of the ley markers with which the British landscape is littered?

■ *Formby is on the A565, to the north-west of Liverpool.*

Gloucester, Gloucestershire

D3/4 SO 8318

When a photograph taken about 1910, inside the empty Gloucester Cathedral, looking from the tomb of Robert of Normandy towards the raised organ, was developed, a mysterious head appeared in it. The photograph was submitted to the Society for Psychical Research in 1935, where it was carefully examined by P.J.C. Hoyle, who came to the conclusion that the 'spirit head' must have belonged to a person or spirit standing at least a foot above the floor of the cathedral aisle itself. The psychic extra has remained a mystery ever since.

■ *Gloucester is off Junction 11 (north) or junction 12 (south) of the M5.*

The interior of Gloucester Cathedral, looking from the Tomb of Robert of Normandy towards the raised organ. The spirit 'extra' on this picture can be seen more clearly on the inset detail.

Great Orme, Gwynedd

C1 SH 7584

It is likely that the church of St Tudno on the Great Orme was built over a simple cell founded by the saint himself. Tudno is said to have owned one of the marvels of Britain – the magical whetstone which could be used only by a truly courageous man. According to Welsh legends Tudno was one of the survivors of the drowned country of Cantref-y-Gwaelod, which, until the 5th century, was on dry land in the middle of what is now Cardigan Bay. He is supposed to have used the large rocking stone, the Maen Sigl, sometimes called St Tudno's Cradle, as an open-air pulpit: the stone no longer rocks, however, as it was fixed with a cement filling in modern times to prevent it from being dislodged. The proximity of several healing wells to St Tudno's church would suggest that in ancient times the Great Orme, with its strange limestone outcroppings, was a centre of great religious significance.

■ *The Great Orme is to the north of Llandudno. St Tudno's church is best approached by following the road which runs alongside the tramway lines up the Great Orme (north-west), and taking the second turning to the right. The church is near the northern end of the Great Orme, to the west of this road. The Maen Sigl is on the headland to the east of the first road to the right of the roadway which runs along the tramway. It is to the southern side of the headland opposite the cafe to the west of the spur road, above the miniature golf field. The pathway is not signposted and signs and indicators have been vandalised, so it is wise to ask for directions from locals. The stone may be identified by a rectangular incision on its northern side, where there was once an inscription plate.*

St Tudno's church and churchyard at Great Orme.

Hay-on-Wye, Powys

C3 SO 2242

The ruinous castle at Hay-on-Wye was said to have been built by the female ogre or witch Malwalbee in the course of a single night's darkness. For a possible origin of this curious witchname, see **Llowes**.

There is a Malwalbee Stone in St Mary's church at Hay, a mutilated effigy, probably of the 12th century.

■ *Hay-on-Wye is on the A4348, west of Hereford.*

Hereford, Hereford and Worcester

D3 SO 5139

The city of Hereford is an important place for believers in ley-lines. The great Alfred Watkins, author of the seminal *The Old Straight Track* which established the theory, was born here on 27 January 1855, in the Imperial Hotel in Widemarsh Street. It is therefore appropriate that we should consider one or two of the ley-lines in the city which Watkins revealed. All Saints' church (which has fine gargoyles) is on an important alignment which begins at Portland Street and continues through the church, to be taken up again by the run of St Owen Street, at the head of which was St Owen's church, demolished during the civil wars, but with its site still preserved on old maps, as in the name of the street. The line is continued through St Giles' chapel, and runs along Eign Road to The Crozen, a house standing on what is said to be an ancient Saxon burial ground. Watkins provided a schematic diagram of this ley, but the information is more clearly set out in the diagram according to Watkins' specification. A historically important ley-line directed on All Saints' is treated under **Dinedor**. It is interesting to observe that as early as 1925 Watkins was reflecting that St Giles' chapel was so awkwardly placed at a cross track, with motors approaching from three directions, that public opinion was demanding its demolition. 'It is,' he writes, 'interesting to reflect that the trouble originated in our ancestors planting a mark stone in the centre of a cross track four thousand years – or more – ago.' In fact, pre-1757

The 'Maen Sigl' at Great Orme linked with the preaching of St Tudno, and formerly a rocking stone.

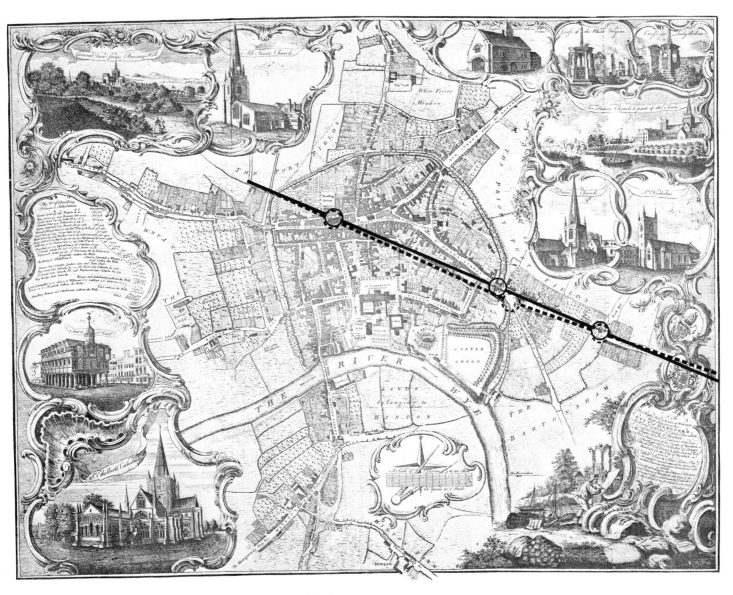

Ley-lines through the city of Hereford revealed by Alfred Watkins.

maps show St Giles on the corner of an ordinary T junction, and the alignment should connect St Giles' chapel (on the almshouse alignment) with the aperture of St Owen's Gate, the north-east corner of All Saints' church, with the run of Portland Street. St Owen's church was destroyed by the Parliamentarians in 1645, and it would seem that Watkins made a mistake about its place in the alignment, since the church occupied the triangular site to the south east of the old gate (itself now destroyed). It is indeed the triangular groundplan of St Owen's in the older maps which accounts for the triangular shape of the present roadway, where the modern Mill Street runs into St Owen's Street. The dotted line in the diagram sets out Watkin's proposed ley-line, while the solid line sets out the amended ley, with a correction for Watkins' error.

Hereford City Museum ♂ △

The museum exhibits a most interesting witchcraft relic in the form of a witch poppet (itemised as a curse doll) along with a written curse which was found at 21 East Street in Hereford, where it had been thrust into a crevice of the brickwork. The curse, which is written in a poor copperplate script, appears to be directed at one Mary Ann Ward (or perhaps Maryan Wand?), and runs 'I ask the spell upon

you from my holl heart wishing you to never rest or eat nor sleep the rest part of your life. I hope you flesh will waste away and I hope you will never gaen another penny I ought to have. Wishing this from my whole heart.'

Also in Hereford City Museum there are some splendid 15th-century roof bosses and carvings of assorted demons, dragons, grotesques and symbols formerly in the chapel roof of Hampton Court, Hope under Dinmore. The highly-coloured figures were probably carved for Sir Rowland Lenthall, who was knighted for bravery at Agincourt in 1415, as a result of which he obtained a licence to build the crenellated, partly fortified manor house (now much altered).

■ *Hereford is on the A438. The street plan in the diagram of Watkins' ley-line is now out of date, but it is sufficiently similar to the street layout of modern Hereford to act as a guide.*

The Imperial Hotel (well preserved, but now a Berni's Inn) is to the west of Widemarsh Street, itself to the north of All Saints' church.

East Street runs from the north end of Broad Street, through to Ethelbert Street. The museum is in Broad Street, opposite the cathedral.

Hollybush, Hereford and Worcester ♂

D3 SO 7636

In 1928 a Hilda Wickstead took a photograph of Hollybush church, on the Ledbury-Tewksbury road, near Malvern. The picture was intended to be a record of the church, with her friend Mrs Laurie standing by the porch. However, when the film was developed, there were two figures, apparently embracing, to the right of the picture. The presence of the ghostly 'extras' was never explained, but Mrs Wickstead recalled that her friend had drawn her attention to the grave of a soldier who had died in the First World War, and to another grave nearby, a memorial to a young woman who had died only a few months later, with the remark, 'I wonder if they were lovers?' She was so impressed by the ghostly pair in the photograph that she contacted the Society for Psychical Research, who investigated the affair, though they were unable to come to any conclusions.

■ *Hollybush lies on the A438 to the east of Ledbury.*

Detail from a spirit photograph taken in 1928 by Hilda Wickstead at Hollybush. It is believed that the two figures are the ghosts of lovers. The poor quality of this print arises from the fact that it is an enlargement (× 20) from a snapshot.

Holywell, Clwyd ◉ ✗

C1 SJ 1875

This is one of the many British towns which takes its name from the healing power of water. St Winifride's Well was probably the best known of all Welsh healing wells, with an output of over 20 tons of water a minute, and without doubt it is still the most beautifully preserved of all mediaeval holy wells in Britain. The water source itself emerges in a mediaeval stepped cistern, surrounded by a beautiful pillared walk, the walls and roof of which display highly symbolic finials, grotesques, memorial inscriptions and reliefs, many of which are treated in a useful and informa-

tive booklet (sold near the site) by Christopher David, one-time curate at Holywell. This water cistern has steps to permit pilgrims total immersion, but the flow is then ducted from beneath the enclosed mediaeval building into what can only be described as an external bathing pool, with steps to enable the infirm to climb down into the waters. Graffiti and lapidary inscriptions on the wall record miraculous cures which have been effected by the waters.

The name Winifride is said to come from the Welsh Gwenfrewi, who was killed by a chieftain: the place where she fell gushed forth water, and it was there that the well was built to contain the flow. The body of St Winifride is said to have been buried in Shrewsbury Abbey in 1138, however, and there are records of the well's therapeutic powers long before that century, for it has been shown that the shrine is virtually unique in having an unbroken history of pilgrimage from the 7th century. Christopher David records that it was once customary for pilgrims to pass through the inner well three times – and suggests that this is a survival of the ancient Christian practice of a triple total immersion (each immersion for one of the Persons of the Trinity) in the baptismal rites. At the end of the last century the well of St Winifride inspired Gerard Manley Hopkins to write one of his most lovely poems in its praise.

■ *Holywell is signposted to the south of the A55(T), west of Chester.*

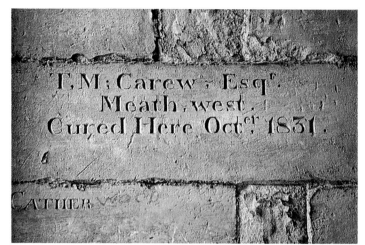

An inscription of 1831 recording the miraculous cure at Holywell, carved into stone above the well.

An 18th-century engraving of St Winifride's Well by Nathaniel Buck.

Hyssington, Powys

C2 SO 3194

The curious story of the monstrous bull of Hyssington is sometimes taken to represent the way in which the Christian religion clashed with the ancient paganism. The cult of Mithras, so popular among the Roman legions that several altars to the god still survive, was involved with zodiacal, planetary and other imagery, and its rituals appear to have revolved around the annual killing of a bull by the god Mithras. It is probably this bull of Mithras which was the source of the Hyssington story, which tells how, in the early days of the Christian faith, a monstrous bull terrorised the countryside around the village, until a priest decided to attempt exorcism. His magic had the curious effect of making the bull grow smaller and smaller, until it was so tiny that he could pick it up in his fingers, and drop it into his shoe. He then buried shoe and bull beneath the church threshold, where they are said to be still. The symbolism of the shoe is probably linked with the secrets of Pisces, which in the astrological image of man has rule over the foot, and is at the same time linked with Christ – the power of Christ has overcome the terrible bull.

■ *Hyssington is signposted to the west of the A489, south-west of Shrewsbury.*

Kilpeck, Hereford and Worcester

D3 SO 4430

The church of Saints Mary and David at Kilpeck is justly famous for its Norman stonework, which is without doubt the finest of any small church in Britain. The extant sculpture is usually dated to 1134, but some of the work definitely belongs to a much later period. Of particular interest to occultists are the demonic grotesques in the lower register of the tympanum arch, the astrological symbol of the Pisces image in the upper register, the ouraboros, the Green Man, and the strange pair of fishes to the north of the church.

The symbolism of the door is usually taken as relating to the temptation and fall in Eden, with particularly fearsome representations of the Old Serpent, to both the left and right of the door: however, it is more likely, in view of the number of alchemical and astrological symbols in the tympanum, arch and columns, that the real subject matter is arcane. This is confirmed by the fact that one of the men sculpted on the inner left pillar wears a Phrygian cap, which is always a sign of initiation, and was ultimately derived from the secret cult of Mithras.

■ *Kilpeck is signposted to the south of the A465 (T), south-west of Hereford.*

The Norman portal at Kilpeck church, with (above right) *the Green Man and* (below right) *a demonic face.*

Llandeilo Graban, Powys

C3 SO 0944

Legend has it that there was once a terrible dragon which made its nest on top of the church tower at Llandeilo Graban. A blacksmith (some say a ploughboy) killed it by making a model of the dragon, inside which was a whole battery of sharp steel spikes. This model he placed in the dragon nest: when the creature returned, it attempted to attack and throw out the interloper, thereby wounding itself fatally on the spikes in the attempt. The only thing at the top of the spire in modern times is an innocuous-looking weather-cock.

■ *Llandeilo Graban is a hamlet (signposted Llandeilo) to the north of the B4594, to the east of the A470(T), south-east of Builth Wells.*

Llandeilo Graban. It is said that the church tower was once used as a dragon-lair.

Llanelian-yn-Rhos, Clwyd

C1 SH 8676

St Elian's Well was said by many to have been the most awful of the many wells in Wales, for its waters had the virtue of granting power of life and death over any enemies. The procedure was to write the name of the person one wished to curse on a piece of paper (sometimes alongside the specific curse), and then to push a pin through the paper. The paper curse was then wrapped around a pebble, and thrown into the waters. Not surprisingly in view of its black magical connotations, the well was closed, and then later destroyed, by a rector of St Elian's Church.

■ *Llanelian-yn-Rhos is signposted off the B5383, south of Colwyn Bay.*

Llanfihangel Rogiet, Gwent

D4 ST 4587

A stone, curiously called the Devil's Quoit, and about 7 feet/ 2 metres high, stands in a field to the west of Llanfihangel Rogiet church. It was said to have been hurled by the Devil, from Portishead (to the south, across the mouth of the Severn), when he was in a fit of temper. The stone appears to be on a ley alignment which connects the fort on Wilcrick Hill with the stone, with Rogiet church, Portskewett church and Black Rock (to the west of Charston Rock).

■ *Llangifhangel Rogiet is signposted to the west of Caldicot, itself best approached from junction 22 of the M4.*

*Two additional ley-lines may be traced in this important part of the countryside, both apparently designed to enclose at their western ends the once-important ancient fort at Wilcrick Hill, and both passing through the standing stone to the west of Llanfihangel Rogiet church. One of these (a ley connecting five points in a straight line) is directed through Rogiet church, then through the ancient well at **Sudbrook**, and across the Severn to the church above Northwick. The second runs slightly further to the north, and after passing through the standing stone, runs through Llanfihangel Rogiet church, through Portskewett church, and on towards the Charston Rock.*

N

R. Wye

M4

A48

Severn Bridge

Caldicot

Llanfihangel Rogiet

Portskewett

Charston Rock

Wilcrick

Rogiet

Sudbrook

Northwick

1 Mile

Llanrhaedr Ym Mochnant *See* Pistyll Rhaeadr

Llowes, Powys

C3 SO 1941

In Llowes church stands the St Meilig Cross or Malwalbee Pebble, linked in popular mythology with the female ogre Malwalbee who was supposed to have built the castle at **Hay-on-Wye** by magical means. This stone is certainly no pebble, for it is about 9 feet/2.75 metres long and weighs 3½ tons. It is said to have stood as an ancient monolith on a hill called Croesfeilig (which is said to mean Melig's Cross, and probably accounts for the modern link with the St Meilig of the Maginogion tales), from where it was transported by Malwalbee. Exactly when the stone was Christianised with the beautiful lozenge-symbol cross is not known: it was however moved from its ancient place in the churchyard (where it is recorded as early as the 12th century) into the church in 1956. If the stone was brought down from Croesfeilig in the 12th century, already carved with its early Christian symbols, it could be that the witch Malwalbee was Maud de Valeri, an entirely historical personage, who was the great landowner in this area.

■ *Llowes is on the A438, west of Hay-on-Wye.*

Llyn Cau *See* Caider Idris

Llyn Cynwch, Gwynedd

C2 SH 6511

It is said that a wild dragon resembling a wyvern used to dwell in these waters, and hunt for its animal or human food in the mountains above. It did not kill in the usual way of dragons, for it had a basilisk eye, and could paralyse with its glance. The monster was killed by a shepherd who chanced to find it sleeping, and cut off its head. There is still a cairn called Carnedd-y-Wiber (Cairn of the Serpent) said to mark the place of this slaying.

■ *Llyn Cynwch is below the precipice walk, east of Llandelltyd, to the north of the A4949(T).*

Llyn Dinas Gwynedd

B1 SH 6149

This lake used to be called Llyn Dinas Emrys (the Lake of the Fortress of Emrys), and calls to mind that one of the names for the magician Merlin was Emrys. From the lake a pathway winds up the hill from which it is possible to see the ruinous walls of the castle called Dinas Emrys, one of the most famous of all mythological sites, linked with the origin of the emblematic Red Dragon of Wales in a series of divergent and confused legends. The essence of the story is that Vortigern (a 5th-century, almost legendary king of the Britons) attempted to rebuild the hill fort at Dinas Emrys, but every night the building material was stolen or removed. By consultation with a magician (whom some insist was Merlin) he discovered that beneath the hill there was an underground lake charged with serpent power, in which two dragons were sleeping. It was necessary to drain the underground lake to wake these dragons, who were then expected to fight. After much difficulty, the task was achieved, and the outcome of the telluric battle was that the Red Dragon killed the White Dragon, as a result of which the Welsh adopted the former as their emblem. It is said that after all his trouble to clear the serpent power, Vortigern finally elected to build a new fortress at Nant Gwynant, rather than at Dinas Emrys, which is why the dragon now bears that name.

■ *Llyn Dinas is a lake in the course of the River Glaslyn, about 2 miles/3 km north-east of Beddgelert, on the south side of the A498.*

Llyn Dywarchen, Gwynedd

B1 SH 5652

Floating islands were a common enough idea in classical times, but are rare in British mythology (at least, until Swift, a student of arcane lore, gave us the flying isle of Laputa in *Gulliver's Travels*), so Llyn Dywarchen has a special place in our lore. It was this which Giraldus of Wales had in mind when he wrote of a floating island, which was wind-carried from side to side of the lake: the Welsh name, which means Lake of the Turf Sod, suggests something of the nature of this curious phenomenon, which apparently has been seen as late as the 18th century. The island, which 'belonged neither to the earth nor to the waters', was said to be the meeting place of a man who had married a fairy, who, on her return to the lake, was condemned never to walk the earth again. Lynn Dywarchen is definitely a holy place, and one can imagine the island in its waters mysteriously floating: it is interesting to record that several locals insist even in modern times that the lake was made by man.

■ *Llyn Dywarchen is in the Nantlle Valley. Take the B4418 from Rhyd Ddu, the lake is visible to the left, from a depression in the road, about half a mile/1 km from the village.*

The lake of Llyn Dywarchen associated in Welsh mythology with floating islands. Could it be that the small island in the centre of the llyn was once believed to float on the surface?

Llyn Pont Rhydden *See* Ffestiniog

Maen Sigl *See* Great Orme

Merlin's Hill *See* Brechfa *and* Carmarthen

Mordiford, Hereford and Worcester

D3 SO 5737

The 19th-century historian Dacres Devlin records that there was once a great dragon in the village of Mordiford. It had begun life innocuously enough as a small creature 'the size of a cucumber and the colour of greenest grass, with wings like a pretty bird', and a small girl who happened to find it in a bramble bush took it home as a pet. She gave it milk to drink, but the dragon grew and grew, and was eventually satisfied only with the blood and flesh of cattle, which it raided from its huge nest in Haugh Wood, by way of its serpent path along the edge of West Hill. Eventually a condemned criminal called Garnstone was promised his freedom if he could kill the dragon, and while he succeeded in despatching it, he himself was killed by its poisonous breath. Garnstone hid himself in a cider-barrel stuck with steel spikes, and the dragon wounded itself fatally trying to get at the man. The story is an old one, of course, and there are many variants to it, but Devlin is worth quoting because he relates that in his day there used to be a replica of the dragon painted on the east end of the parish church – it was 12 feet/3.5 metres long, and had a forked tongue: the attached inscription spoke of it as 'the true effigy of that strange prodigious monster'. The only survivor of the tale in modern times is in the name Serpent Lane, applied to an overgrown cart-track at the base of West Hill, to the south of the village which supposedly was the path taken by the dragon when it crawled down to the river to drink.

■ *Mordiford is on the B4224 to the east of Hereford. Serpent Lane is to the left of the West Hill, which overlooks the village.*

Nant Gwynant *See* Llyn Dinas

Nevern, Dyfed

A3 SN 0839

In the churchyard (which is surely one of the most beautiful in Wales) is an avenue of yew trees among which is found the so-called bleeding tree, the 'blood' of which is really a natural red resinous discharge. It is said that the 'blood' will drip until the day that Nevern Castle (which now exists mainly in name only, the vegetative mound to the north of the church being the insubstantial remains) is in the hands of a Welshman.

In the churchyard is a Celtic cross over 12 feet/3.5 metres high, its surface decorated with interlacings, symbolic forms and undeciphered nordic inscriptions: it is generally regarded as being one of the finest examples in Wales.

Set into a windowsill in the south wall of the church is a 5th-century Ogham stone with a parallel text in Latin, a monument to Maglocunus, the son of Clutarius. In the adjacent windowsill is set an interlace cross of the 8th century.

■ *Nevern is on the B4582, west of Cardigan. The 'bleeding tree' is the second yew on the right, as you walk towards the church porch.*

The so-called 'bleeding yew' in Nevern churchyard. The 'blood' from the tree is a resinous discharge.

Penmaenmawr, Gwynedd

B1 SH 7176

Y Meini Hirion, meaning the Druid's Circle, is the name given to an impressive megalithic circle on the moors above Penmaenmawr. Within the circle is an upright, imaginatively called the 'sacrificial stone', which has a cavity on its top surface. Tradition has it that a newborn child placed in this cradle for a moment or two will have good fortune for the rest of its life. However, not all is well with this stone, for it is linked with witchcraft rites: some say that at one sabbat the noises of sobbing which came from the stone drove away most of the witches, though one was literally frightened to death, and another went mad through fear.

■ *The circle is reached by a difficult trackway some 2 miles/3 km long, which circles above the hills to the south of Penmaenmawr, itself on the A55(T). Directions to the site (which is badly signposted) are best obtained locally: otherwise, an Ordnance Survey map is recommended.*

The Druid's Circle above the town of Penmaenmawr.

The burial chamber at Pentre Ifan.

Pentre Ifan, Dyfed   ☒ ♀

B3 SN 0937

The megalithic tomb called Pentre Ifan is probably the most famous in Wales, and has been mentioned for its great beauty and archaeological interest since the 16th century. It would appear that the word cromlech (from the Welsh *crwm llech*, meaning curved stone or curved slate) was first used by the historian George Owen in connection with this tomb in that century. As the archeologist Jacquetta Hawkes says, the stones (which are really the exposed bones of an earth-covered burial mound) have a slightly fantastic air by virtue of the narrow points of the three upright bearers at the 'open' end, which give the impression that the capstone is floating. Locals insist even to this day that this is a place where the fairies gather: in earlier times it was called Coetan Arthur (Arthur's Quoit).

■ *Pentre Ifan is well signposted down a series of narrow lanes to the south of the A487(T), to the east of Fishguard.*

Pistyll Rhaeadr, Powys   ⟳

C2 SJ 0729

The mighty falls of this the highest waterfall in Wales was once said to be the bathing haunt of a winged serpent, which would drop in on nearby Llanrhaeadr-ym-Mochnant for his human meals. Like most dragons, it could not be vanquished by ordinary means, and so the villagers placed near Pistyll Rhaeadr a stone pillar studded with iron spikes and draped with a scarlet cloth, to attract and infuriate the beast (it is well known that dragons do not like red). Inevitably, the dragon beat itself against the hidden spikes, and eventually died from loss of blood.

■ *Pistyll Rhaeadr is signposted to the north-west of Llanrhaeadr-ym-Mochnant, at the western end of the B4396.*

Portskewett *See* Llanfilhangel Rogiet

Reynoldstone, West Glamorgan   ☒ ✿ ◉

B4 SS 4889

Arthur's Stone at Cefyn Bryn is an enormous capstone (25 tons), part of an ancient burial chamber, still supported by four uprights. There are several legends connected with the chamber, not least of which is that the capstone was a pebble which a giant found in his shoe, and flung away. This is one of the most magical stones in Wales, and the rites attached to it are enhanced by the belief that there is an ebbing and flowing well beneath the chamber, the waters of which are used for making wishes. There is indeed a holy well in the vicinity, about a third of a mile/500 metres along Cefn Bryn, as well as a number of standing stones, involved in a complex series of leys – note for example the ley between Arthur's Stone, running westward through the standing stones (north of Knelston) to the Burial Chambers to the north of Rhossili. This alignment also cuts across the wasteland to the south of Druid's Lodge intriguingly called Druid's Moor. The name Arthur is probably a corruption of a more ancient word, yet it is the same Arthur who was supposed to have split the capstone with his sword, and the armoured spectre which is said to emerge from beneath the stone is also believed to be that of the ancient king – though very many of the traditional demons are said to appear in the form of armoured knights. Women from Swansea are reported to use the stone as an indication of the faithfulness of their men: after a simple ritual with home-made barley bread-making on the stone, the women would crawl around the chamber three times. If the spirit of the lover then appears, he is known to be faithful.

■ *Reynoldstone is signposted to the north of the A4118, to the west of Oxwich Bay. Arthur's stone is signposted to the north, on Cefyn Bryn.*

Rhossili *See* Reynoldstone

Roewen, Gwynedd

C1 SH 7572

The Maen y Bardd cromlech west of Roewen is called locally the Greyhound's Kennel, a name which may be linked with the related standing stone, about 7 feet/2 metres high, about half a mile/1 km to the east. The story runs that a giant's dog, which had been sent to bring sheep from Tal-y-Fan, sheltered instead in the cromlech. Its giant owner was standing on Pen-y-Gaer, and in anger at the dog's disobedience, he threw the stone at the dog; the stone missed, and stuck almost upright in the earth, in the position which it still holds. There are other legends connected with the stone, however, not least of which links it with one of the deeds of King Arthur, as a result of which it is sometimes called Arthur's Spear.

■ *The Maen is to the north side of the Roman Road below Tal-y-Fan, just over 1½ miles/2.5 km west of Roewen, itself signposted to the west of the A5106. Since the roads are single-track, it is advisable to leave vehicles at Roewen.*

Rogiet *See* Llanfilhangel Rogiet

St David's, Dyfed

A3 SM 7525

Cathedral

The Abraham stone set in the wall of the south transept is the oldest part of the existing cathedral. Originally it marked the place where Hed and Isaac, the sons of the mediaeval Bishop Abraham were buried: its particular interest for occultists lies in the curious symbols on the stone – note the alpha and omega sigils on either side of the topmost cross, and the exquisite interlace encircled cross. One wonders if the lower part of the design is intended to point to the story of incarnation through the imagery of the bull, linked in late mediaeval art through zodiacal associations with zodiacal Taurus?

The zodiacal theme is continued in the nearby chapel dedicated to St Edward the Confessor. This lovely chapel was restored in 1920 at the expense of Viscountess Maidstone, whose ashes are beneath her effigy to the north of the altar. The sculptor has worked the four symbols of the evangelists in such a way as to recall the Babylonian and Egyptian astrological origin of their relevant symbols – for example, the image for Matthew (associated with the water-bearer Aquarius) is now a human-headed winged monster, recalling certain Babylonian gate-guardians.

St Non's Well

The waters of the ebb and flow of St Non's Well were for very many centuries regarded as being power magic, and were believed to work most miraculously on St David's day. There is a story that the waters sprang from the ground in a thunderstorm on the day that St David was born (circa AD 500). Nowadays the therapy has been demoted to wish-granting, but the stone structure of the well still preserves

the seats where people would be placed in hope of being cured of their various ills. The last recorded cure at the well was in 1860, though the water was sold widely for its curative power until well into the present century, and there are signs that the well is still used by the faithful.

■ *St David's is at the westerly curve of the A487, west of Haverfordwest. St Non's Well is a mile/2 km south of St David's, overlooking St Non's Bay, signposted from the city.*

The Abraham Stone in St David's Cathedral, Wales. The alpha and omega above the cross are so drawn as to incorporate several secret notions.

Detail of symbol of St John (Scorpio) on marblework of the St Edward the Confessor Chapel, St David's (restored in the 1920s by Viscountess Maidstone).

St Govan's Chapel, Dyfed ◉

A4 SR 9792

This is a tiny chapel wedged into the crevice end of the littoral which tumbles a mass of rocks within a steep-sided crevice to the west of St Govan's Head. The building is much restored, but of a 13th-century design, with many of the fitments cut from solid rock, some of which are ascribed magical properties: one has to pass through the chapel to complete the climb from the cliff top down to the rocks below. The external healing well (again recently restored) just below the chapel, was probably the reason why a chapel was built in this remote place. Legend says that the waters, and indeed the pilgrims visiting the site, were looked after by a 5th-century nun called Cofen, from whom the modern name Govan is derived. The well dried up in the early part of this century, but Chris Barber points to 19th-century records that there were still crutches left by those healed among the rocks. There is a legend that the chapel bell was stolen by pirates, but the undines took it back, and hid it in a rock, which is still supposed to ring when struck: however, no-one appears to know which of the numerous rocks is the famed one, with the result that it is never rung.

The chapel of St Govan's seen through one of the curious rock formations to the south-west of the littoral.

■ *St Govan's chapel is to the south of Bosherston, itself signposted to the south of the B4319, south of Pembroke. Access is sometimes restricted by military training.*

Staunton, Gloucestershire ✾

D4 SO 5412

The Buckstone above Staunton is a curiously-shaped balancing act in stone, which has gathered around it many myths, including the usual attached to curious stones that it was used by the Druids as an altar, and by the witches for their sabbats. However, it is likely that the same occult observations made for the **Brimham Rocks** will be applicable to this Buckstone. The gigantic pile of rocks appear to be so precariously balanced on a small socle pivot 'that a spectator would almost suppose that he could dislodge it . . . with the force of his single arm'. The 18th-century Reverend D. Booker noted that in his day the rocks would move 'in a kind of rocking motion but invariably settling on its ancient pivot'. However, in 1885 a group of people did actually knock it over, seemingly without serious intent. Eventually the pieces of the Buckstone were collected together and rebuilt on its old site, though after this reworking it no longer rocked. Some of the locals refer to it as the Frog Stone, from its resemblance to the bulge-eyed frog. Just above the Buckstone is the so-called Sacrificial Stone, and about a mile/2 km to the north the Suck Stone.

■ *Staunton is on the A4136 to the east of Monmouth. The approach to the stone itself is badly signposted. Take the small road to the left of the post-office, and continue upwards (keeping right) until you are below the covered reservoir, at which point a trackway ascends directly to the stone.*

The Buckstone, or Frog Stone, above the village of Staunton, near Monmouth.

Strata Florida, Dyfed ⚔ ✡

C3 SN 7465

The few remains of this once magnificent abbey in the midst of the deserted region of central Wales speak of the importance of the monastic system as a civilising force during the 12th and 13th centuries. Among the riches once preserved by the Cistercians was a famous cup, once the welsh *Cwpan*, now called the Nanteos Chalice, which is said to have been carved from a piece of the true cross which (according to mediaeval legend) had been discovered by Helena, the mother of Constantine, in the Holy Land. It is claimed by some that this was the famous chalice of the Grail legends, and some recent legends have the monks of Glastonbury placing it in the care of the monks of Strata Florida, despite the difference in religious orders, and despite the historical impossibility (Strata Florida was no longer powerful as a religious centre for many years before the demise of Glastonbury Abbey). Whatever its original source or history, the healing power of the cup was such that whoever drank from it was cured of all illness. After Henry VIII dissolved the monastic system the cup was preserved at Nanteos, where it was still used until comparatively recently for therapeutic purposes. Unfortunately it is now missing, either stolen or locked in some unknown bank vault. The 19th-century historian S.W. Williams wrote while the cup was still at Nanteos, and reports that it was 'supposed to possess healing powers which could only be called miraculous', and observed in passing that the patient had to drink from it wine 'or some liquor', but not being content with such liquids, certain individuals bit at the cup itself, to swallow some of the wood.

The southerly line of old chapels at Strata Florida (now protected by modern roof-systems) are paved with interesting mediaeval tiles, some of which are of a highly symbolic nature – one depicts pride or vanity (and is therefore a most fitting symbol for a monk to kneel on, while at prayer): others depict an eagle-headed griffin, as a sort of prototype of the Welsh dragon.

■ *The abbey is signposted to the east of the B4343, to the south of Devil's Bridge.*

A griffin tile from chapel floor at Strata Florida.

Sudbrook, Gwent → ◉

D1 ST 9744

The remains of St Tecia's chapel are on a rocky island to the south of the Sudbrook end of the Severn Tunnel. This St Tecia was once St Triacle, and some occultists have suggested that the name might be from the Roman word *theriac*, which was a sort of syrup (hence our modern word treacle), made by magical means from the flesh of vipers. Theriac was highly regarded in ancient times, and the Roman Emperor Marcus Aurelius used to take a dose daily: the physician Galen says that it will heal such things as plague and hydrophobia, and will prolong human life. Very often this magical treacle was made into soft pills by mixing it with bread.

The chapel of St Tecia itself is now ruinous, but records point to its being in use during the 13th century. There is no doubt that it was once on land which was joined to the mainland, and that it was built to service a holy well, the remains of which may still be seen: the chapel appears to have been built into what was probably an ancient fort, which may well also have been fortified by the Romans – hence perhaps the Latin corruption discussed above.

■ *Sudbrook is to the south-east of Caldicot, which is best approached from junction 23 of the M4. The remains may be visited safely at low tide.*

Swansea *See* Reynoldstone

Tal-y-Fan *See* Roewen

Teddington Hands, Gloucestershire ✿ ⚔

E3 SO 9633

East of Tewkesbury, five roads meet at Teddington Hands (a picturesque name for the old Teddington Cross): near this spot is a deeply pitted monolith named the Tibble Stone, concerning which there are many local legends. The ley-line expert Alfred Watkins (see **Hereford**) records a story of a giant who lived in those parts, and who sought a stone to destroy the house of his enemy. While he was carrying the stone down the hill his foot slipped, and it was this which made a great furrow in the hillside some way to

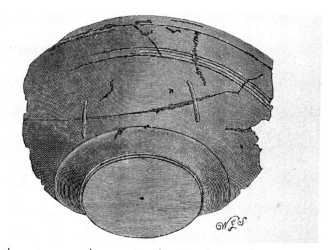
A 19th century wood engraving showing the now lost Nanteos Cup or Chalice which was formerly in the keeping of the monks of Strata Florida, and said to have been carved from a fragment of the true cross.

the east of Teddington Hands. The holes said to have been made by the giant's fingers are still visible in the standing stone. Such pagan stones were often used as mark stones, and almost always lie on important ley-lines: the Christians, who were no longer aware of the ancient use of such stones, often attempted to Christianise them by incising their surfaces with crosses, or by erecting wooden crosses over the top of them, as may well have been the case at Teddington Hands. Alfred Watkins records that he took a rubbing of a Maltese cross which had been cut on the stone at Patricio (in the Black Mountains of Wales) on which the Archbishop Baldwin is supposed to have stood when he preached to persuade men to follow the Crusade of 1188.

■ *Teddington Hands lies east of Tewkesbury, at the junction of the A435 with A438, and a minor road from Beckford, to the north. The Tibble Stone is sunk in the grass, opposite the Teddington Hands public house.*

Tintern, Gwent ♉ ⚔

D4 SO 5005

Above the ruins of Tintern Abbey is an outcropping of limestone, reached by way of a signposted track from Tintern. The weathered rock resembles a pulpit, and it is

entirely understandable why legends have grown to the effect that the Devil preached from this rock to the monks below. There are many stories of the Devil's attempts to persuade the monks from their Christian intent, all of them ending in the rout of the Satanic Majesty due to the superior cunning of the Cistercians in the abbey.

■ *Tintern Abbey is to the west of the A466, south of Monmouth.*

Trellech, Gwent

D4 SO 5005

Three standing stones in a field to the south-west of Trellech are sometimes called the Harold Stones, and are linked with one of the numerous victories over the Britons. However, they are distinctly megalithic: said by specialists to be conglomerate rock, shaped some 3,500 years ago, and in common with such ancient stones, they are merged with the demonological mythology which has them being thrown by the Devil, or by his Welsh adversary, Jack o'Kent.

The so-called Virtuous Well at Trellech was once under the patronage of St Anne. Nowadays virtue is a moral quality, but in earlier times it was the magical quality in a thing – the occult property inherent within a form, which

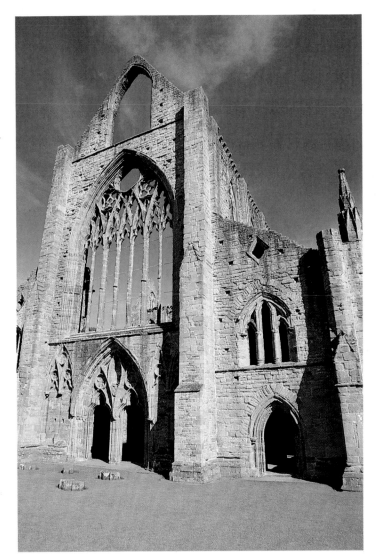

Ruins of the Abbey Church at Tintern Abbey.

The Harold Stones at Trellech dated around 1500 BC.

was generally believed to have come directly from the stars or from the spiritual realm. It is almost certainly this meaning which was intended in the name of the well, though since the 17th century it has gradually been demoted to the role of wishing well: if a small pebble dropped into the water is followed by a rush of bubbles, then the wish will come true. The well is said to gather the waters from four separate springs, three of which bear iron, and all of which are said to cure different illnesses.

■ *Trellech (sometimes marked on maps, or even signposted, as Trelleck or Treleck) is on the B4293. A useful map to the west of the road, by the turning to Llandogo, gives the locations of several of the outstanding remains within the village. The stones are to the east of the B4293, about 100 yards or metres from the turnings to Llandogo. The well is to the north of the Llandogo road, (about 200 yards or metres from the village main street), in pasturage behind a metal gate which is indistinctly signposted.*

Weston *See* Crewe

Wilcrick Hill *See* Llanfilhangel Rogiet

Woolston, Shropshire ◉

C2 SJ 3224

The healing well at Woolston, the waters of which were at one time valued for their magical power to heal wounds and bruises, is perhaps the most beautifully sited in England. The half-timbered cottage over the water flow was originally a meeting hall and court, although it is likely that there was at one time a chapel built over the well.

■ *Woolston is signposted to the west of West Felton on the A5(T), near Oswestry.*

Worcester, Hereford and Worcester ✡ ✿

D3 SO 8555

There is a quite fantastical story that on the 3 September 1651, shortly before the Battle of Worcester, Cromwell and Colonel Lindsey (the 1st Captain of Cromwell's own regiment), went at dawn to a little wood not far from the camp, where they met 'a grave elderly man who held a parchment in his hand'. Cromwell approached him, and the two argued: it seems that the pact was for 'seven years', and not for the 'twenty-one years' which Cromwell had bargained for. Lindsey apparently deserted at the first charge, and did not stop until he reached a friend in distant Grimstone (Norfolk) where he recounted how Cromwell had made a pact with the Devil. The historian of witchcraft, Montague Summers, records that when Cromwell died seven years later, on the 3 September 1658, 'there had raged for many hours a fearful storm round Whitehall; the Devil had come for his own,' folks said. The seven-year cycle was

important to Cromwell, in fact, for his victory at Marston Moor was in 1644, his brilliant victory at Worcester in 1651, and his death in 1658. Some say that Cromwell actually delayed the Battle of Worcester for one day in order that it should fall on the 3 September, to given an exact septenary from the victory at Marston Moor.

The cathedral in Worcester (like almost all the British cathedrals) contains many arcane symbols, among which the most impressive are the zodiacal symbols of the four evangelists in the roof of the cloisters.

■ *Worcester is signposted to the west of the M5, at junctions 6 and 7.*

Zodiacal emblems of the four Evangelists in the cloister roof of Worcester cathedral: probably 15th century.

Worm's Head, West Glamorgan ✡

B4 SS 3887

The inner and outer promonotories of this strangely formed rock, called in Welsh Penrhyn-Gwyr, are linked by the Devil's Bridge. To the north is a blow-hole which creates a bellowing sound, which some say is the sighing of the Devil himself.

■ *Worm's Head is approached by signposted trackway to the south-west of Rhossili, itself at the western end of the B4247.*

The North

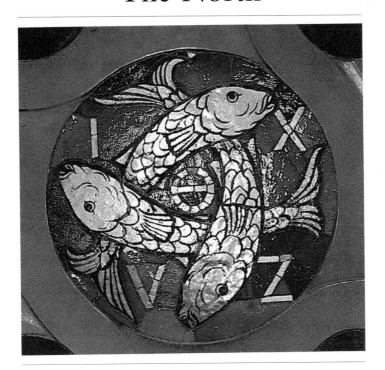

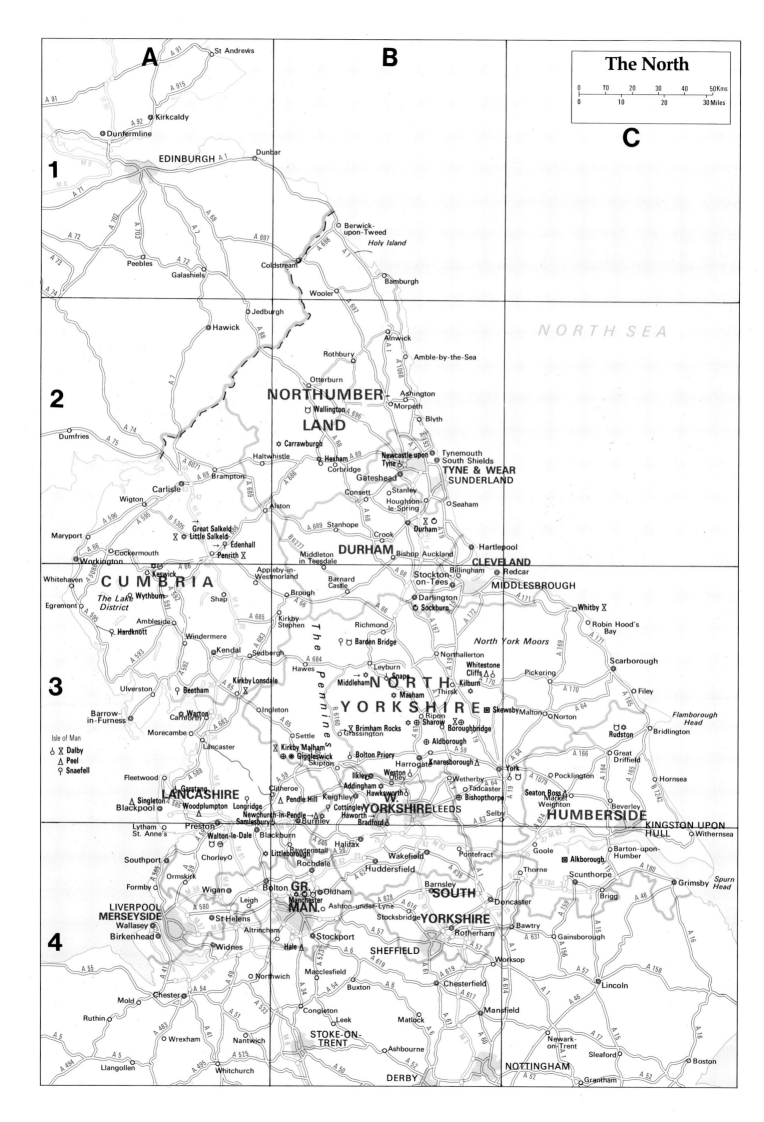

The North

A

B

C

1

2

3

4

St Andrews
Kirkcaldy
Dunfermline
EDINBURGH
Dunbar
Peebles
Galashiels
Coldstream
Berwick-upon-Tweed
Holy Island
Wooler
Bamburgh
Jedburgh
Hawick
Rothbury
Alnwick
Amble-by-the-Sea
Otterburn
NORTHUMBER-LAND
Wallington
Ashington
Morpeth
Blyth
Carrawburgh
Dumfries
Haltwhistle
Hexham
Corbridge
Newcastle upon Tyne
Tynemouth
South Shields
TYNE & WEAR
SUNDERLAND
Brampton
Gateshead
Carlisle
Consett
Stanley
Houghton-le-Spring
Seaham
Wigton
Alston
Maryport
Great Salkeld
Little Salkeld
Edenhall
Penrith
Stanhope
Crook
Durham
Hartlepool
Cockermouth
Middleton in Teesdale
DURHAM
Bishop Auckland
CLEVELAND
Workington
Whitehaven
Appleby-in-Westmorland
Barnard Castle
Billingham
Stockton-on-Tees
Redcar
MIDDLESBROUGH
Keswick
CUMBRIA
Brough
Darlington
Sockburn
Whitby
Egremont
The Lake District
Wythburn
Shap
Kirkby Stephen
Richmond
North York Moors
Robin Hood's Bay
Ambleside
Hardknott
Windermere
Barden Bridge
Northallerton
Scarborough
Kendal
Sedbergh
Leyburn
Whitestone Cliffs
Pickering
Hawes
Middleham
Snape
Kilburn
Filey
Kirkby Lonsdale
NORTH
Masham
Thirsk
Flamborough Head
Ulverston
Beetham
Ingleton
YORKSHIRE
Skewsby
Malton
Norton
A 64
Barrow-in-Furness
Warton
Brimham Rocks
Ripon
Sharow
Boroughbridge
Rudston
Bridlington
Carnforth
Morecambe
Settle
Grassington
Aldborough
Great Driffield
Lancaster
Kirkby Malham
Giggleswick
Bolton Priory
Harrogate
Knaresborough
York
Pocklington
Hornsea
Fleetwood
Skipton
Ilkley
Weston
Otley
Wetherby
Tadcaster
Bishopthorpe
Seaton Ross
Market Weighton
Beverley
Garstang
Addingham
Hawksworth
Singleton
LANCASHIRE
Clitheroe
Pendle Hill
Keighley
Cottingley
W. YORKSHIRE
LEEDS
Selby
HUMBERSIDE
KINGSTON UPON HULL
Blackpool
Woodplumpton
Longridge
Newchurch-in-Pendle
Haworth
Bradford
Withernsea
Lytham St Anne's
Preston
Samlesbury
Burnley
Walton-le-Dale
Blackburn
Halifax
Rawtenstall
Pontefract
Goole
Barton-upon-Humber
Southport
Chorley
Littleborough
Rochdale
Huddersfield
Wakefield
Thorne
Alkborough
Scunthorpe
Ormskirk
Bolton
Oldham
Barnsley
SOUTH
Doncaster
Brigg
Grimsby
Spurn Head
Formby
Wigan
GR. MAN.
Ashton-under-Lyne
Stocksbridge
YORKSHIRE
Bawtry
Gainsborough
LIVERPOOL
MERSEYSIDE
Leigh
Manchester
Stockport
Rotherham
Worksop
Wallasey
St Helens
Altrincham
Stockport
SHEFFIELD
Lincoln
Birkenhead
Widnes
Hale
Macclesfield
Chesterfield
Mansfield
Northwich
Buxton
Chester
Matlock
Mold
Congleton
Leek
Ruthin
Wrexham
Nantwich
Ashbourne
Newark-on-Trent
Sleaford
Boston
Llangollen
Whitchurch
STOKE-ON-TRENT
NOTTINGHAM
Grantham
DERBY

NORTH SEA

The Pennines

Isle of Man
Dalby
Peel
Snaefell

Addingham, West Yorkshire ❀

B3 SE 0749

On the moor's edge above Addingham are two curiously eroded rocks called the Doubler Stones. On the top surface of each, among a proliferation of modern graffiti, are a number of prehistoric incisions, mainly in the form of well-modulated cups. Popular tradition inevitably claims that these strange surfaces were used as slaughter stones by the Druids, and that the cups, with their incised channels, were for collecting blood. While the stones were almost certainly used for some religious purposes which might now be called 'occult', it is unlikely that they were used for blood sacrifice.

■ *The Doubler Stones are best approached from the west of Addingham, to the south of the Steeton Road (A6034). The continuation of this minor road terminates at a (private) road leading to a farm. The rocks are visible on the skyline above the farm, to the east.*

The so-called Doubler Stones on the moors above Addingham.

Ley-lines in northern England

Very often memorials and churches erected in modern times replace much older stone markers, menhirs and circles. The result is that one is often able to trace ley-lines between relatively modern structures. An outstanding example of this (outstanding mainly because it is a quite visible ley) is that between Studley Pike, Heptonstall Church and the war memorial below Pecket Well, which are on a straight line. The photograph (below right) was taken with a long-focus lens over a distance of 3 miles, from a location above the war memorial at Pecket Well, showing Studley Pike on the horizon, above the church at Heptonstall. The desolate stretch of moorlands to the north of this alignment includes Rombald's Moor, which is littered with many ancient remains, standing stones, cairns, stone circles and boulders incised with ancient symbols. It is interesting to observe that almost all of these lie on important ley-lines. The map (below) illustrates three of the most important of these ley-lines, which all cross at the largest of the stones circles, called 'The Twelve Apostles'. The most important ley passes through the Apostles, through another (smaller) circle to the east, and through the exotic Doubler Stones to the west, which have incised upon their surface many ancient symbols, including cup and ring marks. A longer ley-line joins an earthworks at the centre of many tumuli on the edge of Addingham Low Moor, passes through the Swastika Stone (below left), through the Badger Stone, then through the Apostles, to continue in the direction of Reva Hill. A ley-line at right-angles to this connects the White Stones with the Apostles, and continues across the valley to Denton church. It is particularly interesting that these leys have survived, for very many of the stones have in historical times been moved, and are now in local museums, or displayed in other parts of Yorkshire – see for example the fine example in **Keighley** bus station.

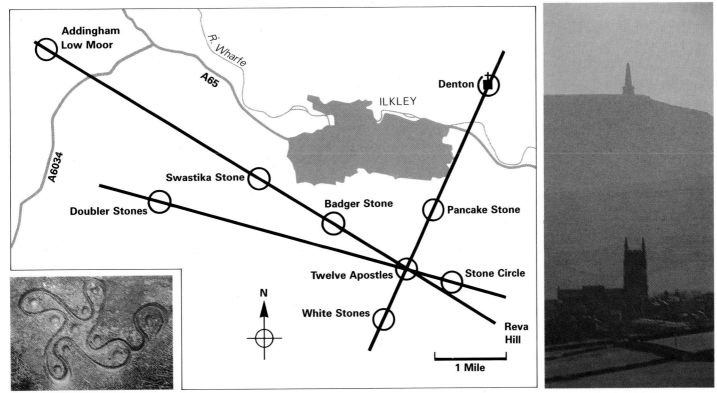

Inset Detail of the carving on the Swastika Stone, on Ilkley Moor. *Above* Map of the most important ley-lines. *Right* Studley Pike (on the horizon) aligned with the church at Heptonstall, seen from above Pecket Well. Such ley-lines are not always so visible.

Aldborough, North Yorkshire ⊕
B3 SE 4066

Aldborough was originally the Roman town of Isurium Brigantum, and St Andrew's church there has a Roman altar in the north aisle on which is carved an image of Mercury, with his magical caduceus of two snakes, twining round a single staff. This symbol was adopted in modern times as the emblem for the medical profession.

The memorial brass to William de Aldeborough in the north wall is perhaps the oldest in any Yorkshire church. The symbols on the thigh armour are quatrefoil crosses, said to be based on the magical three of the clover-leaf design.

■ *Aldborough is signposted to the east of the B6265, which itself is off the A1(T) to the south of Thirsk.*

Alkborough, Humberside 🔲
C4 SE 8821

On the hillside above this village is a depression into which a large turf maze has been cut. Its walls are about five inches/ 13 cm high, and the maze form itself is about 42 feet/13 metres in diameter. Like so many of the late mediaeval mazes, it is not really a maze so much as a dance-pattern, for it is not possible to 'lose' oneself within the formal pattern. The maze is called Julian's Bower locally.

■ *Alkborough is signposted to the north of Burton-upon-Stather, which is on the B1430 north of Scunthorpe.*

The turf maze known as Julian's Bower at Alkborough. It is 40 feet (12m) in diameter.

Barden Bridge, North Yorkshire ♀ ♂
B3 SE 1493

At the enforced narrowing of the River Wharfe into the narrow channel called the Strid, to the south of Barden Bridge, the waters run fierce and deep. The area is infamous for the white horse which is supposed to leap from the waters on May Day. Accounts vary, but along with the horse is said to appear a fairy who will grant humans' wishes or answer questions about the future. The fairy does not have a pleasant reputation, however, for three sisters from Beamsley turned up one May morning, to try their luck with contacting the fairy, and were later found drowned – some say by the demons of the gorge, who disguise themselves as fairies.

■ *Barden Bridge is on the B6160. The Strid narrows about 2 miles/3 km north-west of Bolton Abbey.*

Beamsley *See* Barden Bridge

Beetham, Cumbria ♀
A3 SD 5173

To the west of the old church at Beetham is a pathway leading to the Fairy Steps, which are cut into a crevice of sheer limestone, a reminder that, according to the locals, this whole area is a fairy domain. It is said that if you can climb the steps without touching the walls of limestone on either side, you may make a wish which will come true.

■ *Beetham is on the A6, north of Carnforth, which is to the west of junction 35 of the M6. The pathway to the steps is signposted to the west of the church.*

Berwick-on-Tweed *See* Bearsted (London and Southern England)

Bishopthorpe, North Yorkshire ⊕
B3 SE 5947

One of the earliest references to classical astrology in mediaeval England is connected with Bishopthorpe, the site of the archbishop's palace, near York. In the early part of the 12th century Gerard, the Archbishop of York, who was notorious as one interested in magic, is reported to have died in his private garden with a copy of a famous book on astrology by the Roman Firmicus Maternus under his pillow. Because of this, it is said that his own canons refused to give him decent burial. The story may be spurious, however, for even at that time astrology was widely used in the Church for symbolic purposes – see for example the 12th-century zodiac mentioned under **Canterbury** (London and Southern England).

■ *Bishopthorpe is just over 2 miles/3 km south of York, signposted to the south of the A64.*

Bolton Priory, North Yorkshire ♁

B3 SD 0854

The ghost which haunts the priory has been called by W.R. Mitchell in his book *Haunted Yorkshire* 'the most famous and best-documented of the Yorkshire Ghosts', presumably because it has been sighted by such people as King George V, the Duke of Devonshire and Lord Desborough. The ghost's identity is unknown, but it is that of an old man of middle height, with a heavily wrinkled and unshaven face. He wears the cowled habit of an Augustinian monk. In 1973 a group of amateur archaeologists digging in the grounds of the priory (searching for the burial place of John de Clifford, who was killed in 1461) saw a ghost in mediaeval dress.

■ *The priory is signposted to the north of the A59, east of Skipton.*

The 'Devil's Arrows', megalithic standing stones, near Boroughbridge.

Boroughbridge, North Yorkshire ♂ ✗ ⊕

B3 SE 3966

The Devil's Arrows are three colossal (the tallest is 22 feet/ 6.7 metres high) monoliths of millstone grit, said to be over 3,000 years old. They are not in perfect linear alignment, but it is likely that they are merely the remnants of a much more extensive system, for the antiquary John Leland (1503–52) mentions four uprights. The originator of the ley-line cult, Alfred Watkins, claims that they mark out a ley, but Lockyer held that they were part of an ancient sun-worship avenue (they run on a south-north axis). The southernmost

stone is now fenced off, almost part of a private garden, and, as the modern writer Jacquetta Hawkes says, 'the pagan gods fly from English back gardens.' – even so, the distinctive telluric power of these stones may still be felt. The origin of the name is lost in obscurity, but legends have it that the stones are the remains of a volley shot from the Devil's bow or that the Devil hanged himself from the tallest stone.

■ *The standing stones are visible from the A1(M) to the west of Boroughbridge, which is on the B6265, north-north-west of Knaresborough.*

Bradford, West Yorkshire ♁

B3/4 SE 1633

The old Theatre Royal, in Manningham Lane, is said to be haunted by the ghost of one of England's finest actors, Sir Henry Irving. Irving certainly played his last role in that theatre, in 1905, but he actually collapsed and died in the Midland Hotel, in Cheapside. For the occult 'Bradford heads', see **Haworth**.

■ *Bradford is on the A647, west of Leeds.*

Brimham Rocks, North Yorkshire → ✗

B3 SE 2165

It is mainly the fanciful shapes of these remarkable outcroppings near Pateley Bridge which attract tourists, for some rocks have uncanny resemblances to animals, monsters and the like. Most popular is the 'hanging rock', a boulder of some 200 tons balancing on a rock socle about a foot/30 cm wide, and a weird rock closely resembling a bear.

There is evidence, however, that in the 19th century one or two sculptors aided nature with their art, carving a few of the stones into a close resemblance to the imagined figures. From an occult point of view, however, the stones still retain great interest. The occultist Blavatsky sees the revolving rocking stones on the summits of some of the larger rocks as copies of the divinatory or oracular rocks used by the priests of lost Atlantis. She has in mind the ancient magical tradition recorded by the occultist Olaus Magnus that such rocks were the sites of ancient oracles 'whose voice spoke through the immense rocks raised by the colossal powers of ancient giants'.

■ *Brimham Rocks are to the west of the minor road which runs from the south of the B6265 (to the east of Pateley Bridge) towards Summer Bridge.*

Carrawburgh, Northumberland ✡

B2 NY 8671

Here, among the remains of what the Romans called Brocolitia, to the south of Hadrian's Wall (Northumberland) are the foundation remains of a Temple of Mithras, built in about AD 205. The temple appears to have been savagely destroyed sometime after 297, and the present layout represents the archaeological reconstruction. Mithras was a Persian sun god popular among the Roman armies, with an esoteric lore and symbolism derived from the ancient mystery wisdom with which the early Christians had to contend in the early centuries of our era. There were many interesting parallels in the Mithraic beliefs and those of Christianity – especially in connection with the therapeutic value of the blood. It is argued that some of the Mithraic images have survived into modern symbolism – most notable among these is the zodiacal image of Taurus the Bull, for one of the most important symbols in the Mithraic rites was the annual sacrifice (by Mithras) of a bull, with the esoteric aim of permitting its blood to vivify the earth. Another Mithraic survival into mediaeval symbolism was the strangely shaped initiate cap worn by Mithras. See for example **Coggeshall** (Eastern Counties). The sun-aura around the head of the god recalls the Christian symbolism of the halo. Mithras, like the Christ of early Christianity, was believed to be a sun god. The dedication stones on the site are reproductions: the originals are in the Museum of Antiquities, Newcastle-upon-Tyne.

■ *The temple is signposted from a parking area to the south of the B6318, north-west of Hexham – some signs refer to 'Brocolitia', others to Carrawburgh.*

Castlerigg *See* Keswick

Cayton Bay *See* Rudstone

Cottingley, West Yorkshire ♀

B3 SE 1237

In 1920 Sir Arthur Conan Doyle published some photographs of fairies taken by two young girls, near the beck in Cottingley. These fairy pictures, which were taken in 1917 by Frances Griffiths and Elsie Wright, aged ten and thirteen respectively, soon became with the enthusiastic endorsement of Conan Doyle some of the most famous photographs in the world. For many decades the two women insisted that they had seen fairies in Cottingley Glen, and that the pictures were genuine. However, in 1977 the fairies in the pictures were traced by the writer Fred Gettings to Shepperson's illustrations to a poem by Alfred Noyes called 'A Spell for a Fairy', which was woven around the idea of making a spell to enable one to see fairies!

It transpires that the children had merely copied these pictures, stuck them upright with hat-pins, and photographed them. The clairvoyant Geoffrey Hodson left several descriptions of the fairies he saw in Cottingley between 1921 and 1922. From the description it would appear that the 'bright radiance' which shone over the field, and which was visible to his 'inner eye' some 60 yards/metres away, hovered over the fields beyond Cottingley Beck, in much the same place that the Griffiths and Wright prank was played. See also **Hindhead** (London and Southern England).

■ *Cottingley is now almost swallowed up in the urban spread of Bradford, but is signposted to the west of the A65, between Bingley and Shipley. Cottingley Beck is to the east of the B6269, but lies on private land.*

One of the so-called Cottingley 'fairy photographs' taken by Frances Griffiths and Elsie Wright. It has now been shown that the 'fairies' were cut-outs, copied from an illustration to a poem about fairies. This picture is from a magazine article published by Conan Doyle at the time.

An illustration by Shepperson to the poem on fairies by Alfred Noyes. It was this picture which Frances Griffiths and Elsie Wright used as the basis for their own cut-outs which became the infamous 'Cottingley Fairies'.

The banks of Cottingley Beck, where the myth of the Cottingley fairy photographs began.

Dalby, Isle of Man

SC 2278

The Dalby Spook was what locals called one of the most extraordinary ghosts of modern times, better known on the mainland as 'Gef the talking mongoose'. Gef first intruded on the lives of the Irving family of Doarlish Cashen on the Isle of Man in September 1931 with curious rapping noises, and the sounds of things being dropped. Eventually, still without showing himself, the strange new inmate of the house began to talk, with difficulty at first, but then with great volubility. Asked by one of the members of the family if he were a ghost, he replied 'I'm a ghost in the form of a weasel'. However, when at last the family began to see Gef, they realised that he was rather like a mongoose. He was a friendly mongoose, anxious to learn, and just as keen to help the family with which he lived as any intelligent pet. However, he did not like the father of the household and the story goes that the man tried to kill Gef with rat-poison, though Gef got the better of him by almost bringing the house down with his racket 'in punishment'. The Gef haunting led to unexpected consequences. The well-known psychic researcher Harry Price, and his friend R.S. Lambert, who was then the editor of the *Listener* magazine, investigated the haunting of Cashen gap, and came to the conclusion that this was a true, if bizarre, haunting: after several broadcasts they published a book on the subject. Someone publicly called Lambert 'crazy' for believing in the Dalby Spook. Without hesitation, Lambeth sued for slander, and at the end of a long court hearing eventually won heavy damages.

■ *Dalby is on the A27, to the west of the Isle of Man. The house at Cashen Gap where the spook lived has been removed.*

The demonic sanctuary knocker on the North door of Durham Cathedral. This is in fact a replica; the original is now preserved in the museum.

Eamont Bridge *See* Penrith

Durham, County Durham

B2 NZ 2642

The demon-head knocker on the cathedral's north door, sometimes called the Sanctuary Knocker was originally fixed in place during the 12th century and remounted in 1777. The present knocker is a reproduction, the original being in the cathedral treasury. The use of the knocker by a suspect or criminal summoned specially appointed guardians, who could grant sanctuary, which led eventually to either voluntary trial for the crime, or voluntary exile.

In the cathedral treasury is the Conyers Falchion, a 13th-century sword with a bronze guard and wooden grip. The guard is decorated with interlaced serpents or dragons. The design of the falchion is said to have been derived from that of the scimitar with which the Crusaders became all too familiar during the 13th- and 14th-century campaigns and catastrophes. What is special about the Conyers Falchion (apart from its rare shape) is that it is popularly said to have been the sword used to kill the dragon known as the **Sockburn** Worm.

■ *Durham is signposted off the A1(M), and the cathedral is well signposted within the city.*

Edenhall, Cumbria

A2 NY 5632

The Luck of Edenhall is a 13th-century glass, said to be a fairy cup of the same protective order as the Luck of Burrell Green (see **Great Salkeld**), and is attached to a similar couplet which warns that Edenhall will suffer if the owners part with the talisman. This fairy cup is said to have been left by a group of fairies who had been disturbed by a human while playing and drinking at St Cuthbert's Well near Edenhall. Like the 'Fairy Flag' of **Dunvegan** Castle (Scotland, this cup appears to be Syrian in design, and may have returned with the Crusaders. The historian Hartland points out that there was a Norse belief in such cups, often later used as chalices in the Christian ritual, and that Norse guardian house spirits were eventually materialised into fragile 'Lucks'. Significantly, the magnificent Edenhall was demolished only eight years after the fairy cup left the Musgrave family, on loan to the Victoria and Albert Museum, in 1926.

■ *Edenhall is to the north-east of Penrith, signposted to the east of the A686 – normally, the fairy cup may be seen in the Victoria and Albert Museum, London.*

Garstang, Lancashire

A3 SD 4945

In the country areas around Garstang dwells the boggart, one of the supernatural creatures of the Lake District, which is said to appear in the form of a hooded skeleton. She is scarcely a boggart, however, for in the occult tradition these creatures are elementals, sometimes appearing in a monstrous humanoid form, sometimes as animal spectres. The Garstang boggart is different, for it is said to be the spirit of a murdered woman, who will persuade horsemen to give her a lift, and then drive them to their deaths.

■ *Garstang is on the A6, south of Lancaster.*

Giggleswick, North Yorkshire

B3 SD 8063

Church

On the panels of the pulpit in St Alkelda's church are carvings, dated 1680, of the names of the twelve sons of Jacob, relating to the twelve Tribes of Israel. Each name has a 'badge' – for example, Reuben is symbolised by waves, and Dan by a basilisk. The images correspond to the twelve zodiacal associations drawn up in the mediaeval period, mainly by William Durandus. The waves represent Aquarius, while the basilisk represents Scorpio, and so on. The twelve are not in the usual zodiacal order. For further associations, see Introduction, Page 15, Table 2.

Well

The so-called 'Ebbing and Flowing Well' to the north-east of Giggleswick is said to have magical properties, and to be a healing well, something like the Rag Well of Walton, in Yorkshire: however, it appears to have ceased its regular ebbing and flowing many years ago. A 19th-century stained glass window in St Alkelda's church at Giggleswick shows the 'spirit' of the well in the form of an angel hovering above the waters, the Christianised version of the pagan watersprite, usually called undines by occultists. The dedicatory saint of Giggleswick is Alkelda, about whom nothing is known. Some scholars suggest that the name is from the Old English *haeligkeld*, meaning holy-well.

■ *Giggleswick is signposted to the west of the A65, south of Settle. St Alkelda's is to the north-west of the village, set back from the main street. The well is to the east of the A65, a few hundred yards/metres north of the slip road to Giggleswick.*

Great Salkeld Cumbria

A2 NY 5536

A house called Burrell Green in the parish of Great Salkeld is associated with a brass plate called the Luck of Burrell Green, in this context a luck being a talisman or fairy gift. This embossed metalwork has a twelve-rayed swirl (the so-called wrythen flutes) at the centre of its diameter of 16 inches/40 cm. It is said that there were once two inscriptions, but constant cleaning has made them illegible. However, 19th-century engravings reveal it to be clearly marked (in a 19th-century revival black letter script) with the words 'Mary. Mother. Of. Jesus. Saviour. Of. Men.', and on the next concentric, in a 19th-century grotesque letter, 'If this dish be sold or gi'en, Farewell the Luck of Burrell Green.' Legend has it that the dish was given to the family living in the house by a gnome like 'Hob-i'-th'-hurst' or alternatively by a witch or soothsayer, to whom some kindness had been shown, with the understanding that if the family parted with the gift they would lose the 'Luck of Burrell Green'. A paper read in 1897 by John Lamb at a meeting of the local Archaeological Society in Penrith tells us that on the day Burrell Green last changed owners, the Luck fell down three times in succession from its usual (quite secure) position! It would appear from the inner inscription that the plate may once have been an alms-dish, but some think that it is no older than the 16th century, when such plates were made in Germany, while others have suggested that it was nothing more than an English revival piece, cast for the 1851 Great Exhibition. In spite of this, the Luck of Burrell Green is often quoted as one of the six Lucks recorded in Cumbria, and is almost as famous as the Luck of **Edenhall**.

■ *Great Salkeld is on the B6412 north-west of Penrith.*

Hale, Greater Manchester

B4 SJ 7786

This lovely village is famous as the birthplace and home of the Childe of Hale, a giant of 9 feet 3 inches/2.82 metres. It is said that he did not grow to that size naturally, but was bewitched, so that within a moment he grew from a normal size so rapidly that he split his clothes. He died in 1623, at the height of the witchcraft craze in the Lancashire villages, and so it is likely that the story of his bewitchment is a fabrication: his great size was no invention, however, for his body was exhumed, and it was found that the bones of his hand were 43 cm long, and that he was indeed a giant of over 2.75 metres.

■ *Hale is to the south of Manchester, signposted on the A538, off junction 6 of the M56.*

Hambleton Hills *See* Kilburn

Hardknott, Cumbria

A3 NY 2402

The Roman fort ruins at Hardknott, below Hardknott Pass, appear to have been adopted by the fairies. It is said that Eveling, the king of the fairies holds his invisible court in the ruins. His daughter Modron (who became the *Morgan la fée* of French romantic literature) is the fairy who healed King Arthur, and persuaded Merlin to leave the world behind. Some mythologists say that she is the same as the Irish Murigen, a lake goddess, who changed into a salmon –

but the change from human form to salmon is one of the most frequently used of all symbols for reincarnation, and the story probably has hidden depths to it.

■ *Hardknott is below Sca Fell, to the east of Beckfoot in Eskdale, to the north-east of Ravensglass, to the west of Ambleside.*

Hawksworth, West Yorkshire ♂

B3 SE 1641

In this village is the splendid 17th-century Hawksworth Hall, said to be haunted by three ghosts. One is a fairly conventional 'cowled monk', another a woman who insists on opening doors and leaving them open, while the third is the ghost of a negro page boy, said to be given to leaving dirty handprints on pillows. It seems that the 'witchcraft king', James I stayed here for some time, and the coved ribbed plaster ceiling in the main room still bears his coat of arms.

■ *Hawksworth is signposted off the A6038 to the west of Guiseley.*

Haworth, West Yorkshire →

B3 SE 0337

The curious carving on the roof-end of the last house in West Lane is not a gargoyle, as it does not act as a water spout. The carved head was placed there in accordance with a local tradition that such images will ward off evil spirits. Similar heads, and far more grotesque ones, are often built into the walls near doorways, or over door lintels, and they have been linked with the unpleasant Celtic custom of exhibiting the heads of enemies on spikes at the entrances to towns. It is more likely, however, that they are remnants of the old practice of mounting a fearsome or gruesome head (the so-called Gorgon-head) over a doorway to drive away the evil eye. There is another lintel 'rustic head' above the doorway of the nearby Sun Inn: this was put there during interior restorations in 1972, in the hope of laying the ghosts which had haunted the place for years. For some reason, Ralph Whitlock in his book *In Search of Lost Gods* calls these rustic carvings 'Bradford heads', but they are found in many parts of Yorkshire.

One of the so-called 'Bradford head' amuletic devices on the roof of an ordinary dwelling house in West Lane, Haworth.

■ *Haworth is well signposted to the south of Keighley, or off the A6033, north of Hebden Bridge. West Lane is the continuation of Main Street, at the top of the village, and the carving is on the roof end of the last house to the south of the main village area, just before the entrance to the Brontë Parsonage car park.*

Hexham, Northumberland ✡

B2 NY 9634

The priory church at Hexham has several images and symbols of interest to occultists. Note particularly the famous grotesques on Rowland Leschman's tomb (1491) in what is now a sort of unofficial museum of artefacts inside the abbey. The 15th-century oak screen in the north of the sanctuary has several late mediaeval paintings of the dance of Death. There are several Roman stones built into the walls of the nave, and two Roman pagan altars in the transepts, reminding us that the foundation church and crypt of the priory church (once a cathedral) was built from stones brought from nearby Corstopitum (modern Corbridge). Of particular interest to occultists, however, are the 19th-century mosaic details on the memorial in the interior north wall – among these is a subtle occult play with the image of three fishes (exoterically, the Trinity) and the occult name for Christ in his symbolic form of the fish. The Greek word for fish (here spelled out as IXΘUS) is an ancient acrostic for the Greek phrase meaning 'Jesus Christ, the son of God' (for details of this, and the connection with the pagan mystery tradition, see St Augustine, in the bibliography). What makes this acrostic device especially interesting to occultists is that the letter theta Θ has been placed at the centre of the intertwined fishes. Within the acrostic the theta is the initial letter of the Greek word for God, but in the early Greek and later Roman tradition it was a symbol of death (the Greek words *thanatos*, meaning death, began with the theta). In this form the symbol

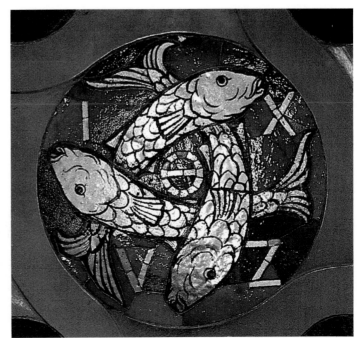

Fish symbols, with the Greek letters for 'fish', inside the Abbey Church, Hexham Priory.

survived as an emblem of death in astrological documents well into the 18th century. Its significance here is that it shows the theta enclosed by the fishes, and is therefore a symbol of the mystery teaching of Christianity, that death was overcome by Christ.

■ *Hexham is signposted off the A69(T) to the west of Newcastle upon Tyne. The priory church is on the hill at the centre of the town, signposted from all entry points.*

Ilkley, West Yorkshire

B3 SE 1147

The parish church has a stone figure said to be that of a water-nymph holding two serpents: inevitably this has been seen as a throwback to some ancient serpent cult.

On the edge of the Ilkley moors above the town are a number of rocks bearing incised designs of occult significance: the most often visited is the Pancake Stone (see also **Keighley**), which has cup and ring marks said by some to point to the stone circles on Rombald's Moor, but perhaps the most remarkable carving is the rock called the Swastika Stone, which is now fenced in. The original design on the surface of this stone is now almost obliterated by wind and weather, but the council has thoughtfully supplied an incised copy nearby, for comparison. The design, which is probably over 3,000 years old, only vaguely represents a swastika, however, and is far more complex in form.

■ *Ilkley is on the A65, north of Bradford. The parish church is in the centre of the town. Rombald's Moor is littered with carved stones and circles, and is best explored with the aid of an Ordnance Survey Map 1:50000 (Sheet 104). The Swastika Stone is to the right of the pathway along the top of Rombald's Moor, in the direction of Addingham.*

Keighley, West Yorkshire

B3 SE 0540

In the central bus station of Keighley, set among a group of other stones, is an extraordinary incised stone design, said to be over 3,500 years old. It has been moved to this site from its original position on nearby Baildon Moor. Related incisions on the Pancake Stone above **Ilkley** are called ring and cup marks, and it is possible that these are ancient pointers, or guides, to stone circles. Those on the Pancake Stone point to horizon markers, in the manner of ley guides, and these in turn point to other markers, which direct one to the stone circle called the Twelve Apostles. Perhaps the more complex design of the Keighley stone is intended as a similar marker?

For a further note on Keighley, see **Knaresborough Forest**.

■ *Keighley is on the A650 north-west of Bradford. The ancient stone is set in a external display south of North Street, almost opposite Lloyds Bank.*

A prehistoric carving on a stone, now ignominiously located in Keighley Bus Station, formerly on Baildon Moor.

Keswick, Cumbria

A3 NY 2623

The Keswick Carles, or Castlerigg, is one of the most remarkable stone circles in the north of England, in the most exquisite natural setting of any circle in Britain, surrounded by a switchback panorama of mountains except to the east. The diameter of the circle is about 100 feet/30 metres, the pattern now being marked out with thirty-nine standing stones or carles.

The clairvoyant Geoffrey Hodson visited this place (which he called a Druid Circle, though, being familiar with the literature of the theosophists, he should have known better) in August 1922, and left a most original record of his experiences there. His gifts enabled him to peer back into the past, and in his entertaining book *Fairies*, he left a record of what he experienced at Castlerigg. With his inner eye he saw a mighty master magician standing within an inner circle of rocks. The magician raised both hands to the heavens, as though to a number of devas who hovered in the skies, and astral beings formed a circle in the air above his head, and by magical means created a sort of fire. This astral fire descended on the stone altar which was in those days raised in front of the high priest, where it continued to burn. Following a prescribed ritual, the observers made obeisance to the flames. Hodson makes the important point that a powerful magnetic insulation existed, and still exists to some extent, round the circle of stones, giving as much seclusion (at least from an occult point of view) as would a solid temple of stone. In the vision, the climax of the ritual is when the heavens appear to open, and there is an enormous influx of forces played into the circle and its immediate neighbourhood: these forces are, as Hodson admits, beyond description, something like a liquid, fiery mother-of-pearl, opalescent yet tinged with an 'inner' colouring of rose. The high priest appears to be one of the few who could see this phenomenon, yet the people gathered there were aware that something remarkable was happening. Hodson observes that since those days, the stones have witnessed other scenes, not all of them so holy and spiritual. For other visionary insights, by Hodson see **Longridge**, **Snaefell** and **Wythburn**.

On a mundane level, the psychic investigator Frederic Henry Myers was born in Keswick, in 1843: he published the first papers in connection with the Society for Psychical Research: see **London – Adam and Eve Mews** (London and Southern England).

■ *The stone circle is signposted to the south-east of Keswick, to the north of the A591.*

Kilburn, North Yorkshire ✡

B3 SE 5179

To the right of the escarpment of the Hambleton Hills 600 feet/200 metres above the village of Kilburn is Roulston Scar, on which is cut a white horse. It was dug out in 1857, under the direction of Thomas Hodgson and his schoolboys, but is not in the tradition of other white horses, for rather than being a chalk figure it is a dug-out which has been filled with white stone. The figure is 228 feet/69.5 metres high and 314 feet/95.7 metres long.

■ *Kilburn is signposted along several minor roads from the A19 and the A170, to the south-east of Thirk, but the Kilburn horse is best seen from the roads to the south-west of the village, around Thrikleby, Carlton Husthwaite and Bagby.*

Kirkby Lonsdale, Cumbria ♉

A3 SD 6178

The so-called Devil's Bridge across the river Lune is still said to bear the claw-marks of the Devil, who built the bridge on the understanding that he should gain the soul of the first creature to cross it. The story is told, with slight variations, of many British bridges, the most famous account being of the triple **Devil's Bridge** in Wales. The Kirkby Lonsdale bridge is said to be haunted by the ghost of a dog, but it is likely that this is a confusion with an old legend.

■ *Kirkby Lonsdale is on the A65(T), signposted to the west of junction 36 on the M6.*

Kirkby Malham, North Yorkshire ♉

B3 SD 8961

In the churchyard of Kirkby Malham there is a tradition of what the locals call the 'banquet of the dead'. Accounts of the feast do not go back beyond 1857, but it seems that the local vicar, the Reverend Knowles, was invited by the Devil to a midnight banquet, laid out on a tomb in the churchyard. The Devil commenced the meal with a curious prayer, but, before eating, the vicar asked for salt, at which

The Kilburn white horse.

point the whole banquet, Devil and all, vanished.

■ *Kirkby Malham is on the road (signposted to Malham) to the north of the A65, and is also similarly signposted from Settle.*

Knaresborough, North Yorkshire △
B3 SE 3557

The cave linked with Mother Shipton (alias, it is said by some, one Ursula Southill, who was born there in 1488) sometimes called a witch, sometimes a prophetess, is less interesting than the nearby Dropping Well, where the lime in the water petrifies objects hung in the water stream. Mother Shipton's well-known prophecies, claimed originally to have been written in the 16th century, and to predict the coming of the railways, motor cars and aeroplanes, and radio, include the verse:

> Carriages without horse shall go,
> And accidents fill the world with woe.
> Around the world thoughts shall fly
> In the twinkling of an eye.

Most interesting however was the supposed prediction for the end of the world for 1891. The verses are not even in a 16th-century style, and it is now known that they were forged by a publisher called Charles Hindley, in 1862. It is interesting to observe that after the dreaded 1891 passed by in relative safety, later publishers of the Shipton prophecies changed it to 1981, and that recently the date has been further amended to read 1991!

Knaresborough Forest

In 1621 the scholar Edward Fairfax charged six old women who lived in the forest with bewitching his children. The charges were not sufficient to stand, but what is of interest is that Fairfax made a manuscript record of the trial, which was illustrated by the vicar of Keighley. These interesting pictures are now in the Manuscript Department of the British Library.

■ *Knaresborough is to the north-east of Harrogate, to the west of the A1(T). The Dropping Well is signposted on the northern banks of the River Nidd, near the Low Bridge, and a short distance from the cave popularly called Mother Shipton's Cave.*

Lancaster *See* Newchurch-in-Pendle *and* Pendle Hill

Littleborough, Lancashire ✡
B4 SD 9316

The gargoyles and grotesques of Littleborough parish church are among the most impressive in the north of England – not merely because of the demonic appearances of these demons and monsters, but because most of the older gargoyles are inscribed with occult symbols on their sides. Among these are spirals, an eye (reminding one of **Newchurch-in-Pendle**), a lemniscate, stars, and the heart (see for example **King's Lynn** – Eastern Counties). The purpose of these symbols has never been adequately explained, as little or no work has been done on the occult system to which they point. It is perhaps significant that one of the most impressive masonic tombs in England is in Littleborough graveyard, and that this also bears a proliferation of occult symbols – in this case entirely masonic in character. It was erected in 1870, to the memory of Laurence Newall, the Deputy Provincial Grand Master, by the Freemasons of East Lancashire.

■ *Littleborough is on the A6033, north-east of Rochdale.*

Little Salkeld, Cumbria ⌛ ⚛
A2 NY 5636

Near the village of Little Salkeld is a large number of standing stones set in a close circle about 350 yards/320 metres in circumference, alongside a square-section monolith to the south-west, popularly called Long Meg. The highest stone, Long Meg herself, is a monolithic Penrith sandstone, over 15 feet 9 inches/4.8 metres high: the angles of the square section are directed to the four points of the compass. In the mythology which attracts itself to such stone circles, Long Meg is said to have been a witch who was petrified with her daughters (some say, indeed, with her circle of demonic lovers), for some crime or other – the most usual account being that well-worn tale of her dancing on the holy Sabbath – though this, of course, has nothing to do with witchcraft. It is said of this circle (as of others) that if one counts their number accurately, then the Devil will appear: not counting Meg there appear to be sixty-seven stones, distributed in what is now called a flattened circle. Yet another piece of traditional nonsense is that if one chips the surface of Long Meg it will bleed. On the surface of the stone are several weather-worn cup and ring marks and concentrics. The popular belief is that the stone was named after a local 16th-century witch, Meg of Maldon.

It was recorded in 1725 that one Colonel Lacy of Salkeld Hall tried to destroy some of the stones, in order to use them as millstones. Almost as soon as the work had begun, however, a terrible storm drove the workmen away: they remained away, convinced that the storm had been raised by the invisible guardians of the circle, or by the Druids (then quite wrongly believed to have been the builders of such circles).

In more modern times (until 1962) church services, arranged from nearby Addingham Church, were held within the circle on the Sunday nearest to midsummer day, a sort of romantic shadow show of the pagan astrological-based rituals which were held there some thousands of years ago.

■ *Little Salkeld is north-east of Penrith, signposted to the east of the B6412. Meg and her daughters are well signposted from the Glassonby road, to the north of the village.*

Longridge, Lancashire ♀

A3 SD 6037

The clairvoyant Geoffrey Hodson gave an interesting description of special kinds of fairies which he saw on one of the hills north-east of Longridge, in November 1922. He called them Red Mannikins from their main colouring. They were 'about' 4 inches/10.15 cm high, but like most elementals they were able to change their forms and heights, so that they could take the full height of a human. Almost in paranthesis, however, Hodson remarks that he did not think that this enlargement was real – it is something of the kind of illusion which occurs when one looks through a telescope, for the mannikins could produce the effect of large size, yet he was aware all the time that they are really small creatures. Their heads were uniquely formed, being axe-like, flattened at the sides, and coming almost to an edge at the vertical centre of the face, through forehead to chin: the eyes were long and narrow, the ears very large, and the nose thin, sharp and curved, the chin being extremely pointed. Some of them wore a 'quaint, pointed, crimson hat', with a tassel or bell on it: clothing (a slashed upper garment) and tights were the same colour. There were thousands of these creatures on the hill, and Hodson was able to ascertain that they are shy, but happy and affectionate towards one another: they gave the impression of being very busy, yet he was unable to see that they were in effect doing any work at all.

■ *Longridge is on the B6423, to the north-east of Preston.*

Manchester, Greater Manchester ✡ ☉ ☿

B4 SJ 8397

Manchester is a surprising place from a point of view of occult symbols, mainly because the Victorian architects who made the city great never hesitated to decorate the interiors and exteriors of their buildings with occult, hermetic and secret symbols. Many of these symbols have been destroyed of late, as the older buildings are removed to make way for the symbol-less (and indeed soul-less) structures considered more appropriate for modern times, yet even now it is still possible to find as many as half a dozen different types of hermetic symbols within a short walk of Victoria Station, near to the centre of the City. In the Station itself, the war memorial is decorated with a splendid base relief of St. Michael fighting the Devil, while to the left of the exit from the station is the Co-operative Building, which has a number of stone-carved symbols below the windows, some of them derived from the winged Caduceus of Hermes, perhaps more Egyptian in style than Greek. A few hundred yards to the right is the Cathedral of Manchester, magnificent in its demonic gargoyles and hermetic symbols, which include (to the eastern end) a splendid mermaid, with comb and mirror, and at the west end a portal with several fine dragons carved upon the external arch. Inside the Cathedral, within the Choir, are some impressive misericords, probably carved towards the end of the 15th century: these include images of the dragon as a devil, a woodwose riding a unicorn, a woodwose fighting a dragon, and a pair of fighting dragons: the most distinctly occult images among these misericords is the initiation image of a man emerging from a welk-shell to fight a dragon, and the magical cockatrice with killing eyes, which the mediaeval artists often used as a symbol of the evil eye. In the evening, when the light of the setting sun works its way directly into the nave, the gilded musical instruments held in the hands of the angels, perched high in the nave roof, glow in a most extraordinary and mystical way: the angels themselves merge so completely into the shadows of the nave that one has the distinct impression that the instruments are hanging magically in space. No doubt this device was intended to refer to the ancient notion of the planetary music of the spheres, which was believed to resonate in the heavenly world, which was the home of the angels.

■ *Manchester centre, near to Victoria Station and the Cathedral, is best approached by car from the M602 to the west of the city.*

One of the demonic gargoyles on the facade of Manchester Cathedral: these are the most impressive series in the north of England.

Masham, North Yorkshire

B3 SE 2280

The so-called Druid Circle, high on the moors to the south of Masham, is a relatively modern though still mysterious structure, somewhat like a walled-in **Stonehenge** (The West Country) of lintel-bearing uprights, half buried in a hillside. It was built by one William Danby in 1820 as a rich man's folly, as some insist, with the main 'circle' measuring at its widest extent about 98 feet/30 metres, at its narrowest 49 feet/15 metres, with a large number of distinctive outliers, and a whole battery of internal altars, standing-stones and recesses. However, Danby's published books (now long out of print) scarcely reveal him as the sort of man who would build a useless folly, even to give work to locals during a period of unemployment. His interest in Neoplatonism

The Druid Circle built at Masham by Danby according to secret principles.

leads us to suspect that the ground-plan of this extraordinary structure is based on secret geometric principles. Many locals claim that the completely buried cell, and the so-called altar stone have been used even in modern times for black magic practices, and for witchcraft. The place certainly has a dark aura around it.

■ *Masham itself is to the west of the A6108, north of Ripon. The circle, which is locally called the Ilton Circle is signposted to the south-west, off the road to Ilton.*

Middleham, North Yorkshire →✡

B3 SE 1287

In 1985, while using a metal detector in a search for treasure in the vicinity of Middleham Castle, Mr Ted Seaton discovered an extraordinary mediaeval gold locket, set with a Roman or early Byzantine sapphire, which was valued (in 1986) at over £300,000. The pendant is diamond-shaped, engraved on one side with an image of the Nativity, and on the other side with a symbolic representation of the Trinity. It is the inscription which has been cut into the border which makes this treasure of interest to occultists, for, after a fairly standard quotation from the opening words of the Eucharist, there follow two magical words – 'Tetragrammaton Ananyzapta'. The Tetragrammaton is the Hebraic name of

god JHVH or YHWH, the four sounds of letters which make up the name of the one god, often pronounced or written 'Jehovah'. It is a commonplace for this four-letter name of God to be treated as a mystical group of characters, each with a numerological value, so that the spoken sound, the appearance of the four letters, and the numerical values of these are each regarded as having a magical efficacy which is often used in magical rituals, and for healing. So powerful was this four-letter name that the occultist Arnold of Villanova wrote a whole treatise upon its meaning: the word (usually in Hebraic characters) appears in a large number of occult and magical symbols (page 9). The other word, which is more usually written 'Ananisapta' in mediaeval charms, is entirely magical. This was also believed to have a profound magical power, as an antidote against death from poisoning, and diseases. Although linked with the Hebraic words, and appearing to be from a foreign language, it is actually derived from no known language, being made up from the first letters of a number of words in a Latin inscription:

'Antidotum Nazareni Necem Intoxicationis Sanctifice Alimenta Pocula Trinitatis Alma'

which translates loosely as 'The Antidote of Christ the Nazarene removes death from poisoning from food or drink, through the benefice of the Holy Trinity.' The remarkable thing is that part of the magical power of the Ananisapta is believed to arise from the fact that it contains 10 letters. These ten give a sentence of 81 letters. If, in accordance with magical practice, you add together the 10 and the 81, you get 91. Following the methods of numerology, you add together these two numbers (a process called 'reduction'):

$$9 + 1 = 10$$

This means that the ten letters and the number of letters combine to point to the magical number ten. But why is the 10 magical? Precisely because it will reduce further:

$$1 + 0 = 1$$

This is the mystic One of Godhead – the mysterious one in three of the Christians, and the equally mysterious four letters in one word of the Hebraic Tetragrammaton. No wonder that the image of the Trinity is engraved on one side of the locket itself. The nativity image on the other side refers to the fact that from this Three there was born a single One. Such levels of occult symbolism were quite normal in the manufacture of mediaeval amulets and other magical devices. If all this seems to be far fetched (as it may do to the modern mentality), then it is perhaps worth while glancing at another Ananisapta, which is seen on a ring found in **Coventry** and now in the British Museum.

■ *Middleham is on the A6108, north west of Ripon. The ruins of the castle are to the south-west of the village.*

Newcastle-upon-Tyne, Tyne and Wear ☿

B2 NZ 2464

Yolande, a 'materialisation', a spirit or ghost living in a partly material body, often appeared in seances held in Newcastle in the late 19th century by a gifted medium called Madame Elizabeth d'Esperance. The photographs of Yolande suggest that she is an attractive fifteen-year-old girl: however, when these pictures were taken she had been dead for some years. Many materialising spirits had been investigated by scientists and doctors, and a large number had even been photographed during such curious antics in the darkened rooms of seances, though exactly how the spirits materialised, where they came from, and what they were remained then (as now) completely unexplained.

During a seance held in 1880 a member of Elizabeth d'Esperance's group began to doubt whether the lovely Yolande was in fact a spirit. As he watched her glide around the semi-circle of people sitting in the eerie half-darkness of the seance room, he began to wonder if she was an imposter in the pay of Madame d'Esperance, and was making fools of all those present? On impulse, the man stood up, ran forward, and made a grab at the girl! The startled Yolande 'dematerialised' – disappearing completely from the view of those present within seconds – leaving only a pile of rapidly-vanishing clothing on the floor. The man himself fell to the floor from shock, as though a powerful electric current had passed through his body. But it was the medium Madame d'Esperance who was most deeply affected by his foolishness, for she was ill for the next seven years!

■ *Newcastle-upon-Tyne is on the A1(T).*

Newcastle-upon-Tyne *See* Carrawburgh

Newchurch-in-Pendle, Lancashire → △ ✡

B3 SD 8239

On the tower of the village church is a stone eye, with a projecting stone eyebrow, and a pupil made from a piece of blue slate. This design, which is locally called the Eye of God, was placed there in the early 16th century as a protection against the power of the evil eye cast by witches. Pendle was an area notorious for its witches (see **Pendle Hill**).

To the south of the church is a flat gravestone which is said to mark the burial place of a local witch called Alice Nutter. In fact, Alice Nutter was hanged, still protesting her innocence of all charges, and buried in Lancaster in that same year. The inscription on the grave is now worn away, and it has probably been popularly assumed to be a witch-tomb because of the grotesque face, originally a standard Christian death's head symbol, but now much weathered. The adjacent upright gravestone does in fact list several members of the Nutter family (a prominent clan in that area), from 1651 onwards, by which time the two main Pendle witchcraft scares (1612 and 1634) were over.

■ *Newchurch is signposted to the north of the A6068, to the north-west of Nelson.*

The so-called witchcraft tomb at Newchurch-in-Pendle, with its grotesque face.

The witchcraft eye, sometimes called the 'Eye of God' on the east side of the church tower at Newchurch-in-Pendle.

Pateley Bridge *See* Brimham Rocks

Peel, Isle of Man △

SC 2484

Peel Castle is famous in witchcraft lore as the prison of the Duchess of Gloucester, who in 1441 had been arrested on suspicion of high treason, her intention being to kill King Henry VI by witchcraft. It would seem that she had intended to employ witches or warlocks to make waxen images of the king, which she could then mutilate or melt to ensure his death. When the plot was discovered, a number of people were implicated. The most severely punished was Roger Bolingbroke, an astrologer in the duke's pay: he was hanged at Tyburn, and his head was displayed on London Bridge. The duchess herself, being of aristocratic blood, got off more lightly, with three penance-trips through London streets, and perpetual imprisonment in Peel Castle.

■ *Peel is on the west side of the Isle of Man, at the junction of the A27, A20 and A1.*

Pendle Hill, Lancashire △
B3 SD 8041

This distinctive hill is maintained by tourism as a centre of 17th-century witchcraft (see **Newchurch-in-Pendle**), though there is little evidence of witchcraft being practised on the hill itself. The Pendle and Lancaster witches are however historically associated with the area, and many of those who were hanged for the alleged crime in Lancaster admitted to practising in the Forest of Pendle to the south of the hill. Anything lacking in historical fact is made up for by the modern tourist industry, and many of the local pubs display traditional witches, in full transvection, on their walls: even a few of the local bus stops bear such evocative emblems. In modern times, however, several clairvoyants and a few ley-line hunters insist that Pendle Hill is the centre for a huge earth-works zodiac, on the same lines as that supposed to exist in the Glastonbury area (see **Butleigh** – The West Country). There are certainly strange earth forces at work on top of this beautiful hill, and it definitely marks the confluence of a number of ley-lines, though it is difficult to trace any ancient zodiac in the surrounding contours, roads and coppices.

■ *Pendle Hill is a distinctive shape from many points on the A59 and the A682, and is perhaps best approached by way of the footpaths from Newchurch-in-Pendle or Barley.*

Penrith, Cumbria ✠
A2 NY 5130

In the churchyard of St Andrew's are two stone uprights, with curiously curved stones joining them at their bases. This strange medley is said to mark the place where the body of the giant Isir was laid. Some insist that this was the same giant who lived in a cave near Eamont Bridge. The 'giant's grave', as it is called locally, appears to be nothing more than two mediaeval cross shafts, with four mediaeval hog-back grave stones (or Viking hump-back tombs) between them.

■ *Penrith is signposted to the east of the M6, at junction 40.*

Rombald's Moor *See* Ilkley

Rudston, Humberside ⚲ ⚚
C3 TA 0967

The highest monolithic standing stone in Britain is in the churchyard at Rudston, dwarfing the graves (and even the church itself) towering 25 feet/7.5 metres above the ground. With a lower girth 6 feet 6 inches/2 metres in diameter, it is said to weigh over 40 tons, but some writers insist that there is a further 25 feet/7.5 metres of stone beneath the ground. There are the usual demonological legends attached to the monolith – the Devil is supposed to have flung the stone at the church, and missed: however, one may be sure that the stone was there for about 2,000 years before Christ came to earth, so the Devil not only missed his aim in space, but also missed his time. Geologists tell us that it probably came from Cayton Bay, some 10 miles/16 km to the north of Rudston. Was it the 'Rude Stone', or (more significantly)

The supposed haunt of the Pendle witches at Pendle Hill.

did it take its name from rood the mediaeval name for the Holy Cross? Was there once a cross affixed to the top, as was certainly the case with certain other ancient stones?

■ *Rudston is on the B1253, west of Bridlington.*

Samlesbury, Lancashire

A3 SD 6128

The 'New Hall Tavern' at Salmesbury, on the road to **Walton-le-Dale,** is one of the few British inns to have a ghost portrayed on its inn-sign. This ghostly image is of a lady in Tudor dress, standing in the gardens of nearby Samlesbury Old Hall, which has been reputed to be haunted for many centuries. The ghost is said to be that of Dorothy Southword, a girl of high birth who dwelled in the Hall, and who died of grief after her lover, a protestant from nearby Hoghton, was murdered because Dorothy's father was a staunch Catholic, and could not bear the notion of the girl marrying outside their religion. The story appears to be fictional, as there is no record of a girl with this name or history connected with the house. Even so, many people have testified to seeing a ghost of a lady wearing what appears to be Tudor clothing, standing on the lawn in front of the manor house, and quite recently (1986), I met two gentlemen who claim to have seen the ghost, wandering disconsolately alongside the river Darwen.

■ *Samlesbury is signposted on the A677 to the west of Preston, off junction 31 of the M6. The 'New Hall Tavern' is to the south of the B6230, south of Samlesbury village.*

Seaton Ross, North Yorkshire

B3 SE 7841

The village possesses an enormous sundial built by William Watson on the wall of one of the cottages.

In the churchyard of St Edmund's is a grave of Margaret Harper, reputed in the 18th century to have been a witch.

■ *Seaton Ross is signposted to the north of the A163, north-east of Selby.*

Sharow, North Yorkshire

B3 SE 3271

In the churchyard of St John's is a gravestone in the form of a pyramid. This was designed by the deceased occupant, Charles Piazzi Smyth, and is intended as a miniature of the Great Pyramid of Cheops at Gîza, Egypt. Smyth was famous for his pioneer work in connection with the magical properties of the Egyptian pyramids, which lead to his complex numerological theories, as well as the study of the astronomical declinations of its interior passageways, especially concerning the orientation of one such passage towards Sirius. The long inscription fixed to the north side of the pyramid tomb is a tribute to Piazzi Smyth's wife, who shared his many adventures in different parts of the world.

■ *Sharow is signposted to the east of Ripon, off the A61.*

Singleton, Lancashire

A3 SD 3838

It was in Singleton that Meg Shelton, sometimes called the Fylde Witch appears to have met her match. She was reputed to be able to turn herself into a hare, and her exploits are now part of local folk-lore. She was really famous for petty thieving, and for turning milk sour, milking other people's cows, and so on. The Singleton miller saw her (in the guise of a hare) cross his yard every night, and in the morning he would find some of his corn missing. One night, having seen the hare, he went into the barn with a pitchfork, but could see nothing. However, he counted his sacks, and discovered one too many, and so, with great gusto, he began to push his fork into each of he sacks in turn. Before he reached the one in which Meg was hidden, she leapt out, grabbed hold of a broomstick, and flew off into the night. For another story about Meg, see **Woodplumpton.**

■ *Singleton is on the B5269, to the east of Blackpool.*

Skewsby, North Yorkshire

B/C3 SE 625719

The Skewsby maze, sometimes called the Brandsby Maze, measures 26 feet/8 metres by 22 feet/6.7 metres and is said to be the smallest turf maze in Britain. However, it is not an original maze in the sense that **Saffron Walden** (Eastern Counties) turf maze is original, for in comparatively recent times it was recorded as being completely destroyed by the cart tracks which ran over it, on the grass verge. It was therefore resited and recut, and it might well be that its formal pattern is not related to the earlier form.

■ *The maze is on the grass verge of the road between Skewsby and Brandsby.*

Snaefell, Isle of Man

NX 3890

In August 1922 the clairvoyant Geoffrey Hodson, while climbing from Sulby Glen on the western slopes of Snaefell, saw with his 'inner eye' a variety of miniature people, from 4 inches/10 cm – 6 inches/15 cm high. Though their features were well modelled, they appeared to wear a perpetual smile, and gave the impression of almost walking in their sleep: most of them had receding chins, and their eyes were elongated. The fairy women wore long dresses, and the menfolk were clothed in shiny, silk-like material, the most common colour being a sort of electric blue. There were countless of these fairy folk, dancing and playing on the hillside: among them was the occasional creature somewhat like a gnome, though with the hind legs of a goat or animal. Hodson, thanks to a most remarkable clairvoyant ability, had been able to make a special study of the elemental creatures, such as the fairies, gnomes and sylphs, and he came to the conclusion that these particular Snaefell creatures were only partly incarnated, living almost a life of dream – they were perhaps part of a race of beings so ancient that it was on the edge of dying out. For an account of the sylphs (water fairies), see **Wythburn**.

■ *Snaefell towers above the junction of the A18 and the A14. Sulby is to the north of the mountain, and the river Sulby runs along the A14 (part of the way) towards the mountain, it was to the east of this river that Geoffrey Hodson was climbing.*

Snape, North Yorkshire

B3 SE 2684

It has been suggested that the ghost seen at intervals in Snape Castle is that of Catharine Parr, the last of the six wives of Henry VIII, whom he had married in 1543, and who lived in the castle for a while. Those who have seen the ghost describe it as being that of a young girl with long fair hair, in a blue dress of the Tudor style.

■ *Snape Castle is to the east of the B6268, south of Bedale.*

Sockburn, County Durham

B3 NZ 3407

It is said that in the 14th century a Sir John Conyers killed the terrible dragon known locally as the Sockburn Wurm. The stone known locally as the Graystone near the village, is said to mark the spot of the slaying, while the 13th-century Conyers falchion, a gift made to the Bishop of Durham by the Conyers' family, is claimed to be the sword with which the dragon was killed – this is still preserved in the treasury at **Durham** Cathedral.

■ *Sockburn is 6 miles/10 km south-east of Darlington, signposted from the B1264.*

Wallington House, Cambo, Northumberland

B2 NZ 0285

The front formal gardens of 17th-century Wallington House are strewn with a line of four curious monstrous stone heads, called the Cambo Beasts, which were almost certainly griffins. These were taken from London's Old Aldersgate when it was demolished in 1761, and arrived in the north as ballast in ships owned by the Blackett family, who then lived at Cambo. After the death of Sir Walter Blackett in 1777 the house was the seat of the Trevelyans, until 1941, when it was given to the National Trust by Sir Charles Trevelyan.

■ *Cambo is on the B6342, near the junction with the B6343: Wallington House is signposted from Cambo. The 'beasts' may be seen ranged near the side of the road which runs to the south of the House.*

The so-called 'Cambo Beasts' – griffin heads on the lawn to the front of Wallington House.

Walton-le-Dale, Lancashire

A4 SD 5528

The churchyard of St. Leonard's is believed by many occultists to have been the site of a famous attempt by the occultist-scholar John Dee, and his rascally friend Edward Kelly, to raise the ghost of a recently deceased man. Engravings of the event have been issued in very many occult books, yet it was not Dee who helped Kelly in this necromancy, but Kelly's assistant Paul Waring. The aim of this necromancy was to persuade the dead man to reveal to them where he had hidden his considerable riches before he died. The reputation of Dee as a necromancer might still appear to be valid, however, for during the reign of Queen Mary he was imprisoned as 'a companion of the hell hounds, and a caller and conjurer of wicked and damned spirits'. The imprisonment was religio-political, however,

A hand-coloured print showing Edward Kelly raising the spirit of a dead man in Walton-le-Dale churchyard.

and Dee's writings betray him as one of the most brilliant esotericists of the sixteenth century. Much of St Leonard's church was restored in the 19th century, but the tower itself is relatively untouched, and still identifiable as the one shown in the picture below left. Many of the symbols in the graveyard are of great interest – in particular the gagged mourner's head on the largest of the Victorian tombs. For further exploits of Dee, see **Mortlake** (London and Southern England).

■ *Walton-le-Dale is to the south of Preston, signposted to the south of the B6230.*

Warton, Lancashire ✡

A3 SD 5071

In this village there is a magical symbol which links Britain with America, and modern time with ancient Egypt. On the church of St Oswald is an old stone tablet on which is inscribed the 15th-century coat of arms of the Washington family, who lived in the parish, and even helped build the church by contributing to the fabric of the tower. John Washington, of the Washington family of Sulgrave, Northamptonshire, emigrated to Virginia in 1657, and was the great-grandfather of George Washington, the first president of the United States. The coat of arms consists of stars and stripes – two horizontal stripes and three stars. The stars are pentagrams which are regarded by occultists as powerful symbols of life, as may be seen in the hieroglyphics from ancient Thebes. In Egyptian hieroglyphics the pentagram, with a sun symbol in its centre, was used to denote the secret power behind all life. No wonder that the alchemists regarded it as one of the most powerful and meaningful of symbols, and used it time and time again in their pictorial art.

This Warton symbolism is a reminder that according to such occultists as Manley Palmer Hall, the Great Seal of America (which, for example, features on the back of the dollar bill) was designed according to secret occult principles. To the east of the church is a headstone dedicated to Thomas Washington.

On Warton Hill are the rocking stones called the Three Brothers. They are set in a line at equal intervals to one another.

■ *Warton is signposted to the north of Carnforth, west of junction 35 of the M6. (This village must not be confused with the other Warton in Lancashire, to the west of Preston.)*

Weston, North Yorkshire ☿

B3 SE 1747

In the early decades of this century the vicarage at Weston (a much haunted house) was occupied by the Rev Tweedale and his family, all of whom were interested in psychic matters. Mrs Tweedale took several photographs of ghosts in the vicarage, but perhaps the most interesting picture was that taken by her husband in 1915. Mrs Tweedale saw a

ghost of a man, 'with a full head of hair and a beard, standing to the left of her son'. The rest of the family could not see the ghost, so the father fetched his camera, pointed in the direction where she indicated the apparition was standing, and took a picture. The developed image showed the face of a man with a beard, and a full head of hair, as Mrs Tweedale had described him. The head is transparent, and the piano may be seen through the features on the picture.

■ *Weston is signposted on the minor road to the west of Otley, to the west of Weston Park.*

Whitby, North Yorkshire ✕

C3 NZ 8910

Writing in the 8th century, the Venerable Bede recorded that when the Abbess Hilda died in her monastery at Whitby, her spirit appeared to the nun Begu at Hackness, near Scarborough. The nun said that the spirit of Hilda was swathed in a great light, and that she was surrounded by a choir of angels. Whitby has marked more than most towns the important stages of the development of Christianity in England. St Hilda, who founded the abbey in 657, was almost certainly not the earliest Christian in the area, for traces of Christian lore have been found in the Roman remains within the area. In 657 the Synod of Whitby dispensed with the indigenous Celtic rituals and vision of Christianity in favour of the imperial-bound versions of Rome. The Danes destroyed Hilda's foundation in 867, and the Benedictines refounded and rebuilt it in 1078, retaining its splendour until the rift with Rome in 1539. Each of these schisms and destructions produced its own heresies, and one could write a curious history of Christianity from what is known of Whitby.

There are few records, but many myths: perhaps the most amusing material remains are the (rare) circular 'adderstones' which may from time to time be picked up on the Saltwick sands below the cliffs. These are ammonites, said by the uninformed to be the snakes which Saint Hilda drove with her magical incantations over the cliffs, beheading them and turning them to stone, in order to rid the area of its numerous adders. Sir Walter Scott, popularised the story in his *Marmion*:

> And how, of thousand snakes, each one
> Was changed into a coil of stone,
> When holy Hilda pray'd;
> Themselves, with their holy bound,
> Their stony folds had often found.

A poetic conceit, yet it is now believed by almost everyone in the town: the local children do not hunt for the common ammonites, but for magical stone snakes. The 19th-century geologist Thomas Brown warned his readers that the beheaded stone snakes were being sold in Whitby by individuals who 'not unfrequently form a head upon the outer volutions in imitation of that of a snake', and sell these products to an unsuspecting public.

■ *Whitby is to the north of the A171, north-west of Scarborough. The Abbey remains are to the west of Saltwick Bay.*

Whitestone Cliffs, North Yorkshire △ ♂

B3 SE 5383

It is recorded that in the reign of the witch-hunter king, James I, a woman named Abigail Carstair, reputed to be a witch, was pursued across the moors to her death over the edge of the Whitestone Cliff crags. A ghost of a white monk is said to wander the edge of these crags, among the many tumuli and dykes above the Whitestone Cliffs, warning travellers of the dangerous drop ahead.

■ *The Whitestone Cliffs are to the north-west of Sutton Bank, which is on the A170 to the east of Thirsk.*

Woodplumpton, Lancashire △

A3 SO 5034

The witch known locally as the Fylde Witch was said to be Meg Shelton of Poulton-le-Fylde (see **Singleton**). Records indicate that she was found dead one night in April 1705, crushed by a heavy barrel, which had rolled against her while she stood by a wall. Because of her reputation, she was buried at night, but legend has it that she tried to scratch her way through the earth, back into the world, and so the local priest exorcised her tomb. One presumes that the exorcism did not work, for it is said that afterwards the body was taken from the grave, and re-buried upside down by the large boulder alongside the path in St Anne's churchyard, Woodplumpton.

■ *Woodplumpton is 5 miles/8 km north-west of Preston, signposted to the south of the B5269.*

Wythburn, Cumbria ♀

A3 NY 3414

The specialist in fairy lore, Geoffrey Hodson, gave a vivid account of the lake spirits which he observed (with his clairvoyant vision) playing on the surface of Lake Thirlmere, from the roadside at Wythburn, in 1922. These nature spirits were seen skimming about 6 feet 6 inches/2 metres above the water (sometimes higher), and to some extent resembled large white birds, though their forms were by no means defined in the sense that physical bodies are, for they could change their appearance with protean rapidity, sometimes appearing more like wisps of cloud than birds. In admitting the difficulty of describing exactly this changing world of forms, Hodson does point out that there appeared to be flow-forces, 'consisting chiefly of whirls, vortices, and wing-like streamers', as though there were some definite organisation within their formations. For elementals of the Earth kind, see **Longridge** and **Snaefell**.

■ *Thirlmere is to the south-west of Keswick: Wythburn is to the south of the long lake, on the A591.*

York, North Yorkshire ♂ ♉

B3 SE 6052

Castle Museum ♂

A rare colour photograph of a ghost was taken in the York Castle Museum by David Card of Rhyl, in 1981. The ghost, about the size of a human, was dressed in a long white dress, with a white cowl hanging over its face. The figure was not seen by Mr Card when he took the picture – he was simply taking a photograph of the model horse and carriage in the 18th-century replica street inside the museum. No explanation was given for the appearance of the figure, but when it was published in the *Yorkshire Post* colour magazine on 9 July 1983, it was printed alongside another supposed ghost-picture, taken in the same replica street. This second 'ghost' was a transparent figure 'with its hands crossed at the wrist above its forehead': it was pointed out that this part of the museum had been a prison 'where inmates were shackled by the wrists'. However, close examination of this imagined ghost reveals it to be a live photographer, with his camera up to his face. He is 'transparent' and out of focus because a relatively long exposure was required to take the supposed 'ghost' picture. This 'ghost' was taking a picture of a little boy (presumably his son), who may be seen seated on the back of the model horse drawing the carriage!

Stonegate ♉

The carved wooden devil near Stonegate is a traditional mediaeval devil with horns, and cloven hooves, his lower parts reminding one of a clean-shaven Pan. The image is said to be the trade sign of the oldest printing shop in York: at one time the 'printer's devil' was the boy who took the printed sheets from the press – a fairly dirty operation. However, there is a chain around the waist of the York red devil, which reminds one of certain Rosicrucian images: perhaps it is indeed a carving of a genuine demon, rather than a printer's symbol?

Trinity Church ♂

This church was famous in the 19th century for its ghosts, which were described by a priest who saw them as apparitions with 'much the same effect as that of a slide drawn through a magic lantern'. He could personally vouch for large numbers of ghosts appearing at the window both before and during services. The ghosts, seen by very many people at different times, and appearing as though walking behind the stained glass, some 5 feet/1.5 metres above the ground, seemingly came from a very old grave in the churchyard. Baring-Gould, who dabbled in occult lore in the last century (see **Lewtrenchard**), records several letters from respectable people who set out their first-hand experiences of the ghostly visitors in detail, even to the point of mentioning the various hypotheses as to how the apparitions might occur. It is said that the church has been haunted in such a way for over 300 years.

■ *The Castle Museum is well signposted off Tower Street, by the castle. The devil is in Coffee Yard, off Stonegate, in the centre of the city. Trinity Church is in Micklegate, in the centre of York.*

Scotland

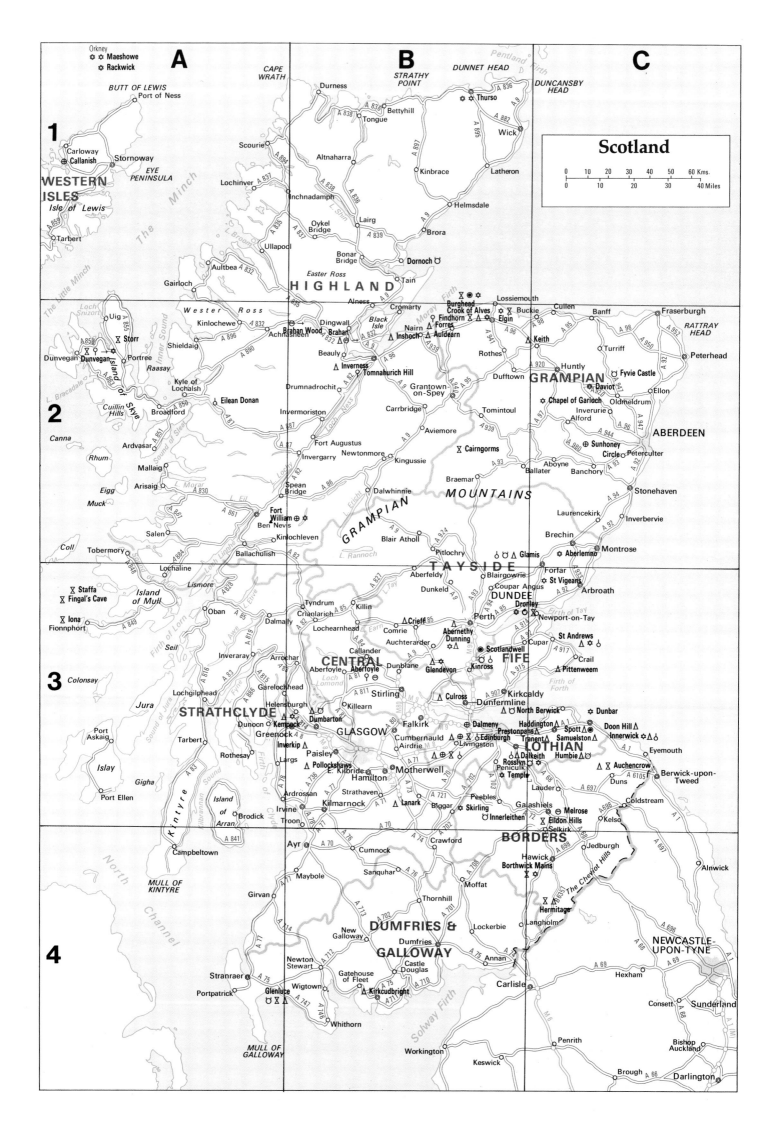

Aberfoyle, Central ♀ ☺

B3 NN 5201

In the old graveyard of Aberfoyle is buried Robert Kirk, the Gaelic scholar and author of a delightful and influential study in fairy lore, *The Secret Commonwealth*, published in 1691, the year before his death. The grave slab is surprisingly well preserved, marked with a coat of arms of crossed dagger and pastoral crook, the memorial inscription in Latin. Many of Kirk's descriptions appear to have been from locals possessed with what is now called second sight. Near the graveyard, to the east, is the hill of Dun-shi, the 'Fairy Hill' where Kirk is said to have died unexpectedly. Local legends have him running around the top of the hill seven times to raise the devil, and dying there on the seventh round. We have it on the imaginative reports of Sir Walter Scott that Kirk did not die, but was made a prisoner by the fairies.

■ *Aberfoyle is on the A81, west of Stirling, north of Dumbarton. The old burial grounds are to the south of the village, on the left of Manse Road. The grave-slab is to the south-east of the ruinous building displaying the interesting metal mortsafes. The fairy hill is visible across the fields to the east of the burial grounds.*

The Fairy Hill at Aberfoyle associated with the legends of Robert Kirk.

Aberlemno, Tayside ❀

C2 NO 5255

Strung along the road in the village of Aberlemno are a series of three of the most impressive local collections of Pictish stones, the occult symbols of which clearly point to three different graphic traditions.

In the graveyard of Aberlemno church is the 'Aberlemno Stone', another 8th-century Pictish stone, its face an interlace cross with flanking dragons and grotesque beasts, its back adorned with curious hunting or battle scenes.

■ *The roadside stones are on the eastern side of the B9134 in Aberlemno. The Aberlemno Stone is in the graveyard of the signposted church, to the east of the B9134.*

One of Aberlemno's 8th-century Pictish stones set along the roadside of the village. The meaning of the symbols is not known.

Abernethy, Tayside △

B3 NO 1916

It is recorded with some grim humour by Samuel Butler that Dr John Brown (1810–82), the local Abernethy author of the internationally important *Dictionary of the Holy Bible* was such a scholar – learning many European and Oriental languages without a teacher – that he was soon suspected by his ignorant neighbours as having acquired his learning from Satan. He gave an almost perfect definition of witchcraft in his great dictionary, and was later required to defend himself against the charge of witchcraft.

There was a tradition of witchcraft in Abernethy, in any case, for the Register of the Privy Council for 1662 shows a commission being established for the trial of Elspeth Young, Jonet Crystie and Margaret Mathie, as confessed witches in the parish. A confessed witch (no matter how the confession was extracted) had only one fate – death.

■ *Abernethy is on the A913, south-east of Perth.*

Alves, Crook of, Grampian ✗ △ ❀

B2 NJ 1362

It is said by some that the southern slopes of the Knock (hill) of Alves is the 'blasted heath' where the witches met Macbeth – perhaps at the place now occupied by the York

Tower. Some writers have identified the place with Duffus Castle, which is not on the Knock of Alves at all, while others have claimed it for Hardmuir near Brodie. It is very unlikely that Dr Samuel Johnson 'drove over the very heath where Macbeth met the witches', as his biographer Boswell claims, but we can imagine him in this place declaiming the Shakespearean passage in 'a grand and affecting manner'. The witches may never have existed of course, for they appear to be Shakespeare's attempt to introduce the notion of the three Fatae, or Roman goddesses of destiny. His phrase 'weird sisters' is definitely a reference to the Anglo-Saxon word 'wyrd' meaning 'destiny'.

Near Forres, at the turning for **Findhorn** is the Suenos Stone, a 20 feet/6 metre high Pictish stone with incised symbols and images, mainly of horsemen in battle.

■ *Alves lies on the A96(T), east of Forres. The York Tower is visible to the south of the road. Duffus Castle is south-east of Duffus village, which is on the B9012, west of Gordonstoun.*

Auchencrow, Borders △ ⚊

C3 NT 8560

There are several witch-stones in the village, only two of which I have been able to locate. In Scotland witch-stones are usually large boulders which mark the place where witches were burned (see, for example, **Elgin**) but at Auchencrow it is believed by the locals that these stones were dropped by witches, carried in their sabbatic transvections. One such stone is built into a retaining wall at the western end of the village street, and another (well hidden behind brambles and nettles) is nearer to the centre of the village. I met one local lady who remembers as a child calling this the Peg Tode stone, and recalls that it was a belief that the stone had been carried by witches from Coldingham (see, however, **Spott**). When passing the stone children were required to say 'I touch Peg Tode, Peg Tode don't touch me.' She also told me of the ancient tradition that in the fields to the north of Auchencrow, witches ploughed the lands and their rats sowed the seeds. The young children with whom I spoke in Auchencrow knew nothing of the witch-stones.

■ *Auchencrow is signposted off the A1(T), south of St Abbs Head. The unnamed witch-stone is built into the wall of the junction of the village street with the B6438, and the Peg Tode stone is along the village street, to the left of the beginning of the southward public footpath.*

Auldearn, Highland △

B2 NH 9255

As the historian Ritchie remarks, the witches of Auldearn were famous in popular legend. He records how a witch plague brought numerous women to trial, and most of them confessed to the most amazing acts. 'Like the witches of Shakespeare's fancy, they sailed in sieves, they rode on broomsticks or "shalties", outstripping the wind in their flight; they took the shape of cats, they worked charms to raise storms, to plague cattle, or to make children fall ill and die'. Ritchie, with his wide knowledge of witchcraft lore, must have taken it for granted that most of these confessions were extracted under torture.

The witch Isobel Goudie (see **Inshoch**) claims to have been 'baptised' as a witch by the Devil in the churchyard at Auldearn, as part of being received into the witchcraft cult. The old church has been replaced by an early 19th-century structure, but its ruins may still be visited, to the east of the modern church. In the graveyard there are some interesting monuments erected shortly after the witchcraft hysteria died down in Scotland.

■ *Auldearn is on the A96(T), east of Nairn. The churchyard is on the hill above the village, to the north of the road.*

Ben Macdhui *See* Cairngorms

Boldragon *See* Dronley

Borthwick Mains, Borders ⚊ ✡

B/C4 NT 43714

In a private garden of a farm here there is a square-sectioned stone on which is incised the simple outline of a fish, with eye, gills and fins clearly marked. This Pictish carving is an indication of how widely spread was the Christian occult or esoteric use of the fish as a symbol for Christ. A tradition insists that it once stood in the waters of the River Teviot, as a marking stone, the flat bottom of the tail marking the level at which the waters were safe to cross.

■ *The farmhouse, in the back garden of which the stone stands, is 4 miles/6.5 km west of Hawick, on the B711.*

Brahan, Highland ◉ △ →

B2 NH 5157

Brahan Castle was the main seat of the Seaforth family, and according to the historian Hugh Miller, it was here in the mid-17th century, that Coinneach Odhar (later called the Brahan Seer) made his detrimental prophecies about the house of the Seaforth Mackenzies between being condemned for witchcraft, and taken away for burning. Although Coinneach was undoubtedly a historical person, and may have been mixed up in wizardry, most of the legends and confusions with older witchcraft stories, appear to begin with Hugh Miller, as late as 1835. (See however **Brahan Wood**). Tradition points to the burial place of Coinneach as Chanonry Point (Fortrose) – but see also **Tomnahurich Hill**. The gift of second-sight, so highly regarded in the Highlands, has been called Deuterosophia, though this word no more explains it than the first.

Brahan Wood

It is maintained in some occult books that in Brahan Wood there is a rock called the Gradhthol with a porthole in it, which is used for divination and for curing sick children: they were passed through the hole a prescribed number of times. However, a thorough search of the area revealed no such stone, though there are a number of cup and ring marked stones – especially that erected as part of the wall facing on to the old stables of the now destroyed Brahan Castle. It is likely that the story of the 'holed stone' is derived from one of the many legends attached to Coinneach Odhar, the Brahan Seer, who is supposed to have been given a tiny stone with a hole in it through which he could peer into the future. When he was near death, he is supposed to have thrown the curious stone into the imprint of a cow's hoof. This then expanded, and filled with water, to form Loch Ussie, which is indeed shaped very much like the imprint of a cow's hoof. One wonders if the 'holed stone' of the Brahan Seer was one of the strange Pictish spindle-whorls, which have survived from the 8th century, marked with the ogham alphabet scripts? These objects are often ascribed magical properties by those unaware of what they were originally used for. See also **Brahan** and **Tomnahurich Hill**.

■ *Brahan Castle (ruinous) is to the south of the A835, south-west of Dingwall. Brahan Wood is north of the remains of the castle. Loch Ussie is north of the A835.*

Brogar, Orkney

ND 3412

On Orkney's mainland is one of the finest stone circles in Britain, the Ring of Brogar, which is some 115 yards/105 metres in diameter. Only twenty-seven of the original sixty stones are left standing, though others are still near their original places. At least one of the broken menhirs is inscribed with ancient (un-deciphered) tree runes, indicating some magical use. The stones appear to have been set with extraordinary precision, their six-degree spacing seemingly connected with orientation points to the geographical north. The numerous surrounding standing stones, and connected smaller circles, have suggested to some occultists that the Brogar circle was intended as a lunar observatory, used for determining calendrical periods and cycles.

■ *The Ring of Brogar, clearly signposted on the A965, is between the lochs of Stenness and Harray.*

Burghead, Grampian

B1/2 NJ 1169

In the old graveyard at the top of the town there is an upright grave slab built into the retaining wall, with a deep hollow in its surface. In his interesting account of a quest for pagan magic, *A Guide to Occult Britain* (1976), John Wilcock tells us that this grave slab was called the Cradle Stone, and records the widely published belief that if one strikes the hollow and listens, one hears the sound of a cradle rocking and a child crying. However, I have been unable to obtain such a sound by knocking on the slab.

Holy Well

The ancient Holy Well, sometimes known as Bailey's Well or the Roman Well was discovered in 1809, and taken to be of Roman origin, as a lapidary inscription still visible on a nearby house wall in King Street testifies. However, it is a mystery. The well is actually a rock-hewn chamber, to which rock steps had been cut (now supplemented by a modern flight, and a certain amount of recutting), to give access from the higher part of the town. The base of the well consists of a rectangular perimeter walkway around a tank fed by springs. A simple platform leading into the waters would suggest that it was used for ritual purposes, perhaps for the total immersion required by the early Christian baptism.

The well, or baptistry, as it should properly be called, lies within the area of the great bailey (hence one of the names) of the promontory fort of Burghead, which was here obliterated during the building of modern Burghead. Artefacts, such as incised bull images (see also **Elgin**) recovered from the site demonstrate that it was used by the Picts, if not actually built by them. It appears that the tank was deepened to increase the water capacity and flow, after 1809. The higher part of the vault, with its central light shaft is also modern. Altogether, the well is one of the most impressive mysteries of the Scottish dark ages.

■ *Burghead lies at the end of the B9013, signposted north of the A96(T), west of Elgin. The graveyard is at the top of the town, to the right of the road. The well is signposted at the top of the town, in a cul-de-sac continuation of King Street, off Church Street.*

Cairngorms, Highland

Parts of the Cairngorms are haunted by distinctive creatures, one at least of which appears to be mythical. This is the *famh* (a Gaelic word pronounced 'fav', meaning mole), though the creature itself is not a mole in any ordinary sense. We are told by the official guide to the area that the *famh* is a little ugly monster, which frequents the summits of the mountains around Glen Avin. It does not appear to be a native of this material world, and we may presume that it is evil, even dangerous. Its head is said to be twice as large as its body. Apparently anyone who crosses over the tracks which it has made (before the sun shines on them) will soon die.

Another Cairngormian is the Great Grey Man, or *Fear Liath Mor* in Gaelic, a ghostly almost human figure, which haunts mainly the summits of Ben Macdhui. There is a story that a local shepherd called Robin Og came across the fairies which dance around the conical hill just above Lochan Uaine, and stole one of their tiny bagpipes. When the morning light came, he found that he had in his hand only a puff ball.

■ *The Cairngorms, perhaps best visited from Aviemore on the A9(T), stretch over too vast an area to designate specifically.*

Callanish, Isle of Lewis

A1 NB 2133

The most remarkable stone circle in Scotland, set in splendid isolation to the west of the Isle of Lewis, is far more than a stone circle – its ground plan reveals it to be a sort of crossed circle, with a north-west avenue, approaching the central circle of thirteen stones, varying in height up to 12 feet/3.65 metres. There are several other (less impressive) circles in the immediate vicinity, all seemingly related to cosmological calculations and effects. Recent research tabulated by Margaret and Gerald Ponting shows that the circle was used for calendrical and astronomical purposes in prehistoric times, and leads one to regard the complex as the ruins of a combined temple and community centre. The circle is well integrated into the geological structure of the vicinity, and the 'skimming' of the moon (every $18\frac{1}{2}$ years – the Sothic cycle) in relation to the stones and the curiously named hills of 'sleeping beauty' to the south, is a spectacular sight even to this day. The parallels of the stone avenue point to the set of the moon at the southern extremes of major standstill. The bibliography provided by the Pontings indicates something of the complexity of the occult structure of this most impressive complex.

■ *Callanish is signposted off the A858, west of Stornoway on the Isle of Lewis.*

The central uprights in the famous stone circle of Callanish on the Isle of Lewis, recently shown to be a calendrical marker.

One of the several stone circles near to the Callanish circle, which forms part of the orientation.

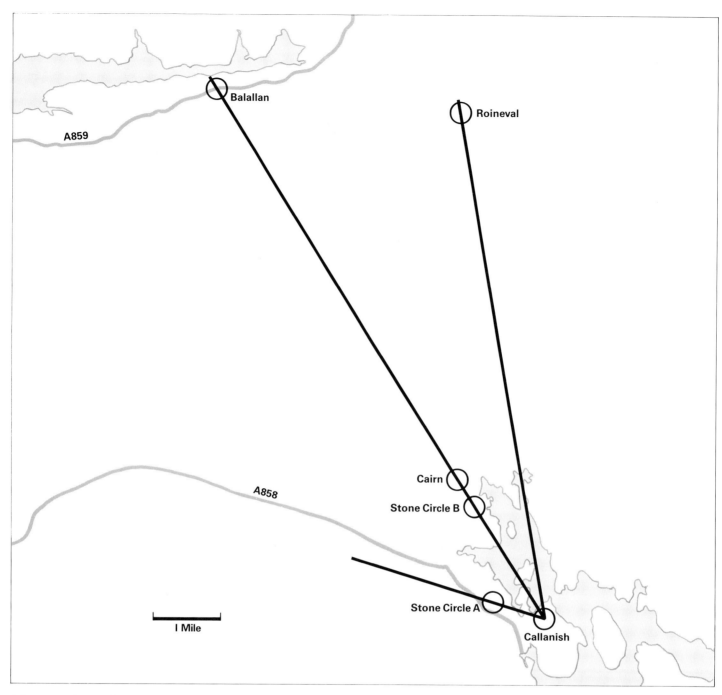

The map above shows the Callanish circle in relation to the surrounding southern countryside. To the east is a second stone circle (A) which itself would be impressive in any landscape, were it not for the proximity of the Callanish circle which is far superior to it. This circle appears to be linked with orientation lines directed towards sunrise and moonrise on certain days (which themselves probably marked important festivals). To the south-east is a simple ley-line, which runs through a third stone circle (B) and a cairn, in the direction of Balallan. This line appears to mark one of the eastern extremities of moonrise and sunrise in relation to the Callanish stone circle (see opposite, bottom). To the west of this line rises the 'peak' of Roineval, which is still in Lewis, but almost merging (visually) with the mountain range which separates Lewis from Northern Harris.

It has been shown that the megalithic circle builders were interested in the position of the moon when it skimmed the mountainous horizon to the south of the Callanish circle. The positions held by the moon during this periodic

skimming are reflected in the diagram shown opposite, top, which shows the silhouette of stones against the southern moon, hovering between Balallan and Roineval. This diagram is based on photographs taken to demonstrate one of the astronomical alignments. The 'skimming of the moon', here represented in degree intervals, marks out the arc, shown here, once every eighteen and a half years. The moon has risen from the east, and we are viewing the circle from the north, along the avenue of stones towards the south. It will eventually set into the midst of the stone circle, leaving a series of lunar segments, gleams and 'after-glow' effects among the stones, and (in rare instances) reflections on some of the stones which have their faces so orientated as to permit one of their vertical sides to throw the lunar light towards the northern observer. This skimming is connected with the fact that during the southern extreme of the lunar standstill, the moon rises from behind Balallan, and sets behind Roineval. This periodic skimming is clearly marked out in the orientation of the major axis and outriders of the Callanish circle. It is possible that the position of the smaller

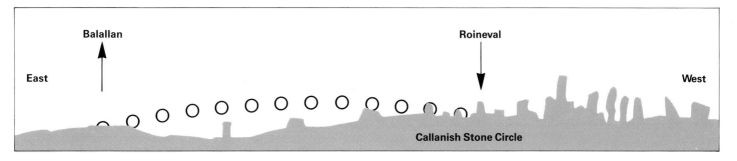

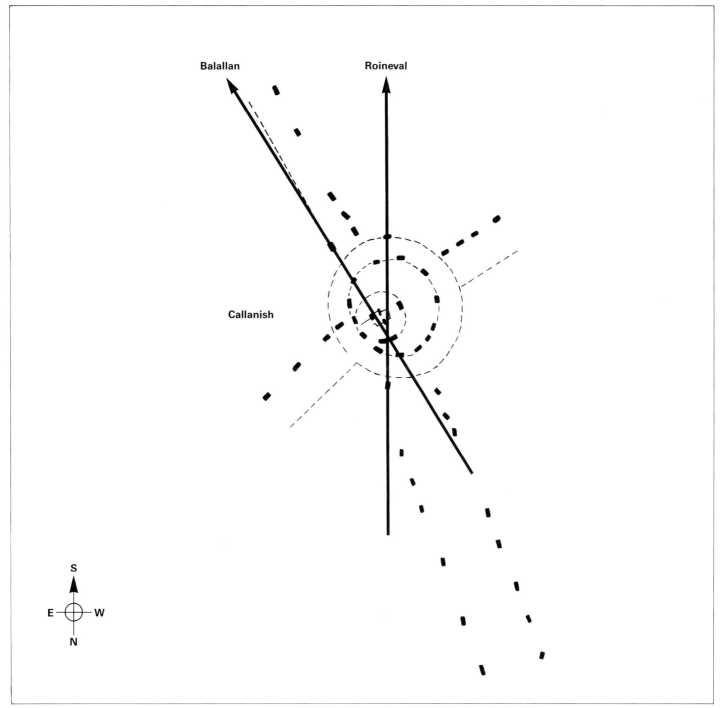

Balallan

Roineval

Callanish

S

E ⊕ W

N

stone circle (B) on the Balallan ley-line is linked with this lunar skimming, and it is quite certain that the distinctive peak of Roineval, almost directly south of the circle, also plays a part in the orientation. The long axis of the Callanish circle is directed to the point of moonrise (Balallan), while a number of stones within the circle are orientated during the period of skimming to several other outriders to fix the point of moonset during this period.

Clearly, the orientation points marked out by the many standing stones indicate a rich variety of lunar and solar positions, but it is evident from this simple plan that the complex was used (among other things) to record accurately the complete lunar cycle. The cyclical phenomenon of moonrise and set would have been of great importance to the megalithic builders who sought to construct and maintain a calendar for religious purposes.

Chanory Point *See* Brahan

Chapel of Garioch, Grampian ✡

C2 NJ 7124

The Maiden Stone, about half a mile/1 km beyond the village called Chapel of Garioch is a 12 feet/3.6 metre-high shaft of a Pictish cross on which have been inscribed a large number of symbols. Many of these symbols are now properly termed occult, though it is clear that at one time they were intended to be Christian.

■ *Chapel of Garioch is signposted to the south of the B9002, to the north-west of Inverurie.*

Cluny Hill *See* Forres

Coldingham *See* Auchencrow *and* Spott

Cool *See* Innerwick

Crieff, Tayside △

B3 NN 8621

The historian of Scottish witchcraft C.K. Sharpe records a tradition, current still in local legends, that a witch who had been a nurse in the family of Inchbrakie was lawfully strangled and burned on Knock Hill (the word is from the Gaelic *cnoic*, meaning hill), near a cave in which she had lived. This woman was said to be called Catharine Niven, which calls into question the story, as in Scotland the word Nicniven was used as the secret name of the Fairy Queen. It is said that as this Catharine was dragged up the hill she spat out a small blue stone, which she gave to one of her Inchbrakie foster-children, telling him that so long as the stone was preserved, then his house would flourish. It seems that this magical stone was set into a ring, and kept as a treasure by the family. The distinctively shaped Knock of Crieff is to the north of the town, and offers splendid panoramic views towards the Sidlaw Hills to the east, the peaks around Loch Earn to the west, and the Grampian foothills to the north, but there are few signs of the ancient witchcraft burnings there: for tangible memorials tourists are usually directed to nearby **Dunning**.

■ *Crieff is on the A5 to the west of Perth. The (signposted) walk up the Knock begins at Hill Street, off the central James Square.*

Culross, Fife △

B3 NS 9885

The 17th-century historian Sinclair records a strange story of this village in his *Satan's Invisible World Discovered*. In 1684 he was told by a friend that he had once walked to Culross to see a witch called Helen Eliot burned at the stake. However, while Eliot was in the stocks in prison the Devil came and carried her off into the air. Surprised at this levitation, Eliot swore, using the name of God, and the Devil dropped her, as a result of which 'she brake her Leggs'. This correspondent told how he had seen the impression left by her heels in the ground, and he noted that no grass would ever grow on the spot. After this fall, Helen Eliot was carried to the place of execution on a chair, and then 'worriet' (strangled) and burned.

■ *Culross is on the B9037, west of Dunfermline. The place where Eliot fell has long been covered over by a dam.*

Dalkeith, Lothian ☿ △

B3 NT 3367

In 1638 a Dalkeith man named James Spalding was hanged for the murder of another local. In his entertaining though horrific *Satan's Invisible World Discovered*, the 17th-century historian Sinclair records that on the scaffold Spalding prayed not to be allowed to die until his soul was reconciled with God. Since it was found 'impossible to hang him', Sinclair relates, he was buried alive (in fact, this was against the law, and we might reasonably doubt Sinclair's account). At this strange burial there was 'such a rumbling and tumbling in his grave, that the very earth was raised . . .' Afterwards Spalding's house at the eastern end of the town was haunted for many years. Some locals say it is haunted still.

Dalkeith was one of the notorious witchcraft centres during the 17th century: for example, we find in the records for August 1661 several suspects under trial, of whom a Margaret Hutchinson was convicted and burned at Wester Duddingstoun, along with four other witches, who were burned in other parts of Dalkeith. The historian Dalyell records that Jonet Ker 'declared at her trial that there were present at a dance with the Devil, beside herself, Agnes Partill, Marjorie Fairwell, John Scott, Margaret Hart, "and uther notorious witches"' In the following month one Janet Cock was found guilty of witchcraft, and was strangled and burned, while six days later, on 16 September, a commission for trial was established to try three who had 'confest the horrid cryme of witchcraft'.

■ *Dalkeith is signposted off the A68(T), south-east of Edinburgh. Sinclair's house is said to be one of those between 216 and 228 High Street, almost opposite Militia House.*

Dalmeny, Lothian ⊕

B3 NT 1477

The 12th-century Romanesque tympanum of St Cuthbert's church at Dalmeny is often described as being decorated with zodiacal symbols. In fact only one of the figures may be said with any certainty to belong to the astrological tradition – this is an image similar to that used in mediaeval times to represent Sagittarius. While astrological imagery is frequently found on surviving Romanesque buildings (especially on the Continent), it is rare to find one zodiacal symbol in isolation (see, however, **Kilpeck**). Perhaps the figure was intended to represent a centaur (though derived from some manuscript image of Sagittarius), in which case it is well fitted into the sequence of curious and fabulous creatures which are cleverly derived from a bestiary collection.

■ *Dalmeny is signposted on the A90, west of Edinburgh.*

Details of Norman carvings on south doorway of Dalmeny church.

Daviot, Grampian

C2 NJ 7528

On a high plateau within the parish of Daviot there is one of the most impressive stone circles of Scotland – the so-called Loanhead Stone Circle, which is a recumbent ring cairn circle, flanked by a smaller circle. The historian Dalyell records that about ten people were burned to death at 'Loanhead' in one single execution for the crime of witchcraft. The place has been confused by some writers with the Loanhead circles, but Dalyell's Loanhead is that in Lothian.

■ *Daviot is signposted to the east of the B9001, north of Inverurie. The circles are well signposted, and are approached through woodlands.*

Doon Hill, Lothian △

C3 NS 3219

The remains of a prehistoric fort are still marked with a neat geometry on Doon Hill, but in the local mythology the place is more famous as the site of numerous executions of convicted witches. Some say that the pile of stones to the north of the fort is a record of such burnings, the number of stones in the pile corresponding to the numbers burned. The place still has an eerie quality about it, for all the breathtaking beauty of the panoramas on all sides. See also **Spott**.

■ *Doon Hill is signposted as an Ancient Site off the A1, east of Dunbar.*

Doon Hill, the site of many witch-burnings in the 16th and 17th centuries.

Dornoch, Highland ♉ △

B1 NH 7989

The cathedral of Dornoch is said to be the oldest church in Sutherland, though most of its fabric is modern reconstruction, with a little surviving work from 1224. The array of exterior gargoyles is fascinating, however, and may be ranked among the best in Scotland. On the front of the west porch is a Green Man, which has been uniquely Christianised by having the tendrils weave the form of a cross over his head. This pagan figure is sometimes confused with the so-called Dornach Imp, which is no longer part of the cathedral fabric however, and is merely a strange, weather-worn grotesque set into the wall of a private house: it is the source of several local stories, but appears to be nothing more than a reject carving from the cathedral fabric.

In a private garden in the area of Dornoch called Littletown is a witch-stone marked with the inscription '1722'. It is said to mark the place where the last Scottish witch was executed in that year. However, the last witch to be executed in Dornoch was Janet Horne, one of two supposed witches (the mother of a mother and daughter team) who was burned in a pitch barrel in June 1727. This woman, who had come from the parish of Loth, was said to have transformed her daughter into a pony, which was shod by the Devil, and then used for riding to a sabbat. The young woman was said to be lame ever afterwards, as indeed was her son after her. The historian Sharpe records that at the time of execution, 'the weather proving very severe, she sat composedly warming herself by the fire prepared to consume her . . .' The severe statutes against witchcraft were repealed in Scotland in 1735. The burning of Janet Horn does appear to be the last official execution of a witch in Scotland, however, though 'mob rule' sometimes resulted in unofficial executions after this time.

■ *Dornoch is at the eastern end of the A9(T), on the spur of the A949. The cathedral is in the centre of the town. The Dornach Imp is on the top of a wall by a gateway fronting on to the main road, about 90 metres to the west of the castle (itself now a hotel). The witch-stone is in the last private garden to the left in the row of houses in Church Street.*

Gargoyle on Dornoch Cathedral.

Dronley, Tayside
B/C3 NO 3437

A boulder marks the spot where a mediaeval damsel-devouring dragon was killed by a gentleman called Martin – at least, this is what the myths insist. The carving on the St Martin Stone, as it is now called, is Pictish, however, and shows a man on horseback spearing a snake-like dragon. The name Martin is something of a puzzle, but perhaps this, like the notion of the dragon itself, has something to do with nearby Strathmartine and the tiny village of Boldragon?

■ *Dronley is signposted off the A923. The Martin Stone is signposted from Dronley.*

Duffus *See* Alves, Crook of

Dumbarton, Strathclyde
B3 NS 3975

The distinctive Dumbarton Rock, which looks over the southern shore of the Clyde estuary, was once the site of the fort which guarded the capital of the Damnonii tribesmen, and the early associations of these pagans have been enshrined in the legends which have developed around the rock. It is said that in the year 388 the whole body of Scottish witches (which is to say, those who followed what even modern Scots call 'the old ways', the pagan worship) rebelled against the work which St Patrick was doing in spreading Christianity. The saint fled towards the Clyde, and set out in a little boat or coracle for the safety of Ireland. The witches, although stopped by the magical power of running water from pursuing, were not content to let Patrick escape: they lifted a huge rock, and threw it after him, but it fell short. This rock was later the land-mass on which Dumbarton castle was built. This same story is also sometimes told of the Devil, who attempted to drive Patrick from Scotland. Perhaps such a link between the Devil and the spur of rock (some 250 feet/75 metres high) is hinted at in the name: for centuries after the Patrick incident, the place was called in Gaelic *Dunbreatan*, meaning 'fort of the Britons', and only after the 11th century became Dumbarton. The older tribes were always linked in mythology with diabolic powers. The fortifications on the rock, while certainly displacing or overlaying older foundations, are now mainly of the 17th and 18th centuries.

■ *Dumbarton itself is off the A82, but the castle and rock are best seen across the Clyde estuary, from the A8, on the south bank of the river.*

The distinctive rocks at Dumbarton, said to have been thrown by the Devil.

Dunbar, Lothian
C3 NT 6878

A surprisingly large Egyptian-type sphinx tops the facade of the huge house designed for the Earls of Lauderdale by Robert Adam in the 18th century.

■ *Dunbar is signposted to the north of the A1(T), east of Edinburgh. Lauderdale House is at the western end of Main Street.*

Dunning, Tayside ✡ △

B3 NO 0114

In the village square, opposite the 13th-century church, is a 19th-century fountain decorated with esoteric images. It is commonplace to find such fountains (and other public memorials) with each of four faces decorated with symbols relating to the four elements of fire, earth, air and water but the Dunning fountain treats them in an unusual way. Each of the four symbols is related to water: the fire element (often symbolised by the salamander) is a newt, the air element (often symbolised by a bird of the air) is a water-fowl, the earth element (often symbolised by an animal) is a frog, an amphibian and the water element itself is symbolised by the image of a fish in the mouth of what is probably a seal.

To the west of the village of Dunning is one of the most dramatic memorials to witchcraft in the British Isles – a cross raised on a rough-built mound of local stone, on which is roughly daubed 'Maggie Wall burnt here 1657 as a Witch'.

■ *Dunning is at the junction of the B8062 and B9141, south-west of Perth. The memorial is on the road to Milhaugh, to the north of the B8062, west of the village.*

The dramatic memorial at Dunning to the witch-burning of Maggie Wall.

Dunvegan, Isle of Skye, Highland ⚥ ♀ → ✡

A2 NG 2547

Dunvegan Castle ♀ ⚥ ✡

In Dunvegan Castle hangs the famous 'Fairy Flag', a fine silken banner which (according to one version of its story) is reputed to have been given to the fourth Lady MacLeod in the 14th century by a woman in a green petticoat, who was supposed to be a fairy. It is tattered and torn now, but one can make out the so-called 'elfen spots', of crimson, which actually look rather like Arabian talismanic sigils. Stories about its talismanic power vary, but it is said to have the power to help the Macleod clan through three crises – the first was in 1490 at the battle of Glendale, the second in 1580 at the battle of Waternish, and the third is still to come. It is said that during the Second World War pilots from the Macleod clan carried its picture as talismans on their flying missions. The flag fabric was made in either Syria or Rhodes before the 7th century, so the tradition that it was brought back to Scotland by crusaders may be well founded. It is unlikely to be the war banner of Harold Hardrada, the King of Norway in the 11th century, as is claimed by another version of its magical origin. The official guidebook to the castle widely lists all the different legends concerned with this curious banner: these include a 'Crusader' version, a 'Fairy Bridge' story, a 'Fairy' version, and a 'Fairy Music' version. The interesting thing is that each of these origins involves a supernatural element. Also of interest to occultists is the 'symbol stone' in the 14th-century kitchens, which is inscribed with a pictograph that appears to portray the lunar and solar influences.

Fairy Bridge → ♀ ✡

The story goes that in mediaeval times one of the MacLeod chiefs married a fairy. The fairy being immortal, and the chief mortal, the liaison had to have a predetermined limit, which was a period of twenty years. When the term was at an end, the chief is said to have taken leave of his fairy wife at a bridge about two miles/3 km to the east of Dunvegan Castle, now called the 'Fairy Bridge'. One version of the tale tells how at the parting she gave to the chief the magic flag, telling him that if he or his clan were in difficulties in a battle, then he should wave it to assure success. This bridge (now of 17th-century design) was on the old road to Dunvegan, but is now used mainly by sheep and tourists.

■ *Dunvegan is on the A863, north-west of Glamaig on the Isle of Skye. The castle is signposted on the A850 about a mile/2 km to the north of the town. The bridge is about 150 yards/metres to the north of the junction of the A850 and the B886, 3 miles/5 km to the north-east of Dunvegan.*

Dunvegan Castle is the most important castle on the Isle of Skye and is associated with the Fairy Flag legends.

Edinburgh, Lothian △ ⊕ Ⅹ ♂

B3 NT 2573

Castle ♂

In July 1689, Lord Balcarras, imprisoned in Edinburgh Castle for having supported James II, was surprised to see his friend John Graham, the Viscount of Dundee, enter his cell, and draw back the curtains of his bed, to gaze down on his face. Graham did not speak, but stayed there for some moments, and then left the room, still in silence. It was only later that Balcarras learned that his friend had died that very day at the battle of Killiecrankie, and realised that the figure must have been his ghost.

Balcarras' first wife was Lady Mauritia de Beverwaert: at their marriage the bridegroom forgot the ring, and so one was borrowed from a friend – this was unfortunately a mourning ring, and had a skull engraved on it. When the young bride saw the ring with which she had been married she declared that she would not live much longer and she did indeed die in childbirth within a year of her marriage.

Castle Hill △

The normal place of execution for witches in Edinburgh was the Castle Hill, as for example on the 7 August 1661 Margaret Bryson and five companions were 'indyted and found guilty of witchcraft and sorcery, condemned to be strangled and burned' on the Hill. However, there are records that in 1614 Robert Erskine and his sisters, found guilty of consulting with witches, poisoning and treasonable murder, were beheaded at the Market Cross in Edinburgh: in this case, the main charge would have been murder. Witches found guilty of murder were usually throttled and burned: burning 'quick', or alive, was reserved only for extreme cases of wickedness. Records for 1678 indicate that five witches were burned in that year on the 'Gallowlee' of Edinburgh. This Gallowlee covered three acres, and is now overbuilt, but the gallows (from which the name took its place) was still being used there well into the 18th century.

The historian of witchcraft, Sharpe, records that after the restoration of Charles II there was so much persecution of witchcraft in Scotland that 'for some years the Castlehill of Edinburgh, and the heights of its vicinity, blazed with the dry carcases of those miserable victims'. Among the most notable victims to die in this dismal place was the beautiful Janet, Lady Douglas (see **Glamis**). Numerous witches were strangled and burned on this hill and some years ago a small fountain was erected on the Castle Esplanade to mark the place where witches and warlocks were burned. In a short address connected with its unveiling the historian Dr Walter Blaikie pointed out that in Scotland witches were persecuted by the clergy, a persecution stopped by the lawyers.

George Street ⊕

On a Victorian building now occupied by the Bank of Scotland in George Street are stone carvings of two different sets of zodiacal images, in ornate and floral surrounds. The sequence of the higher register of images does not correspond in any meaningful way with the lower register, which is ranged from Aries onwards, with a break between Leo and Scorpio, to permit the signs Virgo and Libra to be accommodated in the lapidary ornamentation above the door. The top register begins with Aquarius, and runs in uninterrupted sequence through the twelve signs.

Holyroodhouse Palace △ Ⅹ

The name of this lovely castle means Holy Cross House, and is said to be derived from the exploits of David I, in 1128, while hunting in the forest. He was chased by a stag, but managed to grip the creature's antlers: the moment he touched them, however, the stag vanished, and the antlers turned into a cross in his hands. The story is reminiscent of that told about the vision of St Eustace.

A brass plaque in the palace marks the spot where Mary Queen of Scots' secretary David Rizzio was stabbed to death by her husband Lord Darnley. It is inevitable that legends of hauntings (Rizzio, according to some, Darnley in the view of others) should gather around the palace.

It is however in the gruesome histories of Scottish witchcraft that Holyrood has played a peculiar role. It was here that several of the alleged witches of **North Berwick** were examined by the fanatical King James VI of Scotland in 1592 (see also **Tranent**). The most well-documented of the examinations reads like a horror story, for one of the suspects, Agnes Sampson, a gentle woman, well known in Edinburgh society, denied all the charges against her. The king had the hair shaved from every part of her body, in a search for the Devil's Mark. Such a mark was found on her private parts, so she was fastened to her cell wall with a iron pronged vice (sometimes called a witch bridle) in her mouth, with two sharp prongs piercing her cheeks, and two pushing into her tongue. At the same time she was burned by ropes being drawn over her face. Under tortures she began to confess to many evil deeds of witchcraft, finally admitting that she and her friends had plotted to raise the storm which would destroy the ship carrying King James to Denmark. She and her diabolic friends had gone to sea in sieves to bring about the needed storm.

Holyroodhouse Palace, Edinburgh, steeped in myth and legend.

The Bow ♂

One of the houses in the Bow was once the home of Major Thomas Weir (who was executed for witchcraft in 1670) and is said still to be haunted. The historian Robert Chambers wrote that even when it was deserted, the house was observed 'at midnight to be full of lights,' and emitted 'strange sounds as of dancing, howling, and what is strangest of all, spinning'. Some people claim to have seen the spirit of the major himself emerge from the house, 'mounted upon a black horse without a head, and gallop off in a whirlwind of flame.' Weir's own confession of attempted rape of his sister, incest, adultery and bestiality – crimes which were interlarded with various aspects of witchcraft – are nowadays taken as a sign of intense senile dementia.

Princes Street ⊕

High on one of the imposing buildings to the east of Princes Street is a huge planisphere, with a well-marked zodiacal band, supported by what appear to be cupids.

The zodiacal band on the planisphere on top of the building at the corner of Princes Street and South St Andrew's Street, Edinburgh.

■ *The castle dominates Princes Street to the west, and is perhaps best seen from here, or from the Grassmarket. It is of course possible to visit the castle at certain times of most days. The bank is on the south-east corner of Frederick Street and George Street. Holyroodhouse is best approached (for access to parking) by way of the ring-road around the parklands of Arthur's Seat, to the south of Edinburgh. The Bow is in the Grassmarket. The building with the planisphere faces on to Princes Street, on the corner with South St Andrew's Street.*

Eildon Hills, Borders ⚔

C3 NT 5732

For all their sleepy beauty, the Eildon Hills are said to be haunted, and charged with magic. The story runs that a man walking on the hills penetrated the underground cavern where Arthur and his knights slept, awaiting their call in the hours of England's need, and found hanging from the roof a sword and a horn. He chose to sound the horn, rather than to draw the sword from its scabbard, and a magical wind swept him out of the cavern. It is said that when he told his story to some shepherds, he died within seconds, and the location of the entrance to the cavern was lost.

■ *The Eildon Hills lie to the south-east of Melrose, and are best seen from the A6091 or B6398, or from the minor road which joins these two, north of Newton St Boswells.*

The Eildon Hills which play an important role in Scottish mythology.

Eilean Donan, Highland ☿

A2 NH 8926

This picturesque castle, connected to the mainland by a bridged causeway, was largely destroyed in 1719 by English gunboats seeking to subdue Spanish-backed Jacobites under the fifth Earl of Seaforth who had taken the castle. It is said that the ghost of the Spanish soldier which haunts the castle is from this period. A recent photograph taken inside the castle unexpectedly revealed the appearance of a disembodied head on the print – many people believe that this was an astral image of the Eilean Donan ghost.

■ *Eilean Donan stands at the northern end of Loch Duich, off the A87(T).*

The haunted castle of Eilean Donan.

Elgin, Grampian ✡ ☒

B2 NJ 2162

The museum at Elgin, founded and funded by the Moray Society, is of considerable interest to those involved with esoteric symbolism. The somewhat eccentric collection of a wide variety of different exhibits is largely made up of bequests from notable travellers from the Moray area. The most famous exhibit is the Burghead bull, a Pictish stone carving found during the excavation of the well at **Burghead**. Exhibits range from the curious grotesqued back of a 17th-century chair, through head-hunters' back baskets (replete with monkeys' skulls, in place of the more usual human skulls), ceremonial magic adzes dedicated to the god Tane, from the Cook Islands, to soapstone carvings of Hindu gods and demons.

■ *Elgin is on the A96(T), to the east of Forres. The museum is central, and well signposted within the city.*

Pictish 'Burghead Bull' at Elgin, – possibly 8th century – a stone carving found during the excavations of the Burghead Well. Now in the collection of the Moray Society.

Findhorn, Grampian ♀

B2 NJ 0564

To the south of the village, discreetly signposted, is a small community called the Findhorn Foundation dedicated to a spiritual return to nature, where a concern for the elementals is actively encouraged, and where a search and respect for the harmonious healing processes in nature are cultivated. In the 15th or 16th century the community would no doubt have declared itself interested in 'Natural Magic', and it is significant that in modern times we have no word or phrase to cover adequately the spiritual endeavour of such a community. The stories which have emerged from the work at Findhorn are often exaggerated, and misunderstood – certainly they display misunderstandings of occult terminologies, but this does not appear always to arise from those actively involved in the spiritual researches. The community is regarded as being benign by the locals. In his book on Findhorn, Paul Hawken points to the external view of what the community achieves in terms of people talking

to plants, gardens tended by angelic forms, a place where 'Pan's pipes are heard in the winds', mingled with stories of extraordinary growth, such as huge cabbages, roses blooming in the snow, and so on. As he says, what he personally found at Findhorn seems somehow larger than such cabbages: the fairies and elves are tame stuff in comparison with what one might experience there on a spiritual level. Some ley-line hunters point out that Findhorn is on a powerful ley centre.

■ *Findhorn village is at the termination of the B9011, north of Forres. The Findhorn Foundation is signposted to the east of the road, just before the village.*

Fingal's Cave, Strathclyde ☒

A3 NM 3335

Fingal's cave has the same monolithic significance in Scotland as Stonehenge in England. Fingal's cave, however, was made by nature ('by the daedal hand of Titan Nature', as the Scotsman Blackie wrote in heavy verse), Stonehenge by man. The old myths however insist that both were built by the ancient race of giants. The cave's statistics are remarkable: it has a hollow depth of some 250 feet/75 metres, bored with great beauty into the rock of Staffa, and a height of well over 100 feet/30 metres. The walls of the cave itself are as beautifully articulated as a carved temple. When the poet John Keats visited it in 1818, he wrote to his brother to say that in 'solemnity and grandeur it far surpasses the finest cathedrals', and the old stories of the giant-builders came easily to his mind: 'Suppose now the giants who rebelled against Jove, had taken a whole mass of black columns and bound them together like bunches of matches and then, with immense axes, had made a cavern in the body of these columns.'

Keats' poetic fancy has even found a more scientifically minded supporter in Cope Whitehouse (who was seemingly the first, in the 19th century, to propose the harnessing of the waters of the Nile). Whitehouse maintains that centuries ago refugees from the Mediterranean cut the cave of Fingal into the basaltic columns, in much the same way that their contemporaries rock-hewed the temples of Petra in Jordan and Abu-Simbel in Egypt. The fact is that many of the features in the cave, and indeed on the island itself are a puzzle to geologists. Of course, the cave is famous not only for its association with the mythical Fingal, but also for its music – indeed it is argued that the etymology of the Gaelic name for the cave suggests 'musical cave', rather than 'Fingal's cave', as the expert on the island, Donald MacCulloch points out. The music is probably made from the volumes of air being driven into the interior of the cave by the ebb and flow of the waves, resulting in a booming organ-like noise. For all this ancient meaning in the sound of the name, it is generally believed that Fingal not only lived in the cave (which would have been a physical impossibility), but that he actually built it.

■ *Staffa is most easily reached from Iona, either by private arrangement with local sailors, or by means of tourist boats – in either case, landings are not guaranteed, as the weather is notoriously changeable.*

Fingal's Cave on the Island of Staffa, a place replete with myths and legends.

Forres, Grampian △

B2 NJ 0358

Set in the retaining wall of the A96 is a witch-stone, which marks the place where the mutilated remains of a witch were burned in the 17th century. It was the local practice for witches to be placed in barrels which had sharp prongs on the inside – the unfortunates were then rolled down the hill, and where the barrels came to a halt, the mangled remains were burned. The metal plaque by the stone says it all: 'From Cluny Hill witches were rolled in stout barrels through which spikes were driven. Where the barrels stopped, they were burned . . .' There were once several such witch-stones in Forres, but this is now the last of two surviving, saved (as Richie records) just in time by interested antiquarians. One wonders if it marks the burning place of Isabel Simson, whose execution the Laird of Brodie observed in 1662? In the days of King Duff a party of witches attempted his murder by means of wax-magic. They made an image of the king, and then, while enacting certain rituals, basted it with poisonous fluids over a warm fire. It was supposed that as the wax melted, so would the king die. The witches were apprehended, Duffus recovered, and the witches were burned in the main square at Forres. As Sharpe records, the attempted murder of the king 'occasioned many wonders' – horses in Lothian, remarkable for swiftness and beauty, devoured their own flesh, an owl strangled a sparrowhawk, and the sun was hidden behind the dark clouds for over six months.

■ *Forres is on the A96(T). The witch-stone is on the south side of the road, almost opposite the police station.*

Fortrose *See* Brahan

Fort William, Highland ⊕ ✡

A2 NN 1073

In the West Highland Museum in Fort William is a curious occult device once used in a secret ritual. This device is the so-called 'secret portrait' of Prince Charles Edward Stuart, (otherwise known as the Young Pretender, the Young Chevalier and Bonnie Prince Charlie) painted by an unknown 18th-century artist onto a wooden tray. The painting is a meaningless blur of two crescent forms when viewed directly, but when a polished cylinder is placed in the centre of the upper space between the crescent horns, a perfect image of the prince is reflected in the cylinder. It is said that the device was used to conjure up the image of the prince when toasts were being proposed to his health and success, during those times when it was dangerous to possess a conventional image. The technique of making such secret images appears to have been learned in Renaissance times, but it is claimed that this particular picture was influenced by a Chinese method of occult portraiture, introduced to Scotland in the 17th century. There may be some significance in the choice of a double crescent as the base symbol for the 'meaningless blur', as Scotland is ruled by the zodiacal sign Cancer – a fact which probably also explains the wide use of the unicorn (a Cancerian animal, linked with the ruler Moon) for the mercat (market) crosses in many towns. The crescent moon is of course one of the occult symbols for the moon, and a double crescent may be taken as a reference to the double sigil of Cancer.

■ *Fort William is on the A82T. The West Highland Museum is in Cameron Square, in the centre of the town.*

Demon on pedestal in the castle gardens at Fyvie.

Fyvie Castle, Grampian ♉

C2 NJ 7638

In the forecourt of the chateau-like castle is an interesting symbolic device (probably of the 17th century) incorporating images of the Devil as a Pan-figure, with hooved feet.

■ *Fyvie Castle is well signposted to the east of the A947, north-west of Oldmeldrum.*

Gallowlee *See* Edinburgh – Castle Hill

Glamis, Tayside ♂ ☿ △

B/C 2/3 NO 3846

In both fact and legend the history of this beautiful castle is intimately bound up with the history of Scotland as a whole, and it is therefore inevitable that many legends should have insinuated themselves into the castle fabric. No other castle in Scotland is reputed to be occupied by quite so many ghosts, however, since the list includes Macbeth (in which Shakespearean play Glamis is mentioned by name as the place of the slaying of Duncan by Macbeth), we may reasonably doubt some of the stories attached to this most impressive of all Scottish castles. One rather tenuous story claims that a monster is bricked-up somewhere in the castle but this is more likely to be derived from the supposed secret chamber built into the vast thickness of the crypt walls, where, it is said, one of the Lords of Glamis played cards with the Devil on the sacred Sabbath. As the official guide book to the castle itself records, the result of this heresy was a disturbance which led to the room being permanently sealed. There are however one or two more tangible remains of a past occultism, and at least one historical fact which points, if not to witchcraft, then to the more frequent political use of the laws of witchcraft for personal aggrandisement. The directly 'occult' remain is at the south entrance to the castle, which is by way of the 17th-century Devil's Gate (once located in front of the castle), which is adorned with a pair of demonic or satyr-like supporters and heraldic beasts. The historical fact connected with Glamis

was virtually a political scandal: in July 1537 Jane, Lady Douglas, sister of the Earl of Angus and widow of John, Lord Glamis, was arrested and tried for attempting to bring about the death of James V by poison, witchcraft, or evil charms. As one historian put it, after listing the lands she forfeited as a result of being found guilty, 'it appears that this noble witch, who was as remarkable for her beauty and courage, as for her dismal fate, was hurried from the bar to the stake, where she died with great composure.' The charges were entirely political, of course. The stake at which she died was one of the many set up in that year on Castle Hill in **Edinburgh**.

■ *Glamis Castle is off the A928, south of Kirriemuir, but is well signposted within this region of Tay.*

Glendale *See* Dunvegan

Glendevon, Tayside △ ✡

B3 NN 9904

In 1643 a local man named John Brughe was arrested under suspicion of witchcraft in the area. At his trial in Edinburgh it was claimed that he had met Satan in Glendevon churchyard on three different occasions.

In the west end of the church, set into the fabric of the exterior wall, is a most interesting memorial upon which is carved a skull. This is of course a standard image in 18th-century Scottish memorials, but what is special about this example is that the space behind the eyesockets allows light to fall behind the raised skull. This lends a most eerie quality

Glamis Castle, one of the finest castles in Scotland, with a variety of attached ghost stories.

to the appearance of the skull, for one has the impression that the stone effigy has luminous eyes: it is indeed a symbol of 'resurrection', an occult image of 'death made live'.

■ *Glendevon is on the A823, south-east of Crieff, beyond the intersection with the A9. The churchyard and church are to the right, just visible from the road.*

A skull with 'special' light-effects. From a tombstone to the west of Glendevon church.

Glenluce, Dumfries and Galloway ☿ ⚔ △
A4 NX 1957

According to local mythology, a terrible plague which ravished the area in the 13th century was abated by a wizard, who tricked the demons into one of the vaults of Glenluce Abbey, and locked the door.

In the history of witchcraft, the Devil of Glenluce (nothing to do with the plague demon) appears on the surface to be an early example of a documented poltergeist. From 1654 to 1656 the house of Thomas Campbell at Glenluce was troubled by noises, stones thrown by invisible agencies, nasty tricks around the house, eventually arson, the 'voices' of devils, and so on. Modern specialists in poltergeist activity tend to dismiss the case as trickery by the children of the house (chiefly the son Gilbert), who had a vested interest in dominating their father.

■ *Glenluce is on the A75(T), east of Stranraer. The abbey is well signposted in the area.*

Haddington, Lothian △
C3 NT 5173

The unfortunate Agnes Sampson, made infamous through the witchcraft trials connected with **North Berwick**, lived in Haddington. A rare woodcut from a pamphlet *Newes from Scotland* shows Agnes, along with other supposed witches (including John Fian of Saltpans: see **Prestonpans**) being interrogated in front of judges: it would seem however that the actual interrogation involved far more than beating with a stick.

■ *Haddington is to the south of the A1, between Edinburgh and Dunbar.*

Hardmuir *See* Alves, Crook of

Hermitage, Borders ⚔ △
C4 NY 5095

The severe and ruinous Border fortress of Hermitage is set in some isolation on the left bank of the Hermitage Water. This gaunt building was once the home of James Hepburn, the fourth Earl of Bothwell, who married Mary Queen of Scots in 1567 after her second husband Lord Darnley had been murdered.

However, Hermitage is more famous in the annals of witchcraft as the dwelling of William Lord Soulis, whose career was dramatised by Dr John Leyden, who portrayed him as one of the most evil of all men, and has him boiled to death in a brazen cauldron on the nearby Nine Stane Rig. Soulis was said to be the most wicked wizard that Scotland had ever known, and it is believed that the castle was so weighted down by the dark aura of his evil that it sank into the ground, unable to bear the terrible weight of his deeds. This legend may have grown out of the undeniable squatness of the fortress, which seems to be pressed flat into the bluff of moorland, rather than to stand on it with any real dignity.

■ *Hermitage Castle is signposted to the west of the B6399, which runs directly south of Hawick.*

Hermitage Castle, supposedly haunted by the spirit of a depraved soul.

Home-Cultram *See* Melrose

Humbie, Lothian ☿ △

C3 NT 4562

The modern Humbie parish once included a hamlet called Nether Keith, and it was from this village that the witch Agnes Sampson came. She was often called the 'wise wife of Keith', which has led some people to believe mistakenly that she came from **Keith**. Agnes Sampson is supposed to have confessed in person to King James VI that on one occasion she met 'the devil, in man's likeness' not far from her own house in Nether Keith. The Dark Prince ordered her to be at North Berwick kirk on the following night, where she and her godson, John Couper, went on horse-back. Here in the churchyard, they held a sabbat, along with about a hundred other witches, of whom only six were men. One of the company arranged black candles around the pulpit, and the devil 'like a meikle black man', read out the roster of those present, and then read a sermon. Later they all rifled three graves to get the necessary ingredients for their magical brews: Agnes herself removed part of a winding sheet and two bone-joints. Later, the Devil taught them how to dismember corpses, how to baptise a cat, and then to drown it in order to bring about storms and shipwrecks. For more information on Sampson, see **North Berwick**, which gives some indication of how such stories arose.

■ *Humbie is on the A6137, south-east of Edinburgh.*

Innerleithen, Borders ☿

B3 NT 3336

In the second or third week of July every year the image of the Devil is burnt on a bonfire, followed by bagpipe-led torchlight processions between Caerlea Hill and the town. It is said that the ritual is in commemoration of the manner in which the monk St Ronan overcame the Devil in that part of the world. The ceremony is held at a time close enough to the entry of the Sun into zodiacal Leo to suggest that it is derived from a pagan purification ritual. The ceremony is called locally 'the burning of the Deil'.

■ *Innerleithen is on the A72, west of Galasheils. The ceremony is not fixed to a specific date: contact the Scottish Borders Tourist Board at Selkirk for further information.*

Innerwick, Lothian ✿ ☿ △

C3 NT 7274

Innerwick is famous for a ghost, but should be renowned for the wonderful collection of 17th- and 18th-century gravestones which grace the burial grounds around the kirk. On some of the upright stones there are occult devices and symbols, perhaps the most interesting of which is a mysterious symbol which is something like a prototype for the modern astrological symbol for Uranus.

The Cool Ghost is said to be that of a Mr Maxwell of the village of Cool, who died at the manse in Innerwick in 1724,

and appeared several times to a variety of different people. Among those favoured by his postmortem presence was Ogilvie, the minister of the kirk at Innerwick, with whom he had several conversations which the minister thoughtfully recorded. An account of these conversations was published after his own death, as *A Wonderful and True Account of the Laird of Cool's Ghost*. The Cool Ghost is said to haunt the manse to this day, and is in fact merely one of three ghosts (all benign) which are currently believed to haunt various houses in the village.

The Register of the Privy Council for 1662 shows William Cowan, 'an indweller at Innerweik' under trial as a confessed witch.

■ *Innerwick is signposted off the A1(T), south-east of Dunbar.*

Magic symbols on an 18th-century gravestone at Innerwick.

Inshoch, Highland ☿ △

B2 NJ 9257

The ruinous and romantic castle of Inshoch is where Isobel Goudie, accused of witchcraft in 1662, claims to have first met the Devil, and where she learned to practise wax and clay image-making for purposes of casting spells of evil on people, and for bringing about sickness. See also **Auldearn**.

■ *Inshoch is visible as a romantic ruin on the minor road from Auldearn to the village of Moviston, north of Auldearn.*

Inverkip, Strathclyde △

A3 NS 2072

For all that it is a small parish, Inverkip appears to have been infamous in the 17th century as a centre for witchcraft. In 1662 there are no fewer than four sets of records of trials involving eighteen people being tried on charges of witchcraft. Among the number of women tried in March of that year was eighteen-year-old Marie Lamont, who 'confessed' that she had given her heart and body to the Devil. She said that the Devil sometimes called her Clowts, and required her to call him 'Serpent', that by nipping her he left on her side the Devil's Mark, and that she often had sexual intercourse with him. The Devil was said to sit in at the sabbats which she attended, most often appearing in the form of a brown dog. The purpose of the sabbats was to raise storms to prevent fishing. She, with other witches, also poisoned by enchantment the wife of one Alan Orr.

In the old churchyard above the village there are several gravestones relating to the Orr family. For other accounts see **Kempock**.

■ *Inverkip is on the A78, south-west of Greenock. The old graveyard is on the hillside to the east of the village – on the road from Greenock, turn left at the garage, and then first left. The older part of the cemetery is on the left.*

Inverness, Highland △

B2 NH 6645

In his account of 17th-century witchcraft, the historian Fraser records at the time the visit of a witch pricker to Inverness. His name was Paterson, and his method was to use a long brass pin, 'striping them [the suspects] naked, he alleged that the spell spot was seen and discovered. After rubbing over the whole body with his palms he slipt in the pin, and it seemes, with shame and feare being dasht, they felt it not, but he left it in the flesh, dep to the head . . .' Many witches were 'discovered' in this way, but as Fraser remarks, 'many honest men and women were blotted and broak by the trick'. Two were killed in **Elgin**, two in **Forres**, and one Margret Duff, a 'rank witch' was burned in Inverness. The culmination of the Paterson exploits was at the parish church at Wardlaw, where he pricked fourteen women and one man, first cutting off all their hair. Fraser continues, 'Severall of these dyed in prison, never brought to confession. This villan [Paterson] gained a great deale of mony, haveing two servants; at last was discovered to be a woman disguised in mans cloathes'!

For the Fairy Hill of Inverness, see **Tomnahurich Hill**.

■ *Inverness is on the A9(T), at the southern end of the Moray Firth.*

Iona, Strathclyde ✗

A3 NM 2726

It is said that forty-eight kings of Scotland are buried in the cemetery close to St Mary's abbey established by St Columba in AD 563, and four from Ireland.

Some guidebooks speak of the famous three white marble balls of St Oran. These are supposed to be placed in hollows in a stone slab alongside the chapel of St Oran. Visitors were to turn the balls three times to be granted a wish: the marbles were called fairy stones. However, so far as it is possible to determine, the stones were destroyed under the orders of the Synod of Argyll in 1561 – as well as some 350 Celtic crosses which were either destroyed or removed. It may be that the 'marble' stones were actually green serpentine, for these are still highly regarded as talismans by certain locals. Almost as highly prized as the local seaweed, which is used to fertilise the land and also as one of the most powerful specifics against demons, witchcraft and virtually any evil. The 19th-century historian Cockayne preserves several Saxon beliefs and recipes relating to the magical power of seaweed, and many of these beliefs were held also by the Celts.

■ *The island of Iona is usually approached by way of the Island of Mull, across the Sound of Iona, from Fionnphort, on the A849.*

Kempock, Strathclyde △ ✡

A/B3 NR 2678

A girl called Marie Lamont, who was condemned to burning as a witch in 1662 (see **Inverkip**), had confessed that she, with several other named witches, attended a kind of sabbat at Kempock, with the intention of casting the Longstone into the Clyde estuary, in the belief that it would destroy ships and boats. The Longstone, now called the Granny Kempock Stone, is actually a menhir of the bronze age: since it is still in its ancient place, we must presume that it was not possible for the witches to cast it into the waters below. According to the trial records, however, having held the sabbat, the supposed witches danced around the stone, kissed the devil, and left the spot. The stone is now safely imprisoned behind railings, but with interesting ancient graffiti on its surface still visible. One wonders why certain individuals (identified only by initials) carved alchemical and esoteric sigils near the top of the stone? The menhir, which is about 6 feet/2 metres high, is said to be regarded

The so-called Granny Kempock Stone on the headland above Kempock. It was once called the 'Longstone', and figured in witchcraft trials.

with deep superstition by fishermen, who practise various rites to ensure fair weather, and it is recorded that couples intending marriage would encircle the stone for good luck. The present wall and railings now make such encircling quite impracticable.

■ *Kempock, which virtually merges into Gourock, is on the A770 west of Greenock. Granny Kempock's Stone is on the headland, now surrounded by houses, at the end of the short road to the north of St John's church.*

Keith, Grampian   △
C2 NJ 4350

To the west of the parish church the main road through Keith crosses the river Isla at a 'new bridge' (built 1770), which is close to the 'auld brig', just below the burial grounds. Beneath this new bridge is a pool in the Isla, formerly called the 'Gaun's Pot', where tradition asserts the witches of Keith were 'swum and drowned'. On the south bank is the Scaur or Gaun's Stone from which a man is reported to have used his walking stick to push back into the pool the last old woman to be drowned there for witchcraft.

The Book of the Chronicles of Keith, published in 1880, preserves many interesting snippets of the old lore and primitive occultism. Its author, the Rev Gordon, postulates that the last witch in the area was 'old Alexander Jamieson's Mother', who, however, probably escaped drowning. He tells the true story of how a man, who was being punished in the standard way by having his ear nailed to Keith's communal gallows-tree for a time, was so anxious to see a witch being drowned in the 'Gaun's pot' that he wrenched himself free from the gibbet, left his ear behind, and ran down to the river to watch the spectacle.

■ *Keith is on the A95. The bridge crosses the Isla west of the parish church, just beyond Church Road.*

Kinross, Tayside   ♑ ♀
B3 NO 1102

A very impressive fountain, with four demonic monsters as finials, stands outside the council offices in the town. No-one seems able to give an account as to why this curious quaternary had been so placed but it recalls the old occult practice of setting up triple or quadruple demonic figures at cross-roads, as protective devices.

In 1781 the clergyman's house at Kinross became the centre of an attack of what would now be called poltergeist activity, involving disappearing and moving objects, stone throwing by invisible agencies, the secretion of pins in food, the tearing of personal clothing, and so on. The minister's bible was thrown on the fire by an unknown agency, but would not burn, yet silver spoons and a plate so thrown melted immediately. The tract which was published in 1781 to give an account of this haunting called the agencies 'dreamers, or spirits', and it called the witchcraft phenom- enon 'Endorism', from the biblical 'witch of Endor', who was certainly not a witch in any modern sense of the word.

■ *Kinross is signposted off the M90, north of Dunfermline, to the west of Loch Leven, The demonic monster is in the main street, opposite the signposted turning to the Loch. The clergyman's house appears to have been accommodated into ordinary dwelling houses to the south of the parish church.*

The demonic fountain in the centre of Kinross, at the turning towards Loch Leven. The purpose of the demons is no longer known (the water fount is lower down the pedestal).

Kirkcudbright, Dumfries and Galloway   △
B4 NX 6851

On the 1 March 1698 a commission was established to try the locals Elspeth M'Ewen and Mary Millar for the 'horrid crime of witchcraft'. The former had been charged with having a witch-pin in the end of the beams of her house, by means of which she would cast evil on the animals and poultry of her neighbours. The most 'convincing' evidence against her was that when she was sent for, to appear for trial, the horse she mounted trembled and sweated blood. She was imprisoned at Kirkcudbright, and on the 24 August was strangled and burned. Records show that the expenses for her execution, including fees to the fireman, the cost of the peat, and the barrel of tar in which she was burned, came to about £8.40, a considerable sum in those days. The records of the period contain many petitions from small Scottish villages, complaining that they cannot afford to maintain the many witches languishing in their jails.

■ *Kirkcudbright is on the southern termination of the A711, south of Castle Douglas.*

Knock of Crieff *See* Crieff

Lanark, Strathclyde   △
B3 NS 8843

Under the usual torture inflicted upon witches at the time, a Margaret Watsone testified in 1644 that at a sabbat held in the 'High Kirk' at Lanark, her friend Mailie Paittersone rode on a cat, Jonet Lockie on a cock and her aunt Margaret rode on a thorn tree. She herself transvected (for that is what 'rode' means in this context) on a bail of straw, and Jeane Lauchlan on an elder tree.

■ *Lanark is signposted on the A73(T), south-east of Glasgow.*

Littletown *See* Dornoch

Loanhead *See* Daviot

Lochan Uaine *See* Cairngorms

Locher-Moss *See* Melrose

Maeshowe, Orkney

ND 3213

A mysterious prehistoric chambered cairn, enclosed in a large grassy ditched mound some 24 feet/7.5 metres high and about 115 feet/35 metres in diameter, dated to about 2750 BC, is famous for its collection of runic inscriptions (one of which boasts of the treasure which was stolen from the cairn), carved by Vikings over 800 years ago. Among the rich variety of graffiti on one of the uprights is the famous Maeshowe Dragon. The beautifully built cairn is so orientated that the mid-winter sun shines down the 12-yard/11-metres long entrance passage to light up the inner beehive chamber.

■ *Maeshowe is signposted near Tormiston Far, about 3 miles/5 km on the A965 west of Finstown.*

Melrose, Borders
C3 NT 5434

In Melrose Abbey there is a memorial stone, a flat gravestone (now restored from nine fragments, though still clearly marked with an incised cross), said to be the tomb of the 13th-century wizard, magician and occultist Michael Scot. In his guise as a wonder-working magician Scot is said to have built the road through Locher-Moss in Dumfriesshire in one night and to have made for himself a brass head which could talk, and give details of the future. In fact, as the modern historian Lynn Thorndike has shown, Scot was one of the most remarkable intellectuals of his century, the instructor in the new Arabic lore of magic and astrology to Frederick II in Italy, and the author of the first European book on practical astrology, the *Introductorius*, mediaeval copies of which are preserved in both Oxford (Bodleian) and the British Museum (see **London – British Museum**). Another burial place of Scot is claimed at Home-Cultram, in Cumbria, but the one in Melrose is favoured on the dubious grounds that it was claimed as such by his poetic namesake Sir Walter Scott. In his poem *The Lay of the Last Minstrel* Scott mentions the fantastical tradition that beneath the tomb there is an eternal flame which 'burns a wondrous light, to chase the spirits that love the night'.

■ *Melrose Abbey is signposted to the north of the town, which lies on the A6091. The supposed tomb is one of two set into the floor to the south of the east end of the abbey interior.*

The Abbey at Melrose, where the wizard and occultist Michael Scot is buried.

Nether Keith *See* Humbie

North Berwick, Lothian ⚥ ⚠

C3 NT 5585

The North Berwick witches are perhaps the most famous in the whole annals of Scottish witchcraft. The trials of these suspects, and the later related legal developments, hinged on the notion that a sabbat of witches had attempted to wreck, by raising contrary winds and storms, the ship in which King James VI returned from Denmark with his bride, Princess Anne of Denmark. This treason was said to have been planned in the Old Kirk at North Berwick, where the devil appeared to them 'in the likeness of a man with a redde capp and a rumpe at his taill'. By the harbour are the poor remains of the porch of old St Andrew's church, where (according to some accounts) the Devil preached to the sabbat of witches. Other versions of the story have the witches gathering in the churchyard, however, but the place is now built over, and some of the gravestones have been moved to another churchyard further inland, around a church which is already ruinous. The trial of the North Berwick witches caught the popular imagination largely because of the personal involvement of King James, and the consequent numerous broadsheets and booklets, of which *Newes from Scotland* (1591) was probably the best known, promulgating the notion that the Devil preached to the sabbat of witches from the church pulpit in the Old Kirk. (See also **Prestonpans**).

■ *North Berwick is on the A198. The remains of the Old Kirk stand on a small mound to the east of the harbour. The account of the Berwick Witches given on the official plaque nearby is almost entirely fanciful.*

The Old Kirk porch at North Berwick said to be the site of ancient witchcraft rites.

Pittenweem, Fife ⚠

C3 NO 5402

In 1704 there was a famous witchcraft trial here against a number of local women, on a slight charge of having afflicted a man with a fit. The women were maltreated by their drunken guards until they confessed to deeds which in those days passed for witchcraft. One of these women, Janet Cornfoot, managed to escape her tormentors, and ran from the prison, but she was caught by the mob, hauled down to the rocky beach where there is now the harbour, swung on a rope between the ship and the shore, and then pushed under a heavy door, over which stones were heaped until she was crushed to death. The murderers were never punished.

■ *Pittenweem is on the A917, from which a signposted road runs down to the harbour.*

Pittenweem, the site of one of the last Scottish witch-killings, in 1704.

Pollockshaws, Strathclyde ⚠

B3 NS 5561

In this village in 1677 a number of people, among whom were Jonet Mathie, Jon Stewart, Margaret Jackson, Bessie Weir and Marjory Craig, were strangled and burned as witches. The case was famous in its day, for it involved the supposed bewitching of a local lord, the well-known Sir George Maxwell, and his family.

■ *Pollockshaws is now swallowed up in the conurbation of Glasgow, to the south, in the direction of the A77.*

Prestonpans, Lothian ⚠

B3 NT 3871

This village, with its notable Preston Tower, was once called Saltpans. In 1590 one of its schoolteachers, Dr John Fian (otherwise known as John Cunningham), 'a notable

Sorcerer' according to his detractors, became unwittingly involved with the infamous and unfortunate Agnes Sampson (see **North Berwick**). His story is more an account of courage in the face of incredible torture than one of witchcraft. Fian was tried separately from the others involved in this famous series of trials and tortures, on the main charge of having attempted to bewitch into his bed a woman he was 'enamoured of', by means of treating hairs which he had imagined came from her head. Under the terrible torture of the boot (a sort of metal shoe which was put on the foot of a prisoner, and then hammered with a sledge-hammer) he confessed, like the other Berwick witches, to several incredible witchcraft deeds. He later recanted, escaped, and was tortured again, this time by having his nails torn off, and needles pushed into his fingers 'even up to the heads'. The boot was applied again, until 'his legges were crusht and beaten together as small as might bee . . . that the blood and marrow spouted forth . . . whereby they were made unserviceable for ever'. In spite of this the man would not confess again. His tormentors decided that this inner strength came from the 'devill which entered into his heart', and eventually dragged him off to execution on Castle Hill in Edinburgh.

It is recorded that in 1607 Isobel Grierson was burned to death for witchcraft. Her neighbours in Prestonpans had testified that she would walk around the village at night in the guise of her own cat, and make a terrible feline noise, along with the other cats. She was also accused of entering the house of a local man named Brown, sometimes in the guise of a cat, at other times in the form of a child, and sit by his fireside for hours on end. The death of Brown was eventually ascribed to her, as the direct result of her magical spells.

■ *Prestonpans is signposted off the A198, east of Edinburgh.*

Witches being interrogated at Edinburgh. The text below the illustration lists the witches as 'Agnis Sampson, the elder Witch of them all, dwelling in Haddington, Agnes Tompson of Edinburgh (and) Doctor Fian, alias John Cunningham, maister of the School at Saltpans . . .'

Rackwick, Orkney

HY 2400

Below Ward Hill, on the island of Hoy, is a block of blue sandstone, about 28 feet long and 7 feet high/8.5 by 2 metres, which has been cut by hand into a chamber or passage, about 7 feet/2 metres long. It is said to be one of the two known rock-cut tombs in the British Isles (the other is in Glendalough, Ireland): however, it is of excellent workmanship, and might well be an initiation chamber. In modern times it is called the Dwarfie Stone, a name popularised by Sir Walter Scott in his novel *The Pirate*.

■ *Hoy is most easily approached by way of Stromness, on the mainland. The stone is a few hundred yards/ metres to the south of the Rackwick Road (from Linksness), below Ward Hill.*

The Dwarfie Stone on the island of Hoy, Orkney.

Rosslyn, Lothian

B3 NT 2663

The celebrated church of St Matthew at Rosslyn, the Rosslyn Chapel, was founded in 1446 by Sir William St Clair. The interior and facade is rich in classical and mediaeval imagery, including elements from the bestiaries, mediaeval romances, satires, the dance of death, the seven virtues and sins, and so on. The most famous tourist attraction is the so-called Apprentice Pillar around which a modern myth has been woven, in spite of Apprentice being merely a corruption of Prince: this is the pillar of the Prince of Orkney, Sir William St Clair.

Of special interest to occultists is the collection of grotesqueries and demons inside and outside the church. A pair of striking gargoyles top the north doorway, while a splendid horned demon is to the left of the (interior) window immediately to the right behind this door. The exquisite series of pentagrammic stars in the main roof (so disposed as to proclaim a numerological significance) recall a similar use of stars inside certain of the inner chambers of Egyptian pyramids. It is remarkable that this collegiate church has not been the subject of a published study of its esoteric significance. The chapel is still privately owned by the Earls of Rosslyn.

■ *Rosslyn Chapel is in Roslin, signposted to the west of the A6094, south of Edinburgh.*

Saltpans *See* Prestonpans

St Andrews, Fife △ ✡ →

C3 NO 5016

Market Square △ ✡

Although the normal disposal place for witches was the nearby Witch Hill, the Market Square was also the site of many witch burnings, at what used to be the market cross (now a fountain). Perhaps the grotesques on the fountain which has replaced the cross are grimacing at their agony. Here also one of the early martyrs, Paul Craw (a physician from Bohemia), was burned in July 1433: his name is not one of those listed on the monument now on Witch Hill. As the local historian Fleming remarks, 'A long chapter might easily be written regarding the associations that cluster round the Cross'.

The city abounds in isolated occult symbols – remaining within Market Square, for example, we must note the grotesques and masonic symbols on the walls of the house at the junction of Church Street, and the ten grotesques on the fountain in Market Street. A little further to the west we discover esoteric stars (the pentagram and the hexagram) above the doors of 23 and 25 Murray Park.

North Street →

The tower of St Salvator's College (1450) has inset into its facade a stone which is eroded into the distinctive appearance of a tortured face. This 'face', which is about twenty-four courses up the wall, is said to have been magically formed during the burning of Patrick Hamilton, one of the Protestant martyrs, in front of the College in North Street on the 29 February 1527–28 (Old Style calendar), as the official guidebook for the city says, 'burned into the stone by the psychic power of his martyrdom'.

Witch Hill △

Many of those convicted of witchcraft in St Andrews were burned on what used to be called Witch Hill, to the west of the city. Documented examples abound, but an early case is that of Nic Neville, 'comdamnit to the death and brynt' in 1569. In the same year, William Steward was hanged 'for dyvers pouynts of witchecraft and necromancie'. The old guidebooks point to this execution spot, but record that the name also applies to the ground between the Scores roadway and the sea opposite Graig-Dhu House – however, the

The ruinous cathedral at St Andrews.

hill which was there seems to have been washed away some time before 1819. The area is now much eroded by the sea, and the old 'witch pond' in St Andrew's Bay, formerly called Step Rock, where the unfortunates were swum or drowned, is now a swimming baths. Before being cast into the waters the right thumb of the suspect was tied to the big toe of the left foot, and the left thumb to the big toe of the right foot – otherwise, the proof of the swimming was not regarded as canonical.

There is no memorial to the witches burned or otherwise executed, but a stark memorial to Protestant martyrs, including Patrick Hamilton, Henry Forrest, George Wishart and Walter Mill. It is recorded that the last witch to be burned on St Andrew's Witch Hill was a woman named Young.

Near the Martyrs' Monument there was formerly a complete knoll called Methven's Tower, now half eroded, which was originally believed to be a fairy hill, yet in spite of this, during the witchcraft frenzies, witches were publicly burned on it. A storm which eroded the hill in 1856 exposed a large number of human skeletons, and a stake, all of which were taken to be the remains of burned witches.

One of the towers in the defensive wall around the ruinous cathedral is said to be haunted by a Grey Lady.

■ *St Andrews is at the eastern termination of the A91(T). The fountain is in Market Street, the houses in Murray Park are at the seaward end of the road to the north of North Street. The Martyr's Monument, the Witch Hill and the remains of Step Rock are to the western end of The Scores. The fairy hill is above the band pavilion. The haunted tower (a square tower among the defensive round towers) is to the north-east of the old walls around the cathedral.*

St Vigeans, Tayside ✡

C3 NO 6342

Beautifully displayed in a tiny museum there is a fine collection of 9th-century Pictish stones, bearing some of the symbols which, for all their Christian intentions, must be called occult. 'They demonstrate no artistic or cultural antecedents', says the guide, quite correctly. The so-called Drosten Stone is a 6-foot/2-metre slab, incised with a cross, a serpent, a dragon and a hunting scene, along with an untranslated inscription.

■ *St Vigeans is north-west of Arbroath, signposted off the A933. The museum (which appears to have no permanent curator) is part of the terrace of houses opposite the hill-raised church. Instructions for obtaining the key are (in 1987) given on the door.*

Samuelston, Lothian △

C3 NT 4871

In April 1661 John, Earl of Haddington petitioned parliament on behalf of his tenants to have the witchcraft which 'becomes daylie more frequent' on his lands, stamped out.

There followed in May, June and November of that year a number of commissions and trials of those guilty of 'the abhominable cryme of witchcraft'. Some of those found guilty were executed at a place near Samuelston named Birlie Knowe.

■ *Samuelston is signposted to the south of the A6098, south-west of Haddington.*

Scotlandwell, Fife ◉

B3 NO 1801

This is perhaps the most lovely of the Scottish holy wells. Under the protective wooden structure one may watch the magical bubbling of the waters into the sand-filled cistern, and drink the exquisite waters from the fount from a special metal cup which hangs nearby. The well has a history which merges with myth. It is said to be here that Robert Bruce was cured of leprosy, and records show that Charles II travelled from his Dunfermline Palace to take the waters, while Mary Queen of Scots visited the well, even if she did not drink of its spring. The inscription above the water fount gives the date 1858, but this refers to the reconstruction: the well, like all Scottish holy places, is very ancient.

■ *The well is signposted to the right of the A911, to the west of Kinross.*

The holy well in the village of Scotlandwell, restored in the 19th century, with several cures of historical personages to its credit.

Skirling, Borders ✡

B3 NT 0739

The extraordinary collection of ornate ironwork figures distributed throughout the village of Skirling were commissioned from the wrought-iron craftsman Thomas Hadden by Lord Carmichael, once the Governor of Bengal around the turn of the century. The oriental influence in the shapes of the dragons, lizards and birds and other symbolic forms must surely have come from Lord Carmichael's experience of Indian art and legends.

■ *Skirling is on the A72, north-east of Biggar.*

Spott, Lothian △ ◉

C3 NT 6775

Spott Loan is a road near the village of Spott, which was used in the 17th and 18th centuries as a place for burning those condemned for witchcraft. A witch-stone, set back from the road, marks the place of one such burning. The last witch to be burned south of the Forth died at Spott: her name was Marion Lille, though she was popularly known as the Ringwoody Witch. Other Spott Witches were burned on the nearby **Doon Hill**.

Spott is also the site of a holy well used as a focal point for an annual processional by the Knights Templar, who once had an important foundation at Coldingham, to the south-east of Spott. The processional, said to have been held on St John's day, passed through the churchyard and church (which then had a different orientation) before descending to the well. The medieval arch roof above the well is in reasonably good condition, though the well itself appears to be dry.

■ *Spott is signposted off the A1, south of Dunbar. The witch-stone is at the side of the road (to the south) about 100 yards/metres down the road to the Chesters Fort. The well is approached by a badly-pitted pathway to the west of the churchyard, and is about 150 yards/metres from the road, due north.*

Staffa, Strathclyde ✗

A3 NM 3436

The entire island of Staffa is so magical, so obviously a great natural wonder of the world, that one is at pains to decide which of its many geological fantasies, or which of the numerous myths, one should choose as a guide to its occult value. Anyone who walks on its strange hexagonal-paved walks, or explores the basaltic pillars which seem to support the green sward above like a cluster of exquisitely wrought pillars, will find no difficulty in understanding why the ancients believed that the island was carved by giants. Of course the artist was nature, for the island was born from a massive extrusion of basalt, which rapidly cooled, and was then sea-worn for millennia. Yet the evidence of the senses puts into doubt the romance of its natural formation, and

Fingal's Cave, as well as Clamshell Cave, MacKinnon's Cave and Cormorant's Cave, become giant-wrought cathedrals according to some, with Fingal's in particular a last-bastion castle and place of refuge for long-ships according to others. Myths and legends aside, any occultist must pause and consider the island in terms of the old stories of Atlantis. The fine occultist Blavatsky (along with many other occultists) insists that a few parts of the Scottish Highlands, and surrounding areas, are remnants of the last islands which were left after ancient Atlantis sank beneath the waves of the ocean which still bears its name: these last islands later sank, leaving only the slight traces of the Highlands of Scotland. Are the myths of the giants merely folk-memories of those Atlanteans, and of the early giants who preceded them? The antediluvian giants were the Gibborim mentioned in the Bible, and stories about such giants, Blavatsky says, are not myths: those who laugh at the stories of the giants Briareus and Orion should abstain from going to, or even, talking about, Karnac or Stonehenge. She might also have added, Staffa.

■ *Staffa is most easily reached from Iona, either by private arrangement with local sailors, or by means of tourist boats – in either case, landings are not guaranteed, as the weather is notoriously changeable.*

Storr, Isle of Skye ✗

A2 NG 5152

The old man of Storr, the most remarkable of the free-standing stacks on the Isle of Skye, has had many legends built around it. According to some, it was Baldor of the Evil Eye who is said to have turned the Old Man and his wife into stone.

■ *The stack is visible to the west of the A855 which runs down the east side of the Isle of Skye.*

Sunhoney Circle, Grampian ⊕

C2 NJ 7407

To the north of the village of Echt is a stone circle, one of the several so-called recumbent circles found in this part of Scotland. One of the eleven standing stones, about 8 feet/2.5 metres high, is touched by the recumbent flat stone (is it an ancient altar-stone?), itself about 20 feet/6 metres long, towards the southern end. The stone is said to be directed towards minimum full midsummer moon (230 degrees), and therefore the circle must have been part of a larger calendrical system. The series of twenty-eight cup marks on the recumbent are said by some to represent the asterism of Ursa Major, but this is entirely fanciful. The purpose of the cup marks is unknown, but they may have been linked with establishing orientation points.

■ *About a mile/2 km north of Echt, on the B977, to the right-hand side, is Sunhoney Farm. The circle is above the farm, up an unpaved cart-track, in a distinctive circle of trees. As the circle lies on private land, permission to view must be sought from the farm itself. There is parking to the left of the B977.*

Detail of the recumbent stone in the circle at Sunhoney, to show the ring-marks. These have been erroneously linked with certain asterisms, but are almost certainly intended as orientation marks.

Temple, Lothian

B3 NT 3158

As the name suggests, this charming hillside village was originally connected with the Knights Templar. The ruinous remains of the 13th-century church are testimony to the ancient link with this remarkable order, though from its size one would not imagine that it was the most important within the Scottish order. The church was partly rebuilt after the order was suppressed in 1309. Several of the gravestones and memorials in the burial grounds around the church are of great beauty and historical interest for those interested in secret symbols, the most famous being that showing a sophisticated carving of the deceased with his two children.

■ *Temple is signposted to the west of the A7(T), south of Edinburgh. The ruins of the old kirk are towards the bottom of the village, to the left.*

Teviot *See* Borthwick Mains

Thurso, Highland

B1 ND 1168

In Thurso Museum are some of the most beautiful Pictish carved stones of the 7th century, which contain several esoteric symbols. Among these, the most impressive is the Ulbser Stone, and the Skinnet Stone (probably of the 8th century), both of which are inscribed with crosses, merged with interlacing patterns, dragons and cosmic or Christian symbols. The double crescent (opposite the hippocampus, in the figure below) was later to be adopted into occult symbolism, though its meaning in the 8th-century Pictish culture is unknown. It is sufficiently important to stand at the bottom of the cross in the Skinnet Stone, and its resemblance to the early symbol for Pisces has led some occultists to suggest that it is an early example of the use of this symbol in connection with Christian lore. The crescent symbol occurs again and again in Pictish and Celtic imagery, and is usually linked with lunar forces: at the top right of the Ulbser Stone is a lunar crescent with a broken arrow. Again, a similar symbol was adopted into later occult lore: for example, in alchemy it was used as a symbol for Vitriol, one of the names for the crude matter of the alchemical art – though the meaning of this symbol for the Picts appears to be lost.

■ *Thurso is on the northern coast of Scotland, on the A836, to the west of Duncansby Head. The museum is housed in the public library.*

Early Christian secret symbols on the 'Ulbser Stone', in Thurso Museum.

Tomnahurich Hill, Highland ♀

B2 NH 6343

Tomnahurich Hill now rises above a modern cemetery, to the south of Inverness, but its thick woods still retain much of its fabled feeling for mystery and elemental intrigue. According to Scottish legend this wooded hill was (and perhaps still is) the site where the fairies held court, under the direction of their Queen Nicniven.

Emma Rose MacKenzie tells the story of how Donald the Fiddler fell asleep on this hill, and woke to find a grotesque figure inviting him to play the violin for him and his friends at a party. He accepted the offer, and was taken to an underground palace, where he played and played until he could play no longer, the fairy company dancing without tiring at all. Eventually, he shouted out a holy name, and he found himself lying on a river bank close to his home. Soon, however, he realised that things had changed, and it gradually dawned on him that during his night of fiddling in fairyland, a hundred years had passed in the world around. He died shortly afterwards, and is said to be buried in St Mary's, in Inverness. One can well believe this story (told as it is of many men in many different parts of the world) while sitting in the sheltered magic of this curious hill.

It is said that Thomas the Rhymer, who had the gift of prophecy from the fairies, is buried on the hill, but there were no 'official' burials here until the 19th century.

The famous prophet and magician Coinneach Odhar (see **Brahan**), who is supposed to have had his remarkable gifts of prophecy given to him by fairies, made a prediction that the fairy hill of Tomnahurich would one day be made into a cemetery – a possibility which in his day would have seemed a desecration almost impossible to visualise.

Tomnahurich Hill, the fairy hill near Inverness.

■ *The hill, with its distinctive shape, is visible to the left of the A82(T), a mile/2 km out of Inverness, towering above the signposted cemetery.*

Tranent, Lothian △

B3 NT 4072

In this town began the events leading to the most famous witch trials in Scottish history – those of the so-called **North Berwick** Witches, who were reputed to have gone to sea in sieves to bring about the death of King James VI of Scotland. The deputy-bailiff of the town was David Seaton, who was suspicious of the reputation his young servant girl Geillis Duncan had as a 'healer'. While others saw God at work in the girl, he saw only the Devil. Misusing the power of his office, Seaton tortured her until she confessed to a pact with the Devil. He then turned her over to the proper authorities, and, under more torture, she named many accomplices in her witchcraft. Among these was Agnes Sampson, whose story is told under **Edinburgh–Holyroodhouse Palace**. Barbara Napier, who was a sister-in-law of the Laird of Carschoggill, was among those accused, and charged with attempting to destroy King James by making and mutilating waxen images. The accusations must have been too fanciful even for that time, and the case was dismissed. King James, however, was already personally involved in the trial: he ordered that the court be reassembled, and that Barbara Napier should be strangled before being burned at the stake. Due to a technicality, and presumably also due to lack of real desire for her death, she eventually regained her freedom. Another of these 'witches', Dame Euphemia Maclean, the daughter of Lord Cliftonhall, was less fortunate, however, in spite of enduring the torture and refusing to confess. King James made sure that she was burned to ashes, without the usual mercy of being strangled first. It is said that these experiences of 'witchcraft' were the prime reason why King James wrote his fanatical and influential *Demonology* (1597), which had such a profound effect on witch-hunting in the next century.

■ *Tranent is signposted off the A1(T) south-east of Edinburgh.*

Waternish *See* Dunvegan

Wester Duddingstoun *See* Dalkeith

Bibliography

This is not intended as a guide to reading in the field of occultism, but merely lists the books mentioned in the preceding text.

Atkyns, Folklore Records, 1878

Augustine, St, The City of God,

Barber, Chris, Mysterious Wales, 1983

Baring-Gould, Rev. S., Yorkshire Oddities, Incidents & Strange Events, 1900

Barrett, Francis, The Magus, or celestial intelligencer, 1801

Barrett, W.F., Thoughts of a Modern Mystic, 1909

Begg, E., The Cult of the Black Virgin, 1985

Blake, William, Milton, 1804-8

Bord, Janet & Colin, Ancient Mysteries of Britain, 1986

Braddock, Joseph, Haunted Houses, 1956

Brown, Dr John, Dictionary of the Holy Bible,

Brown, T., Illustration of the Fossil Conchology of G.B. and Ireland, 1849

Chambers, R., Traditions in Edinburgh, 1825

Cockayne, O., Leechdoms, Wortcunning, and Starcraft, 1865

Crocker, W., Far from humdrum: a lawyer's life, 1967

Crowley, Aleister, Magick in Theory and Practice, (no date)

Dacres Devlin, J., Helps to Hereford History, 1848

Dalyell, J.G., Darker Superstitions of Scotland, 1883

Dee, Dr John, Monas Hieroglyphica, 1564

Eyre, Kathleen, Lancashire Legends, 1979

Fleming, D.H., Hand-Book to St Andrews and Neighbourhood, 1902

Fortune, D., Avalon of the Heart, c.1936

Gettings, F., Encyclopedia of Occult Terms, 1987

Gettings, F., Ghosts in Photographs, 1978

Glanvill, Joseph, Saducismus Triumphatus, 1683

Gordon, Rev., The Book of the Chronicles of Keith, 1880

Hall, Manley Palmer, An Encyclopedic Outline of Masonic, etc. Symbolic Philosophy, 1928

Hall, T.H., The Search for Harry Price, 1948

Harris, John, Quainton, Lipscomb's Village,

Hawken, Paul, The Magic of Findhorn, 1975

Hawkes, J., A Guide to the Prehistoric & Roman Monuments in England and Wales, 1973

Hodson, G., Fairies at Work and Play, 1925

Hopkins, G.M., St Winifride's Well – in Poems, 1967

Ishan, G., Rushton Triangular Lodge, 1970

King James VI of Scotland, Demonology, 1597

Kirk, Robert, The Secret Commonwealth, 1691

Laver, J., Museum Piece or the Education of an Iconographer, 1963

Lea, R., Country Curiosities: the Rare, Odd & Unusual in the English Countryside, 1973

Lewis, L.S., St Joseph of Arimathea at Glastonbury, 1955

Lytton, Sir Edward Bulwer, Zanoni, 1842

Lytton, Sir Edward Bulwer, The Coming Race, 1871

MacCulloch, D.B., Staffa, 1975

MacKenzie, Emma Rose, Tales of the Heather, 1892

Maltwood, K., A Guide to Glastonbury's Temple of the Stars, 1929

Maxwell, A Wonderful and True Account of the Laird of Cool's Ghost, (no date)

Miller, Hugh, Scenes and Legends of the North of Scotland, 1835

Mitchell, W.R., Haunted Yorkshire, 1969

Munn, P., The Charlotte Dymond Murder, 1978

Owen, G. & Sims, V., Science and the Spook, 1971

Pevsner, N., Derbyshire, 1953

Ponting, Gerald & Margaret, New Light on the Stones of Callanish, 1984

Scot, Reginald, The Discovery of Witches, 1584

Scott, Sir Walter, The Lay of the Last Minstrel, 1805

Sharpe, C.K., A Historical Account of the Belief in Witchcraft in Scotland, 1884

Shuttleworth, Arthur, The Warminster Mystery, 1973

Sinclair, Satan's Invisible World Discovered, 1685

Sinnett, A.P., The Pyramids and Stonehenge, 1893

Summers, M., The Geography of Witchcraft, 1927

Thorold, H., A Shell Guide: Derbyshire, 1972

Watkins, A., The Old Straight Track, 1925

White, A., A History of the Warfare of Science with Theology in Christendom, 1955

Whitlock, R., In Search of Lost Gods, 1979

Wilcock, John, A Guide to Occult Britain. The Quest for Magic in Pagan Britain, 1976

Williams, S.W., The Cistercian Abbey of Strata Florida, 1886

Acknowledgements

The pictures were all taken by Charles Walker, and supplied through Images Colour Library Ltd, Leeds and London. Several of the black and white pictures are printed from colour transparencies. The drawing by William Blake on page 69 is reproduced by permission of the Tate Gallery and the zodiacal picture on page 71 by courtesy of the Trustees of the British Museum. Charles Walker would like to thank all those individuals who have helped him during his travels and researches throughout Britain.

Index

Figures in italics refer to captions

Aberfoyle 159, *159*
Aberlemno 159, *159*
Aberlemno Stone 159
Abernethy 159
Abingdon 64
Abraham, Bishop 132
Abraham Stone 132, *132*
Adam and Eve Mews 69
Addingham 139, *139*, 148
Agglestone 57
Ahriman 49
Akelda, St 144
Alchemy 6, 7, 8, 9, 11, 12, 22, 26, 36, 49, 53, 58, *58*, 70, 74, 91, 112, 155, 185
Aldborough 140
Alfred, King 59
Algol 11
Alkborough 20, 140, *140*
Allen, Ralph 42-3, *43*
Alpha and omega 132, *132*
Alsop, Dr 42
American Museum, Claverton 43
Amulets 9, *10*, 20, 22, 23, 24, 36, 39, 45, 70, 105, 108, 109, 111, 117, *117*, 123, *145*, 151
Ananyzapta 105, 150, 151
Ancient Mysteries of Britain (Bord) 52
Angels 12, 16-17, 36, 58, *104*, 122, 144, 149
Anne, St 135
Annunciation 90
Anthroposophical Society of Great Britain 77
Apollyon 71
Aquarius 15, 132, 144, 170
Arabian Bird *see* Phoenix
Archangels 16, 45
Archer (writer) 82
Aries 14, 15, 57, 70, 71, 170
Arkville maze 92
Arnold of Villanova 150
Arthur, King 37, 38, 39, 41, 46, 48, 51, 53, 57, 80, 84, 118, 119, 122, 132, 144, 171
Arthur's Quoit 131
Arthur's Spear 132
Arthur's Stone 122, *122*, 131
Ascendant 22
Asenora, Princess, of Brittany 60
Astrology 6, 7, 8, 11, 12-15, 25, 74, 75, 79, 83, 91, 98, 109, 140, 179
Atlantis 17, 22, 28, 51, 53, 141, 184
Aubrey, John 70, 112
Auchencrow 7, *7*, 160
Augustine, St 41-2
Auldearn 160
Ault Hucknall 103
Avebury 17, 32, *32*, 54
Avin, Glen 161
Ayrton, Michael 92, *92*

Bacon, Francis 64, 79
Baildon Moor 146, *146*
Bailey's Well 161
Balcarras, Lord 170
Baldor of the Evil Eye 184
Baldwin, Archbishop 135
Barber, Chris 122, 133
Barden Bridge 140
Barfreston 64
Baring-Gould, Rev 49, 156
Barrett, Francis 69, 71, 77
Bartholomew, St 70
Bartholomew's Hospital, St 69-70

Basilisk *13*, 15, 22, 32, 72, *72*, 108, 112, 144
Basingstoke 64
Bath 14, 18, 36, *36*, 42
Beamsley 140
Bearsted 64
Beattie, John 40, *40*
Bede, Venerable 155
Beetham 140
Begg, Ean 106
Begu, nun 155
Behal *71*
Bell-man 103, *103*
Belvoir Castle 104
Bench-ends 11, *11*, 16, *16*, 26, 37, 43, 44, *44*, 48, 49
Bendigeidfran 80
Bere, Abbot 46, 47
Berkeley 116
Berkeley Square 69, 70
Besant, Annie 78
Betws-y-Coed 116, *116*
Betyles 107
Beverwaert, Lady Mauritia de 170
Bexley 65
Bideford 37, *37*
Binsey 103
Birlie Knowe 183
Birmingham 14
'Birthing places' 20
Bishop's Lydeard 37
Bishopthorpe 140
Bisterne Dragon 66
Bisterne Park 66
Black Rock 128
Black Virgins 106
Blackett, Sir Walter 154
Blackie, John 172
Bladud, King 36
Blaikie, Dr Walter 170
Blake, William 65, 68, 69, 77
Blavatsky, Madame 55, 74, 81-2, 94, 141, 184
'Bleeding tree' 130, *130*
Blond, Frederick Bligh 46
Bloomsbury 70
Bloxham 27, 103
Bodmin 37
Bodmin Moor 37-8, *38*, 39, 41, *41*, 53, 58
Boehme, Jacob 72
Boggarts 144
Boleyn, Anne 79, 92
Bolingbroke, Roger 151-2
Bolton Priory 141
Bolventor 38
Book of the Chronicles of Keith, The (Gordon) 178
Booker, Rev D. 133
Booker, John 90
Bord, Colin 52
Bord, Janet 52
Borderland 76
Borley 87
Boroughbridge 141, *141*
Borthwick Mains 160
Bosbury 116
Boswell, James 160
Botha, Piet 76, *76*
Bothwell, James Hepburn, 4th Earl of 175
Bottesford 7, 8, 103-4, *103*
Boudicca 90
Bourn 20, 87
Boursnell, Robert 76
Bracken, Lord 72
Braddock, Joseph 82
Bradford 141
'Bradford heads' 145, *145*
Bradsby maze 153
Brahan 160-61
Bran, the Blessed Raven 80
Brannock, St 39
Brantham 87, *87*
Braunton 39

Bread Street 70-71, *72*
Brechfa 116-17
Bretforton 117
Brewham Forest 39
Briareus 184
Brightling 65
Brighton 68
Brimham Rocks 133, *141*
Brinsop 117
Bristol 40, *40*, 46
British Museum 20, 71, *71*, 179
British Theosophical Society 64
Brock, Mr 120, *120*
Brodie, Laird of 173
Brogar 161
Bromfield 117
Brown, Dr John 159
Brown, Thomas 155
Brown Willy 53
Browne (esotericist) 72
Brudenell, George 109
Brudenell House 26
Brughe, John 174
Brutus of Troy 79, 80
Bryson, Margaret 170
Buck, Nathaniel *19*, *126*
Buckstone 133, *133*
Bull symbol 15, 91, 132, 142, 161
Bunbury 117, *117*
Bungay 88
Burghead 19, 161
Burghead bull 172, *172*
Burley 66
Burne-Jones, Sir Edward 108
Burton, Sir Richard 83
Burwash 66
Bury St Edmunds 88, *88*, 95
Bussell, Frederick Vernon 108
Butleigh 40
Butler, Samuel 159
Buxton (clairvoyant) 120
Buxton, Mrs (psychic assistant) 45

Cabbala 72
Cader Idris *see* Caider Idris
Caduceus of Hermes 149
Caerlea Hill 176
Caerleon 84, 118
Caider Idris 118, *118*
Cairngorms 161
Calendrical computers 55
Callanish 17, 40, 55, 162, *162*
Callow End 118
Calne 42
Cambo Beasts 154, *154*
Cambridge 88, 99
Camelford 37, 41, *41*
Campbell, Gilbert 175
Campbell, Thomas 175
Cancer 15, 173
Cannon St 72, *72*
Canterbury 66, *66*, 140
Cantref-y-Gwaelod 124
Capricorn *13*, 15, 74, 79
Caractacus Stone 60
Card, David 156
Carew Cross 119, *119*
Carmarthen 119
Carmichael, Lord 184
Carnedd-y-Wiber 129
Carrawburgh 141-2
Carreg Cennen 119
Carstair, Abigail 156
Catherine of Aragon 93
Cave of Merlin 116
Cayton Bay 152
Cefyn Bryn 131
Cerne Abbas 41-2
Cerne Abbas Giant 41, *41*, 42
Chakra 22
Chalfont St Giles 20, 104, *104*
Chambercombe Manor 48, *48*
Chambers, Robert 170
Chanonry Point 160

Chapel of Garioch 166
Charles Edward Stuart, Prince 173
Charles II, King 75, 170, 183
Charlotte St 72-3, *73*
Charms *17*, 20, 24, 67, 88, 150
Charnock, Thomas 36
Charston Rock 128
Chartres Cathedral 106
Cheapside 73, *73*
Cheesewring 38, *38*, 42, 50
Chelmsford 89, *89*, 92, 96
Cheltenham Ghost 119
Cherhill 42
Chesterton, G.K. 111
Chetnole 42
Chichester 67, 105
Childe of Hale 144
Chriomantia 18
Christ, symbols for 9, 12, 13, 23, 26, 42, *42*, 57, 160
Christchurch 12, 13, 27, 42, *42*
Chronos 107
Chun Castle 50
Chun Quoit 50
Churchill, Sir Winston 72
City (of London) 74
Clairvoyance 22, 77
Clamshell Cave 184
Clarke, Elizabeth 95
Claverton 42-3, *43*
Clederus, St 52
Cleopatra's Needle 81
Clerkenwell 74
Clifton House 93
Cluny Hill 173
Clydach 119
Cobham 67
Cock, Janet 166
Cock Lane 74
Cockatrice 84, 149
Cockayne (historian) 177
Coggeshall 89, 142
Coinneach Odhar 160, 161, 186
Coirbridge 145
Colchester 90
Coldingham 160, 184
Cole, Francis 58
Colebrooke 43
Coleman-Smith, Pamela 73, *73*
Collen, St 46
Columba, St 177
Coman, Old Widow 89
Combermere 120
Combermere, Lord 120
Combermere Ghost 69, 120, *120*
Coming Race, The (Lytton) 94
Cony, Joan 89
Conyers, Sir John 154
Conyers Falchion 143
Cook, Florence 65
Cool Ghost 176
Corbet, Sybell 120
Corineus 75
Cormoran 52-3
Cormorant's Cave 184
Cornfoot, Janet 180
Cosmi Utriusque Maioris (Fludd) *18*
Cottingley 69, 142, *142*
Couper, John 176
Coventry 104-5, 151
Cowan, William 176
Cox, Julian 39
Cradle Stone 161
Craig, Marjory 180
Craw, Paul, 182
Crewe 120, *120*
Crewe Circle 120
Crickhowell 120
Crieff 166
Crocker, Sir William 87
Croesfeilig, 129
Cromlechs 122, *122*, 131, *131*, 132
Cromwell, Oliver 65, 136
Cromwell House 65

Crook of Alves 159-60
Crookes, Sir William 65, 69
Crowborough 69
Crowcombe 43-4
Crowcombe Worm 44
Crowland 90
Crowley, Aleister 68, 73, 112
Crown symbol 9
Crystie, Jonet 159
Cuckney 105
Culbone 44, 51
Cullender, Rose 95
Culross 166
Cunningham, John see Fian, Dr John
Curse-dolls, 20, 22
Curses 125, 128
Curzon, Elizabeth 70

Daedalus 92
Daiyta 51
Dalby 143
Dalkeith 166
Dalmeny 166-7, 167
Dalyell (historian) 166, 167
Damer, Anne 106
Damnonii tribe 168
Dan (Israelite tribe) 13, 15, 144
Danby, William 149-50, 150
Dance of Death 108, 145, 181
Dance patterns 20, 20, 25, 52, 87, 112, 140
Darandus, William 13
Darnley, Lord, 170, 175
Dartford 67
Dashwood, Sir Francis 112
David, Christopher 126
Death's head 11, 151
Dee, John 40, 70, 72, 77, 82-3, 154, 155
Deerhurst 121
Demonology/demons 6, 7, 12, 16-17, 16, 21, 22, 24, 40, 48, 50, 71, 75, 77, 81, 83, 84, 88, 91, 94, 95, 96, 100, 104, 105, 108, 122, 122, 125, 140, 148, 173, 177, 178, 178, 181
Demonology (James I) 186
Denbigh 121
D'Esperance, Elizabeth 151
Deuterosophia 160
Deva 22
Devil, the, 17, 26, 28, 32, 37, 37, 39, 42, 48, 57, 60, 65, 88, 93, 98, 100, 100, 103, 111, 112, 116, 118, 121, 121, 128, 135, 136, 141, 147-8, 149, 152, 160, 166, 168, 168, 173, 174, 176-7, 180, 186
Devil of Glenluce 175
Devil's Arrows 141, 141
Devil's Bridge, Cumbria 147
Devil's Bridge, Dyfed 121, 121
Devil's Bridge, W. Glamorgan 136
Devil's Door 45, 52, 58
Devil's mark 23, 28, 95, 170, 176
Devil's Punchbowl 121
Devil's Quoit 128
Devil's teat 23
Devlin, Dacres 130
Dinas Emrys 129
Dinedor 18, 121, 124
Dinton 105
Discovery of Witches (Hopkins) 95
Discovery of Witches, The (Scot) 83
Diseworth 12, 105
Divining rods 81
Doarlish Cashen 143
Dolphin symbol 13
Doniert, King 37-8, 52
Doniert Stone 37
Doon Hill 167, 167, 184
Doré, Gustave 104

Dornoch 167-8, 168
Dornoch Imp 168
Dorstone 122, 122
Doubler Stones 139, 139
Douglas, Lady Jane 170, 174
Dover 67-8
Doyle, Sir Arthur Conan 68-9, 142, 142
Dozmary Pool, 37, 38, 39, 39, 52, 53
Dragon Hill 111
Dragons 6, 21, 21, 23, 25, 32, 39, 43-4, 45, 49, 51, 53, 59, 66, 89, 93, 96, 103, 105, 108, 111, 112, 116, 117, 121, 125, 128-31 passim, 128, 143, 149, 154, 159, 168, 179, 183, 184, 185
Draper, Hugh 79, 80
Dronley 168
Dropping Well 148
Drosten Stone 183
Druid Stone 88
Druids 55, 56, 133, 137
Druid's Circle, Gwynedd 130, 130
Druid's Circle, N. Yorkshire 149, 150, 150
Druid's Lodge 131
Druid's Moor 131
Drury, William 83, 84
Du Maurier, Daphne 39
Dubricius, St 51
Duff, King 177
Duff, Margaret 177
Duffryn 122
Duffus Castle 160
Dumbarton 168, 168
Dun Cow 112
Dunbar 168
Duncan, Geillis 186
Dundee, John Graham, Viscount 170
Dunning 166, 169, 169
Dunvegan 169, 169
Dunvegan Castle 143
Duny, Amy 95
Durandus, William 144
Durgan 44
Durham 143, 143, 154
Dwarfie Stone 181, 181
Dymond, Charlotte 41
Dymond Monument 41, 41

Eagle as symbol 9, 13, 15, 46, 91
Eamont Bridge 152
Earth-zodiac 40, 40
Earthworks 32, 66, 121
East Quantoxhead 26, 27, 44, 44
Ebbing and Flowing Well 144
Echt 184
Edenhall 143
Edgehill 105, 105, 106, 112
Edinburgh 8, 8, 170-71, 170, 171, 174, 181, 181
Edington 45
Edward, the Black Prince 66
Edward II, King 104
Edward III, King 66
Edward the Confessor, St 132
Edwards, Susanna 37
Egloskerry 45
Eildon Hills 171, 171
Eilean Donan 171, 171
Elementals 22, 144, 149, 153-4, 156, 172
Elements 22, 23, 27, 91, 103, 169
Elfrida, Queen 84
Elgin 160, 172, 172, 177
Eliot, Helen 166
Elizabeth I, Queen 70, 77, 82, 92, 100
Elmswell 9, 10, 90, 90
Ely 20, 25, 91, 91
Erlestone 9, 45
Erskine, Robert 170

Erwarton 92
Etheric 23, 26, 44, 52
Eusebius 107
Evans, David 75
Eveling 144
Evil eye 36, 111, 149, 151
Excalibur 37, 38, 53
Exmouth 44, 45
Eye of God 151, 151
Eyre, Kathleen 123

Fairfax, Edward 148
Fairford 122, 122
Fairies 6, 22, 40, 46, 68, 69, 131, 140, 142, 142, 143, 144, 149, 153-4, 159, 161, 169, 186
Fairies (Hodson) 146
Fairwell, Marjorie 166
Fairy Bridge 169
Fairy Flag 169, 169
Fairy Hill 159, 159
'Fairy photographs' 69, 142, 142
Fairy Steps 140
Famh 161
Fauns 28
Fawkes, Guy 80
Felpham 68
Ffestiniog 122, 123
Fian, Dr John (John Cunningham) 175, 180-81, 181
Findhorn 160, 172
Fingal's Cave 172, 173, 184
Fish symbol 12-13, 15, 23, 25, 26, 46, 57, 72, 73, 73, 111, 127, 145, 145, 146, 160, 169
Fitzgerald, Edward 95
Fitzjames Arch 7, 8, 109
Flamstead, John 75, 75
Fleming (historian) 182
Fletcher, Elizabeth 148
Floating islands 129, 129
Fludd, Robert 18, 18, 64-5, 64, 109
'Fool, The' 11, 48, 73
Formby 123
Forres 17, 28, 160, 173, 177
Forrest, Henry 183
Fort, Charles 96
Fort William 173
Fortune, Dion 46
Foster, Ann 108
Four Evangelists 13, 13, 46, 92, 132, 136
Francis, Elizabeth 89, 92, 93
Fraser (historian) 177
Frideswide, St 103
Frog Stone 133, 133
Fulcanelli (occultist) 89
Fuller, Mad Jack 65
Furry Dance 48
Fylde Witch 153, 156
Fynee, William 92
Fyvie Castle 173, 173

Gabriel, Archangel 16, 45
Gardener, Sir Robert 9, 90
Gargoyles 8, 8, 17, 37, 42, 46, 49, 98, 99, 99, 103, 103, 108, 108, 111, 122, 124, 149, 167, 168, 181
Garnstone 130
Garrow Tor 53
Garstang 144
Gaun's Stone 178
Gemini 15, 72, 74
Genethlialogia 18
Geoffrey of Monmouth 55, 75
Geomancy (geomantia) 18, 18, 23, 88
George, Sir Ernest 108
Gettings, Fred 110, 142
Ghost Writer (Archer) 82
Ghosts see Hauntings
Giants 41, 41, 42, 52-3, 55, 75, 97, 99, 132, 134-5, 141, 144, 152, 184

Gibborim 184
Giggleswick 13, 13, 15, 144
Giraldus of Wales 129
Glamis Castle 174, 174
Glanvill, Rev Joseph 36, 39, 53, 60, 83, 84
Glastonbury 13, 20, 46, 47, 134, 152
Glastonbury Thorn 46, 109
Glastonbury Tor 20, 40, 46, 47
Glastonbury Zodiac see Earth-zodiac
Glendalough 181
Glendevon 11, 174-5, 175
Glendurgan House 44
Glenluce 175
Gloucester 123, 123
Gloucester, Duchess of 151
Gloucester Place 74
Gnomes 22, 23, 154
Goat symbol 13, 15
Goat-fish symbol 13, 15
Godstone 123
Goello, King 60
Goemot 75
Gog 75, 81, 97, 97, 99, 99
Gordon, George, 2nd Earl of Huntly 120
Gordon, Rev 178
Gorgon 23, 36, 84
Goudie, Isobel 160, 176
Gradhthol 161
Grange Hill 109
Granny Kempock Stone 177, 177
Gravestones/graveyards 7, 8, 8, 9, 11, 20, 42, 42, 43, 103, 151, 152, 153, 161, 176, 176, 177, 180, 185
Great Bear constellation 18
Great Fire of London 74, 74, 75
Great Grey Man 161
Great Orme 8, 9, 124, 124
Great Rollright 106, 106
Great Salkeld 144
Great Seal of America 155
Green-Children of Woolpit 100
Green Man 24, 24, 37, 43, 48, 96, 106, 111, 111, 127, 127, 167-8
Greenwich 75
Grey, Lady Jane 48, 80
Greyhound's Kennel 132
Grierson, Isobel 181
Griffins 134, 134, 154, 154
Griffiths, Frances 142, 142
Grimoires 24, 40
Grimstone 136
Grotesques 48, 49, 53, 57, 91, 94, 94, 99, 111, 125, 126, 127, 145, 148, 168, 181, 182
Guata, Stanislas de 9
Guide to Occult Britain, A (Wilcock) 161
Guildford 68
Guildhall 75
Guinevere, Queen 46
Gurney (psychic researcher) 69
Guron, St 37
Guy of Warwick 112
Gwyn ap Nudd 46

Hackness 155
Hackwood Park 64
Hadden, Thomas 184
Haddington 175, 181
Haddington, John, Earl of 183
Hadrian's Wall 141
Hadstock 20, 92, 92
Hale 144
Hall, Manley Palmer 155
Hall, Trevor 87
Hamilton, Patrick 182, 183
Hardknott 144-5
Hardmuir 160
Hardwick Hall 103

Harkstead 92, _92_
Harold Stones 135, _135_
Harper, Margaret 153
Hart, Margaret 166
Hartland (historian) 143
Hastings 68, 73
Hatfield Peverel 92-3
Haunted Yorkshire (Mitchell) 141
Hauntings 6, 20, 36, 39, 48, 49,
    53, 58, 67, 69-70, _69_, 74, 75,
    77, 79, 80, 82, 83-4, 87, 93,
    93, 105, _105_, 106, 109, 112,
    116, _116_, 118, 119, 141, 143,
    145, 153-6 _passim_, 166, 170,
    171, 174, _175_, 176, 178, 183
Hawken, Paul 172
Hawkes, Jacquetta 50, 54, 131, 141
Hawksworth 145
Haworth 145, _145_
Hay-on-Wye 124, 129
Hayward, William 106
Hecataeus 55
Helena, mother of Constantine
    134
Heliopolis 81
Helith 41, 84
Hell-Fire Club 112
Helston 48
Hemans, Felicia 118
Henley on Thames _10_, 106, _106_
Henry VI, King 94, 151
Henry VII, King 88
Henry VIII, King 79, 92, 93, 103,
    134, 154
Heraclius 54
Herd, Annys 96
Hereford 18, 59, 121, 124-5
Hermes 49
Hermes Bird _see_ Phoenix
Hermetic Order of the Golden
    Dawn 72-3
Hermitage Castle 175, _175_
Hexham 145-6, _145_
Highclere 68
Highclere Grampus 68
Highgate 75
Hilda, Abbess 155
Hill figures 42, 59, 84, 99, _99_,
    111, _111_, 147, _147_
Hilton 93
Hindhead 68-9
Hindley, Charles 148
Hobbes, Thomas 103
Hodgson, Thomas 147
Hodson, Geoffrey 142, 146, 149,
    153, 154, 156
Holeway, Prior 36
Holland, Lord 75
Holland House 75
Holloway Road 76, _76_
Hollybush 126, _126_
Holst, Gustav 98
Holy Grail legends 13, 46, 48,
    81, 134
Holy Well 161
Holyrood House Palace 170, _170_,
    171
Holywell 18, 126, _126_
Home-Cultram 179
Hope (clairvoyant) 120
Hope, William 44, _45_
Hope under Dinmore 125
Hopkins, Gerard Manley 126
Hopkins, Witch-finder Matthew
    89, 95, _95_, 108
Horne, Janet 168
Horoscopes 8, 12, _12_, 40, 65, 75,
    _75_, 79, 81, 90, 105, 109
Horseheath 69
Horseman symbol 13, _15_
Horseshoe symbol 20-21, 109
Horus 106
Hoy 181, _181_
Hoyle, P.J.C. 123
Hudson (spirit photographer) 76

Humbie 176
Humphrey, John 90
Huntingdon 99
Huntly, George Gordon, 2nd
    Earl of 120
Hurless 38, 50
Hutchinson, Margaret 166
Huw Lloyd's Pulpit Stone 122, _123_
Hyde-Lees, Georgie 73
Hyssington 127

I Ching 70, 72
Ilfracombe 48, _48_
Ilkley 146
Ilkley Moor 139, 146
Images House 117, _117_
In Search of Lost Gods
    (Whitlock) 145
Incantations 24, 117
Inchbrakie family 166
Initiation 23, 25, 55, 72, 73, 89,
    99, 106, 117, 127
Innerleithen 176
Innerwick 176, _176_
Inshoch 176
Introductorius (Scot) 179
Inverness 177, 186
Inverskip 176-7
Iona 177
Irving, Sir Henry 141
Irving family 143
Ishan, Sir Gyles 110
Isir 152
Isis 106, _106_

Jack o' Kent 135
Jackson, Margaret 180
Jackson, William 67
Jamaica Inn 39
James (psychic researcher) 69
James I, King 65, 83, 95, 145,
    156, 170, 176, 180, 186
James V, King of Scotland 174
Jamieson, Alexander 178
Jerome, St 104
Joan of Arc 112
Jocelyn, Bishop 59
John, St 46, 90, _132_
John, St, of Jerusalem 77
John de Clifford 141
John of Nottingham 104
John of the Thumbs, Sir 121
Johnson, Dr Samuel 74, 160
Jones, Richard 36, 53
Joseph of Arimathea 46, 47, 48,
    _48_, 109
_Journal of the American Society
    for Psychical Research_ 40
Judge (theosophist) 74
Julian's Bower 140, _140_

Kandinsky, Wassily 77
Keats, John 172
Keighley 146, _146_
Keith 178
Kelly, Edward 154, _154_
Kemp, Ursley 96
Kempock 17, 28, 177-8
Kennet Avenue 32
Ker, Jonet 166
Keswick 146-7
Keswick Carles 146
Kilburn 147, _147_
Kilkhampton 11, _11_, 48, _48_
Kilpeck 13, 25, _25_, 26, 127, _127_,
    167
Kimbolton 93, _93_
King Arthur's Hall 37
King Arthur's Tomb 53
King James Bible 65
King Stone 107
King's College Chapel
    (Cambridge) 88
King's Lynn 24, 93, _93_
King's Men 107

Kinross 178, _178_
Kirby Lonsdale 147
Kirby Malham 147-8
Kirk, Colonel Sir Lewis 105
Kirk, Robert 159, _159_
Kirkcudbright 178
Kirklington 107, _107_
Knapp 122
Knaresborough 148
Knebworth 28, 94
Kneelers, church 12-13, 20, 97
Knelston 131
Knights Hospitallers 57, 110
Knights Templars 38, 81, 96,
    184, 185
Knock Hill 166
Knock of Alves 159, 160
Knock of Crieff 166
Knowles, Rev 147

Lacy, Colonel 148
Lady Well 100
Lake spirits 156
Lamb, John 144
Lambert, R.S. 143
Lamont, Marie 176 _177_
Lanark 178-9
Lang, Andrew 69
Lanyon Quoit 50
Lauchlan, Jeane 179
Lauderdale House 168
Launceston 26, 49, _49_
Laurie, Mrs 126
Laver, James 68
Law, William 72
Lay of the Last Minstrel, The
    (Scott) 179
Lea, Raymond, 112
Leadbeater, C.W. 77, 78
Leamington Spa 68
Leeds Castle 82
Leland, John 141
Lemniscate 24, 98, 148
Lenthall, Sir Rowland 125
Leo 14, 15, 46, 170, 176
Leschman, Rowland 145
Lethbridge, T.C. 99, _99_
Leverson, Mrs 120, _120_
Leviathan (Hobbes) 103
Levitation 36, 53, 166
Lewannick 49, 49
Lewis, Isle of 162, _162_
Lewis, Rev L.S. 46
Lewtrenchard 49
Ley-lines 18, 24, 32, 50, 55, 59,
    121, 122, 124, 125, _125_, 128,
    131, 135, 141, 152, 172
Leyden, Dr John 175
Libra _12_, 15, 170
Liddell, Dean 108-9, _109_
Ligonier, Lord 67
Lille, Marion 184
Lilly, William 12, 74, _74_, 81, 90,
    105
Lily as symbol 90
Lincoln 94, _94_, 106
Lincoln Imp 94
Lincoln's Inn 77
Lindsey, Colonel 136
Lion as symbol 9, _10_, 11, 15, 46,
    91, 92
Little Oakley 96
Little Rollright 107, _107_
Little Salkeld 18, 148
Littleborough church 8, _8_, 16,
    17, 148
Llandeilo Graban 128, _128_
Llanelian-yn-Rhos 128
Llanfihangel Rogiet 128, _128_
Llanfihangel-y-pennant 118
Llanrhaeadr-ym Mochnant 131
Llowes 129
Lloyd, Huw 122
Lloyd, Temperance 37
Llyn Cau 118

Llyn Cynwch 129
Llyn Dinas 129
Llyn Dywarchen 129, _129_
_Lo!_ 96
Loanhead Stone Circle 167
Lockie, Jonet 178
Lockyer, Norman 50, 141
Lohan 70
London
    Adam and Eve Mews 69
    Bartholomew's Hospital, St
        69-70
    Berkeley Square 69, 70
    Bloomsbury 70
    Bread Street 70-71, 72
    British Museum 20, 71-72, _71_,
        179
    Cannon Street 72, _72_
    Charlotte Street 72-3, _73_
    Cheapside 73, _73_
    City 74
    Cock Lane 74
    Gloucester Place 74
    Greenwich 75
    Guildhall 75
    Highgate 75
    Holland House 75
    Holloway Road 76, _76_
    Lincoln's Inn 77
    London Stone, The 79
    Marble Arch 77
    Marylebone 77
    Muswell Hill 77
    Park Road 77
    Parliament Hill Fields 20, 77
    Pond Square 79
    Temple 81
    Tower of London 79-80, _79_,
        _80, 81_
    Victoria Embankment 81
    Westminster Abbey 81-2
    Wilton Row 82
London Stone, The 79
Lonely Shepherd 119
Long Man, The 84
Long Marston 94, 99
Long Meg 148
Longridge 149
Longstone 177-8, _177_
Lowestoft 95
Lucas, Sir Charles 90
Luck 24, 144
Luck of Burrell Green 143, _144_
Luck of Edenhall 143, _144_
Luke, St 46
Lunar clock 93
Lunar-solar cycles 55
Luppitt 49-50
Lyonesse 51, 53
Lytton, Lord 70, 94

Macbeth 159, 160, 174
MacCulloch, Donald 172
Macdhui, Ben 172
MacKenzie, Emma Rose 186
MacKinnon's Cave 184
Maclean, Dame Euphemia 186
MacLeod clan 169
Madron 50
Maen Sigl 124, _124_
Maeshowe 179
Maeshowe Dragon 179
Magi, the 67, 105
Magick in Theory and Practice
    (Crowley) 68
Maglocunus 130
Magog 75, 81, 97, _97_, 99, _99_
Maiden Stone 166
Maidstone 82
Maidstone, Viscountess 132, _132_
Maltwood, Catherine 40
Malwalbee (ogress) 129
Malwalbee Pebble 129
Malwalbee Stone 124
Manchester 149

Manningtree 149
Mansfield Woodhouse 108, *108*
Marble Arch 77
Margaret, St 117
Margate 82
Mariteut, King 119
Mark, St 46
Mark stone 25, 116, 124, 135, 160
Marlborough 50
Marmion (Scott) 155
Mars (planet) 17
Marshall, Robert 104
Mary Queen of Scots 82, 170, 175, 183
Marylebone 77
Masham 149-50, *150*
Masons 8, *8*, 43, 81, 148
Massey, Charles Carleton 64
Massey, Gerald 64
Maternus, Firmicus 140
Mathers, Liddell (MacGregor) 73
Mathie, Jonet 180
Mathie, Margaret 159
Matthew, St 46, 132
Maud de Valeri 129
Maxwell, Mr 176
Maxwell, Sir George 180
Mazes 6, 20, *20*, 25, 36, 44, 49, *49*, 52, 84, 87, 91, *91*, 92, 92, 93, 97, *97*, 112, 140, *140*, 153
Medlycott, Sir Hubert 53
Medusa 84
Medusa Mask 36
Mee, Arthur 53
Meg of Maldon 148
Megalithic tombs *see* Cromlechs
Meilig, St 129
Melothesic Man *12*
Melrose Abbey 179, *179*
Men-an-Tol 50, *50*
Men-fish 108
Menhirs 17, 55, 177-8
Merlin 50, 117, 119, 129, 144
Merlin's Cave 57
Merlin's Hill 117, 119
Mermaids 25, 45, 60, 98, 99, 103, 108, 149
Merton 95
Merton College, Oxford 7, 8, 13, 109
Methven's Tower 183
M'Ewen, Elspeth 178
Michael, Archangel 16, 45, 49, 52, 58
Michael, St 75, 111, 149
Middleham 150-51
Milgate House 64
Mill, Walter 183
Millar, Mary 178
Miller, Hugh 160
Milton (Blake) 68
Milton, John 104, *104*
Milton's House 20, 104, *104*
Minions 37, 38, 42, 50
Mitchell, W.R. 141
Mithraic cult 89, 127, 142
Mithras 25, 80, 142
Modred 53
Modron 144
Monas Hieroglyphica (Dee) 82-3, *82*
Monks of Medmenham 112
Moon *18*, 20, 21, 49, 79, 91, 173
Moon Clock 93
Morax 17
Moray Society 172
Mordiford 21, 130
Morgan la fée 144
Mortlake 82-3
Morvah 51
Moyse's Hall Museum 88, *88*
Mumler, William 76
Munn, Pat 41
Murigen 144

Musgrave family 143
Music of the spheres 149
Muswell Hill 77
Myers, Frederic Henry 69, 147
Mysterious Wales (Barber) 122
Myths 6, 8, 18, 42, 51, 53, 54, 116, 155, 168, 184

Nant Gwynant 129
Nanteos Chalice 134, *134*
Napier, Barbara 186
Necromancy 154, 182
Nether Keith 176
Nevern 130, *130*
Neville, Nic 182
Newall, Laurence 8, 148
Newark-on-Trent 8, 108, *108*
Newbury 83
Newcastle-upon-Tyne 151
Newchurch-in-Pendle 151, *151*
Newes from Scotland (James I) 180
Newquay 51
Newton, Isaac 75
Nicniven, Queen of Fairies 186
Nine Maidens 50
Nine Stane Rig 175
Niven, Catharine 166
North Berwick 170, 175, 176, 180, *180*, 186
North Brentor 51
North Tidworth 83
Northampton 108
Norwich 96, *96*
Nostradamus 68
Notre Dame, Paris 89
Nottingham 14
Noyes, Alfred 142, *142*
Nutter, Alice 151

Og, Robin 161
Ogham 25, 49, 53, 99, 130
Ogilvie (minister) 176
Ogma 99
Olaus Magnus 17, 141
Olcott, Henry 74
Old Straight Track, The (Watkins) 122
Oran, St 177
Order of the Holy Cross 9
Orion 184
Orr, Alan 177
Osbornes of Long Marston 94, 99
Ossington, Viscountess 108
Ouraboros 25, *25*, 52, 127
Owen (psychic investigator) 67, 82, 118
Owen, George 131
Oxford 8, 13, 108-9, *109*

Pacy, Deborah 95
Pacy, Elizabeth 95
Paittersone, Mailie 178
Pancake Stone 146
Paracelsus 9, 94
Paradise Lost (Milton) 20, 104, *104*
Paradise Regained (Milton) 20, 104, *104*
Paris, Matthew 96
Park Road 77
Parker, Jonathan 97
Parkes, Thomas 40
Parliament Hill Fields 20, 77
Parr, Catherine 154
Parsons, Elizabeth 74
Partill, Agnes 166
Partridge, John 83
Pateley Bridge 141
Paterson (witch pricker) 177
Patricio 135
Patrick, St 168
Paycock House 89
Pearce, Alfred 75, *75*

Peel Castle 151-2
Peg Tode Stone 160
Pelican symbol 26, 39, 58, *58*
Pen-y-Gaer 132
Pendle Hill 151, 152, *152*
Penmaenmawr 130, *130*
Penrith 152
Penryhyn-Gwyr 136
Pentagrams 9, 23, 26, 49, *49*, 51, 90, 155, 181, 182
Pentre Ifan 131, *131*
Perranuthnoe 22, 51
Perranzabuloe 51
Perrault, Charles 99
Perrers, Alice 66
Peterborough 96
Petroc, St 37
Pevsner, Nicholas 103
Philosopher's Stone *11*
Phoenix 26, 27, 49, *49*
Physiognomia 18
Pimperne 112
Piran, St 51
Pirate, The (Scott) 181
Pisces 12, 13, 15, 23, 26, *26*, 27, 38, 42, *42*, 57, 72, 73, *73*, 79, 111, 127, 185
Pistyll Rhaeadr 131
Pittenweem 180, *180*
Planets, The (Holst) 98
Pollockshaws 180
Poltergeists 74, 82, 83-4, 119, 175
Pond Square 79
Ponting, Gerald 162
Ponting, Margaret 162
Poole, Alice 92
Poppets 17, 20, 22, 26, 27, 77, 88, 88, 104, 117, 125
Porlock 44, 51
Portishead 128
Portskewett 128
Poulton-le-Fylde 156
Prentice, Joan 89
Prestonpans 180-81
Price, Harry 87, *87*, 143
Prime, Mathias 98
Prior Court 118
Pub signs 9, *10*

Quainton 9, *10*, 20, 26, 109, *109*
Queen's College, Cambridge 88, 99
Quintessence 26, *26*, 27, 44, 91, 103, 112

Rackwick 181
Rag Well 144
Ragley Hall 36
Rahere 69, 70
Raleigh, Sir Walter 64, 79
Ramsay, David 81
Ramsbury 51
Raphael, Archangel 16, 45
Ravens 80, *81*
Rebus 26, 48, 58, 109
Red Dragon of Wales 129
Redgate 37
Reincarnation 26, 27, 145
Reuben (Israelite tribe) 144
Reynoldstone 131
Rhinoceros 9, *10*, 90
Rhossili 131
Rich, Lady Diana 75
Richard de Sowe 104
Richie (writer) 160, 173
Ridgeway 111
Ring of Brogar 161
Ringbom, Sixten 77
Ringwoody Witch 184
Ripley Scoll (manuscript) 72
Rizzio, David 170
Robert Bruce, King 183
Robert of Normandy 123, *123*
Roche 52
Rock of the Evil One 118

Rocky Valley 20, 52
Roewen 132
Rollright Stones 107, *107*
Roman Well 161
Rombald's Moor 146
Ronan, St 176
Rose symbol 9, *9*, 65
Rosicrucians 9, 64-5, 70, 94
Rosslyn Chapel 181
Rosy Cross 9, 65
Rough Tor 38, 41, 53
Roulston Scar 147
Round Table 84, 118
Royal Observatory, Greenwich 75, *75*
Royston 96
Rudston 152-3
Runes 25, 27, 161, 179
Rushton 9, *10*, 90, 110, *110*
Ruta 51
Rutland, Earl of 104

Sabbats 27, 36, 39, 60, 87, 103, 130, 133, 168, 176, 177, 178, 180
Sacrificial Stone 133
Saducismus Triumphatus (Glanvill) 36, 53, 60, 83, 84
Saffron Walden 20, 97, *97*, 153
Sagittarius 13, 14, 15, 166, 167
St Albans 96
St Alkleda's Church *13*
St Andrews 27, 182, *182*
St Catherine's Hill 84
St Clair, Sir William 181
St Cleer 19, 38, 52
St Clether 18, 52
St Cuthbert's Well 143
St David's 132, *132*
St Elian's Well 128
St Govan's Chapel 133, *133*
St Guron's Well 37
St Ive 52
St John's College, Oxford 109
St Loe, Sir William 79
St Martin Stone 168
St Meilig Cross 129
St Michael's Mount 52-3
St Non's Well 132
St Osyth 90, 96-7
St Paul's Cathedral 58
St Tudno's Churchyard 8, 9
St Tudno's Cradle 124
St Vigeans 183
St Winifride's Well 19, 126, *126*
Salamanders 22, 23, 27, 53, 169
Saltpans *see* Prestonpans
Saltwick 155
Samlesbury 153
Sampson, Agnes 170, 175, 176, 181, *181*, 186
Samuel, Gammer Alice 99
Samuelston 183
Sanctuary Knocker 143, *143*
Sandford Orcas 53
Saros cycle 55
Sarsens 32, *32*
Satan's Invisible World Discovered (Sinclair) 166
Saturn 107, 112
Scaur 178
Sciomancy 27
Scorpio 13, *13*, 15, 46, 66, *66*, 132, 144, 170
Scot, Michael 179, *179*
Scot, Reginald 83
Scotlandwell 18-19, 183, *183*
Scott, John 81, 166
Scott, Sir Walter 155, 159, 179, 181
Seaforth, Earl of 171
Seaforth family 160
Seal of Aemeth 83
Seal of Solomon 8, 9, 27, 44, 103
Seances 40, 46, 65, 73, 120, 151

Seaton, David, 186
Seaton, Ted 150
Seaton Ross 153
Second sight 27, 95, 160
Secret Commonwealth, The (Kirk) 159
Selkirk, Earl of 70
Senara, St 60
Serpent stones 107
Shakespeare, William 64, 160
Sharow 153
Sharpe, C.K. 166, 168, 170, 173
Shax 17
Shelton, Meg 153, 156
Shepperson (illustrator) 142, *142*
Shepton Mallet 36, 53
Shervage Wood 44
Shiney Night (Tonshow) 117
Shipton, Mother 148
Shorteley Park 104
Shuttleworth, Arthur 59
Sible Hedingham 97, 98
Sidbury 28, 53
Sigils 12, 13, *16*, 17, 24, 27, 42, *42*, 77, 79, 80, 83, 112, 132, 173
Silbury Hill 32, 33, *33*
Sims (psychic investigator) 67, 82, 118
Simson, Isabel 173
Sinclair (historian) 166
Singleton 153
Sinnett, A.P. 32
Skewsby 20, 153
Skirling 184
Slaughter Bridge 41, 53
Smeeth 83
Smith, Ellen 89
Smith, Emma 97
Smith, Thomas 12
Smyth, Charles Piazzi 153
Snaefell 153-4
Snake symbol 25, *25*, 32, 52, 112, 140
Snape Castle 154
Society for Psychical research 64, 69, 123, 126, 147
Sockburn 154
Sockburn Worm 143, 154
Soulis, William Lord 175
South Hill 53
South Tidworth 83
Southey, Robert 116
Southwell 16, 111, *111*
Southword, Dorothy 153
Spalding, James 166
Sparrow, William 93
'Spell for a Fairy, A' (Noyes) 142, *142*
Spells 20, 24, 66, 67, 88, 95, 108, 176
Spenser, Edmund 64, 116
Spirit photographs 20, 40, *40*, 44, 45, 65, 69, 76, *76*, 120, *120*, 123, *123*, 126, *126*, 151, 155, 156, 171
Spirit-writing 46, 73
Spiritual Magazine 76
'Splendor Solis' (manuscript) 71
Spott 184
Staffa, Isle of 52, 172, *173*
Standing stones 17-18, 32, 119, 120, 131, 135, *135*, 141, *141*, 148, 149, 152
Star stones 107
Staunton 133, *133*
Stead, W.T. 76, *76*
Steiner, Rudolf 77
Steiner House 77
Steward, William 182
Stewart, Jon 180
Steyning 83
Stone circles 17-18, 32, 40, 50, 54, *54*, 55, 56, 107, *107*, 146, 161, 162, *162*, 167, 184, *185*

Stone Magic 6, 81-2
Stone of Scone 81
Stonehenge 17, *17*, 32, 40, 50, 54-6, *54*, *56*, 172
Storr, Isle of 184
Stow, John 79
Stow Longa 98
Strata Florida Abbey 121, 134, *134*
Studland 57
Suck Stone 133
Sudbrook 134
Suenos Stone 160
Summers, Montague 95, 96, 99, 136
Sun *12*, 49, 91, 97, 176
Sundials 93, 107, *107*, 153
Sunhoney 18, 184-5, *185*
Swaffham 16, 98
Swallow Falls 116, *116*
Swansea 131
Swastika Stone *139*, 146
Swift, Jonathan 82, 129
Swifte, Edmund 79, 80
Swinhoe, Mrs 119
Sylphs 22, 23, 27, 154
Sympathetic magic 27, 37, 104

Table-rapping 65
Tackley 111
Tal-y-Fan 132
Tarot 11, *11*, 48, 68, 73, *73*
Taurus 11, 15, 25, 132, 142
Tecia, St (Triacle) 134
Teddington Hands 134-5
Tedworth Drummer 36, 83-4, *84*
Temple (Cornwall) 38
Temple (London) 81
Temple (Lothian) 185
Temple of Mithras 141-2
Tetractys 110
Tetragrammaton 105, 150, 151
Thaxted 98
Theosophical Society of Great Britain 74
Thirlmere, Lake 156
Thomas the Rhymer 186
Thorndike, Lynn 179
Thorpe le Soken 96
'Thoughtform of Music' 78
Thought-forms (Besant and Leadbeater) 78
Three Brothers 155
Three-Ways-to-Nowhere Bridge 90
Thriplow 98
Throckmorton, Sir Robert 99
Thurlow, Davy 96
Thurlow, Grace 96
Thynne, Lady Elisabeth 75
Tibble Stone 134
Tintagel 57, *57*
Tintern Abbey 135, *135*
Tode, Peg 7
Toller Fratrum 12, 57
Tomnahurich Hill 186, *186*
Tompson, Agnes *181*
Tonshow, Beatrice 117
Tower of London 79-80, *79*, *80*, *81*
Tramur, Ralph 58
Tranent 186
Tree of Life 9
Trefoil 9, *10*, 110
Tregeagle, Jan 38, 52
Trellech 28, 135-6, *135*
Trendle earthwork 41
Tresham, Sir Thomas 9, *10*, 57, 110
Trethevy Quoit 38
Trevelyan, Sir Charles 154
Trewhella, Matthew 60
Trewortha Tor 37
Triangular Lodge 9, 110, *110*
Tring 27, 99

Troy Town 112
Truro 58
Tudno, St 124, *124*
Tweedale family 155
Twelve Apostles 146
Twelve Tribes of Israel 13, *13*, 15, 144
Tyburn gallows 77

Uffington 42, 59, 111, *111*
UFOs (unidentified flying objects) 59, 96
Undines 22, 23, 28, 144
Unicorns 45, 72, *72*, 149, 173
Upney, Joan 89
Uranus 176
Uriel, Archangel 16, 45
Ussie, Loch 161
Uther Ben 80

Varley, C.F. 65
Varley, John 65, 77
Venus, 45, 112
Verulamium 96
Vesica piscis 28, 91
Victoria Embankment 81
Virgin Mary 13, 106
Virgo 13, 15, 72, 170
Virtue 28
Virtuous Well 135-6
'Vision, A' (Yeats) 73
Vortigern 129
Vril 17, 28, 94

Waite, A.E. 73
Wall, Maggie 169, *169*
Wallington House 154, *154*
Walter of Coventry 41
Walton 144
Walton Ashes 96
Walton-Le-Dale 27, 153, 154-5, *154*
Walton-on-Thames see Diseworth
Wandelbury 99, *99*
Warboys 99
Ward, Mary Ann 125
Ward Hill 181
Wardlaw 177
Waring, Paul 154
Warleggan 58, *58*
Warminster 59
Warminster Mystery, The (Shuttleworth) 59
Warren, Earl 117
Warton 155
Warwick 112
Warwick, Earl of 112
Warmington 112
Washington, John 155
Washington, Thomas 155
Waterhouse, Agnes 92-3
Waterhouse, Joan 92, 93
Watkins, Alfred 18, 24, 25, 116, 121, 122, 124, 125, *125*, 134, 135, 141
Watson, William 153
Watsone, Margaret 178-9
Waves symbol 144
Wayland's Smithy 111
Weeks, Matthew 41
Weir, Bessie 180
Weir, Major Thomas 170, 171
Welbourn 99, *99*
Wellington, Duke of 82
Wells 6, 18-19, *19*, 36, 37, 41-2, 46, 48, 52, 59, 77, 92, 100, 103, 106, 119, 126, *126*, 128, 132-6 *passim*, 143, 144, 148, 161, 183, *183*, 184
West Kennet long barrow 32
West Walton 100, *100*
West Wycombe 112
Westbury 59, *59*
Wester Duddingstoun 166

Westminster Abbey 81-2
Weston 120, 155
Wheeler, Sir Mortimer 118
Wherwell 84
Whispering Knights 107
Whitby 155
White, Andrew 58
Whitehouse, Cope 172
Whitestone Cliffs 156
Whitlock, Ralph, 145
Whittington, Dick 75
Wickstead, Hilda 126, *126*
Wilcock, John 161
Wilcrick Hill 128
'Wildemen' 92, *92*
William de Aldeborough 140
William of Malmesbury 46
William, S.W. 134
Wilmington 84
Wilton Row 82
Wincanton 36, 60
Winchester 84
Windmill Hill 32
Windover Hill 84
Wing, Bucks 112
Wing, Leics 112
Winifride, St 126
Winsford Hill 60
Wishart, George 183
Wisley Labyrinth 20, *20*
Witch-bottles 88
Witch Hill 182, *183*
Witch pricking 28, 53, 177
Witch scratching 28, 53, 99
Witchcraft/witches 6, 7, 17, *17*, 26, 27, 28, 36, 37, *37*, 53, 66, 74, 77, 79, 83, 87, *87*, 88, 89, *89*, 90, 92-3, 93, 95, 96-7, 98, 99, 103, 104, 108, 112, 130, 133, 144, 150, 151, 152, *152*, 153, 156, 159, 160, 166, 167, 169-72 *passim*, 174-8 *passim*, 180-84 *passim*, 186 see also sabbats
Witchcraft eye 151, *151*
'Witchcraft Tomb' 7, 8, 103-4, 151, *151*
Witch-stones 7, *7*, 17, 28, 160, 168, 172, 184
Withersfield 100
Wonderful and True Account of the Laird of Cool's Ghost, A (Ogilvie) 176
Wonderful Head, The 80
Wood, John 42
Woodplumpton 156
Woodwose 28, 43, 92, *92*, 149
Woolpit 16, 100, *100*
Woolston 136
Worcester 65, 136, *136*
Worm's Head 136
Wormenhert Dragon 96
Wright, Elsie 142, *142*
Wybrant Viper 116
Wythburn 156

Yeats, W.B. 72, 73
Yolande 151
York 156
York Tower 159-60
Yorkshire Oddities, Incidents and Strange Events (Baring-Gould) 49
Young, Elspeth 159

Zanoni (Lytton) 94
Zennor 52, 60, *60*
Zodiac 7, 8, *8*, 12-13, *12*, *13*, 22, 25, 27, 28, 40, 66, 73, 79, 88, 109, 136, 166, 167, 170, 171, *171* see also individual names of signs
Zodiacal clock 72, *72*
Zodiacal Man 12, *12*, 28, *28*, 57
Zoroastrianism 49